The Other Campaign

Soft Money and Issue Advocacy in the 2000 Congressional Elections

Edited by
David B. Magleby

ROWMAN & LITTLEFIELD PUBLISHERS, INC.
Lanham • Boulder • New York • Oxford

ROWMAN & LITTLEFIELD PUBLISHERS, INC.

Published in the United States of America
by Rowman & Littlefield Publishers, Inc.
A Member of the Rowman & Littlefield Publishing Group
4720 Boston Way, Lanham, Maryland 20706
www.rowmanlittlefield.com

12 Hid's Copse Road, Cumnor Hill, Oxford OX2 9JJ, England

British Library Cataloguing in Publication Information Available

Library of Congress Cataloging-in-Publication Data

The other campaign : soft money and issue advocacy in the 2000 congressional elections / edited by David B. Magleby.
p. cm.
Includes bibliographical references and index.
ISBN 0-7425-1771-3 (cloth : alk. paper)—ISBN 0-7425-1772-1 (paper : alk. paper)
1. Campaign funds—United States. 2. Pressure groups—United States. 3. United States. Congress—Elections, 2000. I. Magleby, David B.
JK1991 .068 2003
324 . 973'0929—dc21

2002001445

Printed in the United States of America

∞™ The paper used in this publication meets the minimum requirements of American National Standard for Information Sciences—Permanence of Paper for Printed Library Materials, ANSI/NISO Z39.48-1992.

To
Alma Woodruff Magleby Jr.
and Marydean Curtis Magleby

Contents

Figures

Tables

Preface

Field research is an important part of political science, but the tradition of "soaking and poking,"[1] as Richard Fenno has described it, is not as much a part of the discipline as it once was. In the area of money and politics, researchers for a time were able to rely on the data from the Federal Election Commission (FEC) to test ideas and develop theories about this topic. With the demise of the Federal Election Campaign Act (FECA) and the rise of unlimited and often undisclosed money in federal elections, researchers must face the reality that the data needed to understand money in politics are no longer available online.

The research reported in this book is an effort to begin discovering the full range of campaign communications, disclosed and undisclosed, in competitive congressional races. In our study, we deploy a field research methodology, with academics closely monitoring campaign communications in competitive congressional races. This study builds on a similar project during the 1998 congressional elections[2] and 2000 presidential primaries.[3]

This research was funded by a grant from the Pew Charitable Trusts. Sean Treglia, program officer at Pew, has offered just the right mix of support and candor about this and other proposals. I am indebted to him for his professionalism and trust. Michael Delli Carpini, a fellow political scientist, has also been wonderfully supportive, as has Pew President Rebecca Rimel.

I have also had the good fortune of working with four extraordinary research associates, all recent Brigham Young University graduates. Anna Nibley Baker, Jason Beal, Michelle Reed, and Eric Smith all worked tirelessly on this project. Anna Nibley Baker helped launch this study, both designing the database and coordinating academic training for the project. She managed editing and production while coordinating academic needs. Jason Beal worked out of Washington, D.C., coordinating and attending most of the elite interviews I conducted. He also attended numerous PAC and interest group meetings on this topic. He was our primary liaison with the Federal Election Commission (FEC) and Federal Communications Commission (FCC). Michelle Reed, before she left to attend law school, helped launch this study and design our secure Web site for data entry from the seventeen contests we monitored. Eric Smith, who joined the team upon Michelle's departure, helped design and streamline the data entry, managed the dataset, and provided the first cuts of data analysis. Anna, Eric, and Jason each worked with a group of the academics during the study and provided editing assistance for the entire report. Nate Moses, a BYU undergraduate, created the database and Web site, managing them on a daily basis. We all benefited from his knowledge of Microsoft Access and his ability to translate our ideas into a working computer program. We appreciate the excellent editorial assistance provided by Catherine Matthews Pavia. Stephanie Perry Curtis, Christopher Fillmore, Jenny Jensen, Eric McArthur, Christopher Rees, and Charles W. Ross provided more general research assistance. Marianne Holt, from the Center for Public Integrity, read the report and provided valuable comments. Bob Biersack, of the Federal Election Commission, helped us navigate 2000 election spending reported to the FEC.

I wish to thank all of my colleagues who joined this project as fellow investigators. We became data scavengers, hunting for mail from parties and interest groups, tracking down telephone banks, interviewing others who monitor campaigns for tips on what was happening in a particular contest. Unfortunately, space constraints mean that not all of the seventeen case studies in our project can be included in this book. However, all of the academics did a superb job of following the races, entering their data into our common database, and writing up their findings. I gratefully acknowledge the contributions of Ola Adeoye, Sandra M. Anglund, David C. Barker, Harold F. Bass, Adam J. Berinsky, Christopher Jan Carman, Sue Carter, Chris Christenson, Todd Donovan, Julia Dowse, Bob Dudley, Eric Freedman, Donald A. Gross, Allison Hayes, Rebekah Herrick, Robert Holsworth, E. Terrence Jones, Scott Keeter, Kathryn A. Kirkpatrick, Robin Kolodny, Kyle Kreider, Martha E. Kropf, Susan S. Lederman, Drew Linzer, Maureen Gilbride Mears, Steven Medvic, David Menefee-Libey, Penny M. Miller, Dale Neumann, Joanne M. Miller, Charles Morrow, Charlie Peaden, Joseph A. Pika, Barry Rundquist, Anthony Simones, Randy Smith, Sandra Suarez, Michael W. Traugott, Amber E. Wilson, Craig Wilson, and Harry Wilson. The investigators created their own reconnaissance networks in their districts or states involving colleagues, students, residents of retirement centers, political reporters, and others. In addition, we acknowledge the support of the League of Women Voters and Common Cause, who provided access to their members, many of whom assisted in monitoring campaign communications in 2000. Specifically, we appreciate the efforts of Betsy Lawson at the League of Women Voters and Ed Davis and his assistant Laura Williams at Common Cause.

Following outside money begins with identifying the contests where it will likely be spent. Our research design included frequent interviews with party, interest group, and political professionals who work in this environment. I am especially indebted to David Hansen, political director at the National Republican Senatorial Campaign Committee; Jim Jordan, Executive Director of the Democratic Senatorial Campaign Committee; John Guzik, Deputy Executive Director at the National Republican Congressional Committee; and Karin Johanson, Political Director at the Democratic Congressional Campaign Committee, all of whom met with me often and identified likely targets for party soft money and interest group issue advocacy activity. Bernadette Budde, senior vice president of the Business and Industrial Political Action Committee, and Karen Ackerman, deputy political director of the AFL-CIO, provided insights from the interest group community on which races to monitor. Finally, I carefully read the newsletters of Stu Rothenberg and Charlie Cook and occasionally interviewed them to get their assessments of campaign dynamics in the relatively few competitive races of 2000.

Jennifer Knerr, executive editor at Rowman & Littlefield, provided timely support and helpful advice on the book. Jehanne Schweitzer, production editor, and Sharon DeJohn, copyeditor, were thorough and professional in their work on the book.

I have a supportive and understanding wife and great kids. Frequently during the time I was doing this research, my father would ask about how much soft money was being spent and whether studying the flow of so much money might not help my ability to make money. I assured him that this was an academic project only. I appreciate his interest in my work and the love he and my mother have always shown me. I dedicate this book to them.

NOTES

1. Richard Fenno, "U.S. House Members in Their Constituencies," *American Political Science Review* 71, no. 3 (September 1977): 884.
2. David B. Magleby, ed., *Outside Money: Soft Money and Issue Advocacy in the 1998 Congressional Elections* (Lanham, Md.: Rowman & Littlefield, 2000).
3. See David B. Magleby, ed., "Outside Money in the 2000 Presidential Primaries and Congressional General Elections," <www.apsa.com/PS/june01/outsidemoney.cfm>, June 2001, [accessed June 2001]. The full monographs are included in David B. Magleby, ed., "Getting Inside the Outside Campaign in the 2000 Presidential Primaries," <www.byu.edu/outsidemoney/> [accessed 6 August 2001].

1

The Importance of Outside Money in Competitive Congressional Campaigns

David B. Magleby

Competitive congressional elections have seen a dramatic change in campaign communications since 1996. Outside money—party soft money, election issue advocacy, independent expenditures, and internal communications within organizations—now rivals and often exceeds candidate spending in these contests. Noncandidate campaigns use all modes of communication, almost always involve campaign professionals, and are concentrated in competitive races. The candidates in these contests generally spend record-setting amounts of hard money on their own campaigns. When the millions of dollars of outside money are added to candidate spending, the election becomes a deluge of information from multiple campaigns, much of it negative.

Outside money has become crucial in competitive races, but its effects are varied and occasionally backfire. The purpose of this book is to explore the importance of outside money along with some of its positive and negative effects on congressional campaigns. We report on data gathered from twelve U.S. House and five U.S. Senate races in 2000. All of the races were projected to be highly competitive.

Our methodology relies on academics from the state or congressional districts where the races occurred. They assembled reconnaissance networks to gather mail; record telephone contacts; obtain data from television and radio stations on advertisements run in their particular race; and conduct extensive interviews with candidate campaign staff, party and interest group officials, and other knowledgeable observers. In addition, we acquired data on broadcast television advertising in any of the top seventy-five media markets that were in our sample races. This comprehensive approach to gathering data on all forms of campaign communication permits us to assess a set of important questions: How much noncandidate campaigning exists? Who does more of this activity, the parties or the interest groups? Are the issue agendas of the parties and interest groups congruent with the candidates' issue agendas? Is noncandidate campaigning more negative in tone? What, if any, impact does outside money have on competitive races? Our aim in this book is to answer these questions, assessing the extent and nature of noncandidate campaigning in competitive races.

TYPES OF CONGRESSIONAL CAMPAIGNS

Congressional campaigns can be divided into two broad types: safe-seat and competitive races. Although money is a factor in almost all congressional campaigns, it typically reduces competition because it largely goes to incumbents. In competitive races candidate spending is more balanced, and outside money plays a much larger role.

Safe-Seat Races

These races typically pit well-funded incumbents against underfunded challengers and constitute the vast majority of House and Senate races in any given election cycle. They fit the candidate-centered model widely accepted in political science as typical congressional elections.[1] Furthermore, in these contests incumbents receive the lion's share of political action committee (PAC) donations, raising on average in the 1990s and in 2000 over seven dollars from PACs to every dollar raised by challengers.[2]

Competitive Races

The second type of race is a competitive contest in which both candidates are adequately funded and equally matched. It is in these few competitive races that the political parties and interest groups do battle for control of Congress, and it is in these competitive races that candidates must compete with interest groups and parties for control of the campaign agenda. In 1998 and 2000, only about one in ten House races fit this description. Although the proportion of competitive Senate races is higher, most Senate races are also not competitive.

MODES AND LEVELS OF SPENDING

Competitive races help explain the noticeable increase in campaign expenditures as well as the development of new and innovative ways to raise and spend campaign money outside the intent of the campaign finance laws. The following sections discuss some of the ways in which money is spent on campaigns, with special reference to the 1999–2000 election cycle.

Hard Money

Under the Federal Elections Campaign Act (FECA), individuals and PACs can make limited and disclosed contributions to candidates and political parties; this is called *hard money*. Individuals can give up to $2,000 per election cycle (primary and general election) and PACs can give up to $10,000. Despite these low limits, congressional candidates in the 1999–2000 cycle raised more than $1 billion from individuals, PACs, and contributions from their own personal funds. This figure is over 30 percent higher than in 1998. Because of contribution limits, hard money is harder to raise and is the only kind of money that federal candidates can spend on their own campaigns. There are no restrictions on how hard money is spent by candidates.

Soft Money

In contrast to hard money, nonfederal money, or *soft money*, has no contribution limit, and only parties are legally allowed to raise and spend it. Parties are limited in what they can contribute to candidates and what they can spend in coordinated campaigns with them. However, with soft money the parties can allocate the money as they choose.

Party soft money has grown dramatically in amount and influence in recent years. The growth came about because of Federal Election Commission (FEC) efforts to empower the political parties to engage in generic party-building activities such as thematic advertising, voter registration, and get-out-the-vote (GOTV) efforts. Soft money was not intended to directly benefit federal candidates. Today, however, its main focus is to provide another means to promote the election or defeat of particular candidates. Because soft money contributions are unlimited, party committee leaders understandably saw soft money fundraising as a priority, and interest groups and wealthy individuals responded by making very large soft money contributions. For example, the American Federation of State, County and Municipal Employees (AFSCME) gave $6.46 million in soft money in 1999–2000 to the Democrats, while Phillip Morris Companies, Incorporated contributed $2.4 million to the Republicans.[3] In 2000, in the aggregate, the parties spent nearly half a billion dollars in soft money, with both parties setting new records in raising and spending soft money.[4]

To facilitate the collection of both hard and soft money from the same donors, parties have created joint fundraising committees, or Victory Funds, in select states. These funds effectively permit large donors to contribute hard and soft money at the same time as well as allowing them to earmark their soft money to particular races.[5] Hillary Clinton's 2000 campaign made especially good use of joint fundraising. Other individuals, such as Mel Carnahan, John Ashcroft, Dianne Feinstein, and Richard Gephardt, also used Victory Funds. The Democrats typically made better use of this 2000 innovation than did the Republicans.[6]

Some methods for raising soft money might be new, but parties have been spending soft money on generic party building since 1980 and more recently have used soft money for "issue advocacy," which typically promotes or attacks particular candidates.[7] We discuss soft money in more detail in chapter 2.

Election Issue Advocacy

Groups or individuals who engage in electioneering may now avoid the FECA's regulatory regime through issue advocacy. Relying on a distinction made between electioneering (express advocacy) and communications about issues (issue advocacy) in the 1976 Supreme Court decision in *Buckley v. Valeo*, parties and interest groups now spend unlimited amounts on advertisements while avoiding disclosure, as long as they do not participate in express advocacy. The court defined express advocacy as the use of the magic words "vote for," "elect," "support," "cast your ballot for," "Smith for Congress," "vote against," "defeat," and "reject."[8] For a number of years the court's distinction had little effect on campaign advertising, but since 1996 parties and interest groups have devised ways to advertise "for" and "against" candidates without using the language of express advocacy. Despite the absence of an explicit voting reference, the message of support for or opposition to a federal candidate is clear in election issue advocacy.[9] For example, these communications often show the image or likeness of a candidate, occur a few weeks before an election, mention an election, and mention a candidate's name.

The unions expanded the extent and use of this means of influencing elections with their substantial broadcast blitz against Republicans in 1996 and again in 1998, when they applied issue advocacy to voter mobilization. Parties also engage in election issue advocacy, which can be partially funded by soft money. The use of soft money to fund issue advocacy was pioneered by President Clinton in his 1996 campaign.[10] The Annenberg Public Policy Center of the University of Pennsylvania conservatively estimates that parties (national and state) spent $161.9 million on issue advocacy in 2000 and that interest groups spent an estimated $509 million overall in issue advocacy (election and pure issue advocacy) in 1999–2000.[11]

Pure Issue Advocacy

Individuals and groups sometimes communicate about issues without regard to a particular candidate, adhering to the intent of the *Buckley* ruling; we call this "pure issue advocacy" to differentiate it from candidate-centered election issue advocacy. We saw very little pure issue advocacy in the period between Labor Day and Election Day 2000. Issue advocacy in the 2000 congressional elections is discussed in chapter 3.

527 Organizations

Named for Section 527 of the tax code, these political organizations could avoid FECA disclosure until July 2000 because they engage in issue advocacy and therefore are not required to report to the FEC; they are also not required to report to the Internal Revenue Service (IRS) as long as their funds are in non-interest-bearing accounts. Legislation signed into law in July 2000 requires a group that organizes itself under section 527 to register with the IRS within twenty-four hours of being established and to report monthly spending and receipts during an election. The legislation requires disclosure of receipts of more than $200 and expenditures of more than $500, if the group plans to spend more than $25,000 to affect the election of any candidate. Many groups, like the Sierra Club and the National Association for the Advancement of Colored People (NAACP) National Voter Fund, used their 527 accounts to accept large donations from undisclosed donors before the legislation took effect. As part of the money and politics story in 2000, 527 organizations became one of several ways noncandidate money was spent on elections. An examination of approximately twenty soft money-funded 527s—those that avoided disclosure and were new in the year 2000—saw expenditures of around $40 million.[12]

Independent Expenditures

As a result of the *Buckley v. Valeo* decision in 1976, groups and individuals can spend unlimited amounts of money advocating the election or defeat of a candidate as long as those expenditures are not coordinated with the candidate or party campaigns. Although independent expenditures may be spent in unlimited amounts, their sources and amounts are reported to the FEC. Some groups prefer issue advocacy to independent expenditures because of the absence of FEC disclosure. Nevertheless, membership organizations such as the National Rifle Association (NRA) and the League of Conservation Voters (LCV) rely heavily on independent expenditures. They often communicate outside their membership and prefer using express advocacy terms like "vote for," and "vote against." The FEC reported total independent expenditures in all federal races in 1999–2000 as $36.5 million.[13]

Internal Communications

Membership organizations such as trade unions; some business organizations; and environmental, gun, and other groups also communicate with their members using internal communications, a form of electioneering rarely noticed nationally since it is directed to members only. Internal communications can be paid for with union dues or from an organization's treasury. When a membership communication expressly advocates the election or defeat of a federal candidate and the communication costs are more than $2,000 per election, the organization must report the expenditure to the FEC. When election endorsements are not the primary intent of a communication, or if they avoid the magic words of express advocacy from the *Buckley v. Valeo* decision, the expenditures are exempt from reporting. This means of electioneering was important in competitive contests in 2000. The aggregate total of internal communications reported to the FEC in 1999–2000 equaled $17.9 million.[14] Independent expenditures and internal communications in the 2000 congressional contests are the subject of chapter 4.

Candidate Self-Financing

Candidates face no constraints other than disclosure when financing their own campaigns. Both parties welcome self-financed candidates who are electorally viable, because it permits them to target their party resources to other races. None of the contests we monitored had substantial candidate self-financing, but in the 1999–2000 election cycle candidates for Congress invested a total of nearly $90 million in their own campaigns.[15] The largest self-financing by far came from John Corzine, the New Jersey Democratic candidate, who spent over $60 million of his own money on his successful 2000 Senate race.[16]

A COMPETITIVE AND UNCONSTRAINED ELECTION

Soft money and issue advocacy were not new in 2000, but changes in the electoral environment forced candidates, parties, and interest groups to alter their strategies and expand the extent to which they are used. Two major factors have shaped these recent changes in campaign financing in competitive contests. First, the highly competitive nature of recent elections has made higher expenditures a necessity and encouraged the flow of outside money to those races; second, to spend more on campaigns, candidates, parties, and interest groups have all looked for new ways to circumvent the FECA regulations.

The Competitive 2000 Elections in Context

There was a lot at stake in the 2000 elections. With no incumbent running for the White House, narrow majorities in both houses of Congress, and state legislatures poised to take up redistricting after the election, the 2000 elections provided ample incentives for candidates, political parties, and interest groups to invest in the outcome.[17] For example, four of the five U.S. Senate races we monitored (Delaware, Michigan, Missouri, and Montana) set spending records for Senate races in their states. The most expensive House race in U.S. history was the contest in the Twenty-seventh Congressional District in California, where over $19 million was spent by candidates, parties, and interest groups. "In the end, the candidates raised and spent over $11.5 million, political parties spent approximately $5.5 million, and outside organizations spent over $2 million, bringing the total price tag to over $19 million."[18] Part of the explanation for the high level of candidate spending, $11 million, was the visible role Republican incumbent James Rogan had played in the Clinton impeachment and Senate trial, helping him raise money from those who disliked Clinton's performance as president. Rogan spent $6.9 million in his race; Democratic challenger Adam Schiff, who may have benefited from Clinton supporters eager to defeat one of the most visible proponents of impeachment, spent $4.65 million.[19] But the Clinton issue does not explain the heavy levels of party and interest group spending, which nearly doubled the candidate spending and made this a $19 million race. The reason so much money went to this race, and to a lesser extent other competitive races, is that there were comparatively few battlegrounds for the parties and interest groups to influence in 2000.

Most groups, political parties included, stratified their campaigns, providing separate communications for the candidates in different races in the same state. Even in states like Montana and Michigan, which had intensely fought campaigns for the U.S. Senate and House, the candidates, groups, and parties mounted largely separate campaigns. For the most part, the two congressional campaign committees and the national party committees operated in their own spheres, minimizing the extent to which more than one race was mentioned in candidate commercials and much of the political mail. In only about 10 percent of the campaign communications we observed did interest groups and parties push more than one candidate in the same communication.

A Slim Majority with Few Competitive House Races in 2000

The number of competitive House races declines at the end of a decade in part because incumbents get established after the reshuffling following redistricting. The advantages of incumbency—PAC contributions, constituency services, and name recognition—discourage serious would-be challengers. Often therefore, races are not competitive until an incumbent steps down, leaving an open seat. In 2000 there were relatively few open seats, because the close party balance prompted leaders in both parties to push their incumbents to run again. Democratic Minority Leader Dick Gephardt (D-Mo.) did better than his Republican counterpart in keeping retirements and incumbents seeking other offices to a minimum.[20]

As in 1998, there were relatively few competitive U.S. House races in 2000—too few, according to Linda Lipson of the Trial Lawyers Association, because all the groups and parties paid attention to a small number of contests.[21] The number of competitive races declined dramatically after 1996. Figure 1.1 shows the number of races seen by one prominent authority as competitive in July of each of the last five elections. This small number of competitive contests meant that the interest groups and parties were forced to compete in races that may have already had an abundance of money on both sides or where the candidate profiles were not well suited to the groups' interests. Because of the limited range of competitive races, the groups or parties felt they needed to spend on the race anyway.

In addition, the 1998 and 2000 cycles saw the reality that a net shift of roughly a half-dozen seats could make in the party balance. Both parties and allied interest groups were therefore forced to compete in a set of contests that were not always the preferred battlegrounds.

House Republican Open-Seat Challenge

In 2000, the Republicans were in a more difficult strategic position than the Democrats in House elections because of the larger number of Republican retirements resulting in competitive seats. Of the thirty-three open seats in 2000, twenty-four were Republican, and seven of these were rated toss-ups. In contrast, the Democrats only had nine competitive open seats to defend, two of which leaned Republican and one of which was a toss-up.[22]

Going into the 2000 cycle, Democrats were optimistic about their chances of regaining the majority; successful fundraising reinforced this optimism. The Democratic fundraising operation was in full swing in both congressional campaign committees. As Karen Johanson, of the Democratic Congressional Campaign Committee (DCCC), observed, "The Democrats had enough money [this election cycle]. Money was not a factor."[23] Republicans were even more flush than the Democrats, having raised record-setting amounts of hard money and continuing to enjoy a substantial hard money lead over the Democrats. As we discuss in chapter 2, the laggard in party fundraising in 2000 was the National Republican

Figure 1.1. Competitive U.S. House Races Over Time

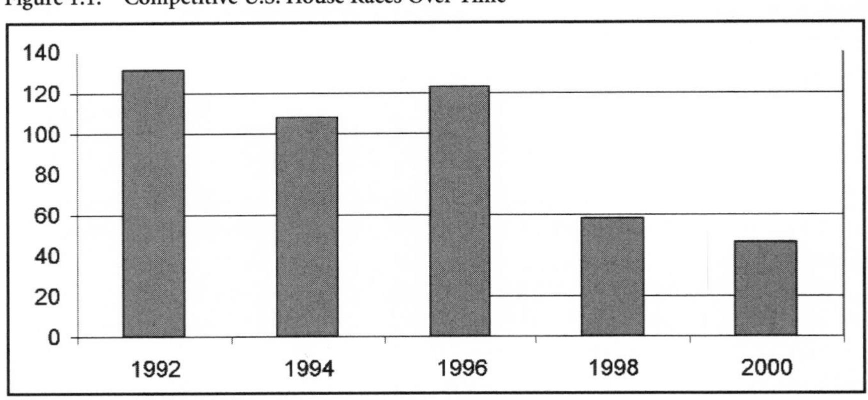

Source: Charlie Cook, "How Big Will the Republican Gains Be?" *National Journal* (26 September 1988): 225; Charlie Cook, "National Overview," *The Cook Political Report* (23 June 2000): 6.

Senatorial Committee (NRSC), whose rate of growth was the lowest for any congressional campaign committee.

Senate Takeover Possible

The competitive environment for control of the U.S. Senate changed on 19 July 2000 with the unexpected death of Georgia Republican Senator Paul Coverdell and the appointment of a popular Democratic successor, former Governor Zell Miller. Miller's appointment reduced the Republican margin in the Senate to 54/46. With Democrats hoping to pick up vulnerable Republican seats in Delaware, Florida, Michigan, Minnesota, Missouri, Montana, Pennsylvania, and Washington, a Democratic majority was more attainable. Part of the apparent Republican vulnerability stemmed from the perceived weakness of some of the senators first elected in the Republican surge in 1994: Abraham in Michigan, Ashcroft in Missouri, Grams in Minnesota, and Santorum in Pennsylvania. Candidate recruitment was therefore important, and Democrats aggressively courted candidates such as Governor Mel Carnahan, Representative Debbie Stabenow, and millionaire Mark Dayton. Virginia Senator Chuck Robb, who narrowly defeated Oliver North in 1994, was seen as the Democrats' only seriously vulnerable incumbent. In terms of open seats, Republicans saw Nebraska, Nevada, and New York as viable targets in which to pick up seats, while Democrats focused on picking up Florida. The death of Missouri's Mel Carnahan in an airplane accident twenty-two days before the election seemed to stymie the Ashcroft campaign. Voters narrowly elected Jean Carnahan, the late governor's widow.

The competitive nature of the 2000 elections and the increasing ability of individuals, candidates, parties, and groups to avoid the constraints of the FECA combined to elevate the importance of money in the 2000 elections. Voters in competitive House and Senate races saw extraordinary levels of hard money, soft money, and issue advocacy spending. In most of our sample races, outside money spending by parties and interest groups equaled or exceeded candidate spending and essentially eroded the efficacy of the FECA regulations.

Outside Money in Congressional Primaries

Even though the national parties did not invest soft money in the presidential primaries, congressional elections were a different story. Because of the declining numbers of competitive races, party committees and interest groups became involved in contested party primaries. Traditionally, party committees wait until after contested primaries are decided to endorse or support particular candidates. However, in 2000 the party committees, not wanting to go into the general election with anything less than the most electable candidate, were occasionally involved in primaries. The outgoing Republican congressman in the Illinois Tenth Congressional District, for example, successfully promoted Mark Kirk in the district primary, and the DCCC unsuccessfully endorsed Matt Mangino in the Pennsylvania Fourth Congressional District primary. Bernadette Budde of the Business and Industry Political Action Committee (BIPAC), when speaking of the preprimary GOP involvement in the Illinois Tenth, observed, "They couldn't wait until after the primary in Illinois Ten. You can't do that anymore—you have to go in early."[24]

The Demise of the Federal Election Campaign Act

The Federal Election Campaign Act (FECA) regulates the federal election process. Originally passed in 1971, the FECA has been amended in 1974, 1976, and 1979 and challenged in court in the landmark *Buckley v. Valeo* decision. The key provisions of the act that have withstood judicial scrutiny include contribution limits on the amounts individuals, parties, and PACs can give to federal candidates and national party committees. Individuals also have an aggregate contribution limit. When combined with public financing, the act also limits candidate expenditures, a provision that only applies to presidential elections. Table 1.1 provides these limits, which have not been increased or indexed for inflation since they were put in place in 1974.

The heavy use of outside money in the last election clearly violates the intent of the post-Watergate reforms in that it permits unlimited contributions to the parties for electioneering purposes (soft money) and unlimited and largely undisclosed spending to influence an election (election issue advocacy). Voters generally attribute the flood of campaign communications to the candidates,[25] even though in some instances candidates disavow party soft money communications on their behalf. Our electoral system assumes that candidates are responsible for campaign content, but in races funded by outside money that assumption is false. Not only are candidates not responsible for campaign content, but often they cannot control the level of negativity in noncandidate communications. In 1998 and again in 2000, we found that noncandidate communications are more inclined to be negative in tone and that groups that hide behind innocuous names are even more harshly negative.[26] For example, in the Michigan Eighth Congressional District contest in 2000, the party played good cop/bad cop, with the state party playing the good cop by being positive in communications and the National Republican Congressional Committee (NRCC) the bad cop by attacking the Democrats.[27]

Escaping Limits and Avoiding Disclosure

The simple fact that outside money violates the intent of campaign finance reform did not stop campaign participants from finding creative ways to circumvent FECA limitations in 2000. Although soft money and issue advocacy have been campaign elements for several election cycles, both were substantially

Table 1.1. FECA Contribution Limits

Donors	Candidate Committees	PACs	Local Party Committees[a]	State Party Committees[a]	National Party Committees[b]	Special Limits
Individuals	$1,000 per election	$5,000 per year	$5,000 per year combined limit		$20,000 per year	$25,000 per year overall
Local Party Committees[a]	$5,000 per election combined limit	$5,000 per election combined limit	Unlimited transfers to other party committees			
State Party (multicandidate)[a]			Unlimited transfers to other party committees			
National Party Committees (multicandidate)[b]	$5,000 per election	$5,000 per year	Unlimited transfers to other party committees			$17,500 to Senate candidate per campaign[c]
PAC (multicandidate)	$5,000 per election	$5,000 per year	$5,000 per year combined limit		$15,000 per year	
PAC (not multicandidate)	$1,000 per election	$5,000 per year	$5,000 per year combined limit		$20,000 per year	

Source: Federal Election Commission, *Campaign Guide for Political Party Committees*, August 1996.

[a]State and local party committees share limits unless the local party committee can prove its independence.

[b]A party's national committee, Senate campaign committee, and House campaign committee are commonly called the national party committees and each has a separate limit. See the "special limits" column for the exception.

[c]The Senate campaign committee and the national committee share this limit.

changed by the 1996 election cycle. The use of soft money for candidate definition purposes by the Democratic National Committee (DNC) for the Clinton/Gore campaign and the expansion of soft money spending by both national parties in the 1996 races helped set the stage for the surge in soft money electioneering in 1998 and its further expansion in 2000. Soft money is no longer a tool simply meant to help strengthen party organization; it has become an integral part of presidential elections and competitive congressional contests and has allowed parties to increase expenditures that avoid express advocacy but still support or attack specific candidates.[28]

The Shift to Issue Advocacy

Similarly, the nature of independent expenditures has also changed. Some groups have long used the unlimited independent expenditures allowed under the *Buckley* decision, but the recent surge in election issue advocacy, which avoids the FEC disclosure constraint, can be mostly attributed to organized labor's $35 million in advertising against congressional Republicans in 1996 and the predictable response of the business community in that cycle.[29] Labor's bold move in 1996 may have been prompted by a court ruling that communications by the Christian Action Network in 1992 had not been express advocacy and therefore fell out of the reach of the FECA.[30] In 1996, labor's lead was followed by other groups with obscure names like "Triad" and "The Coalition: Americans Working for Real Change" who also ran ads for and against candidates.[31] The latter group was affiliated with the U.S. Chambers of Commerce.[32]

In 1998 issue advocacy grew and diversified to include more widespread use of mail, telephone, and person-to-person contacts, while still including substantial amounts of television and radio.[33] Here again, organized labor took the lead. These ground war efforts successfully mobilized voters and helped explain why the House Democrats didn't lose seats, despite the long-standing pattern of presidential party House seat losses in midterm elections.[34]

In the 2000 election cycle, issue advocacy continued to grow in importance. Campaigning in 2000 showed greater congruence in issue agendas between party committees and candidates and between allied groups and candidates than in 1998. In this cycle Republicans and allied groups concentrated their messages on Social Security, prescription drug benefits for senior citizens, and education, in part to deny Democrats an advantage on those traditionally Democratic issues. Republicans emphasized taxes and guns more than Democrats, and Democrats emphasized the environment more than Republicans; because of the greater congruence in issue agendas, it became increasingly difficult to distinguish between candidate ads and issue ads funded by parties and interest groups.

The 2000 election cycle also saw new groups involved in issue advocacy. Some Democratic-leaning groups, like the NAACP and Emily's List, had been active as interest groups or in funding campaigns through hard money contributions but in 2000 decided to add issue advocacy to their activities. Most groups already involved in issue advocacy expanded their involvement. On the Republican side, the Republican Majority Issues Committee (RMIC) campaigned for Republicans, and business and pharmaceutical interests funded Citizens for Better Medicare and Americans for Job Security.

527 Organizations: A New Issue Advocacy Tool

Interest groups also had a new issue advocacy tool early in 1999–2000, the "527 Organization," which permitted them to do issue advocacy anonymously, at least until July 2000. Groups that picked this strategy included the NAACP National Voter Fund and the Sierra Club.

Issue Ads in the 2000 Presidential Primaries

The 2000 presidential primaries also provided interest groups with an opportunity not only to influence the choice of both parties' standard bearers but also to influence the campaign agenda. Growing out of their ground war strategy of 1998, organized labor and the teachers' unions mounted a substantial grassroots mobilization for Al Gore, giving special emphasis to the Iowa caucuses and New Hampshire primary.[35] More than 25,000 union households in Iowa, for example, received a videotape cassette with an endorsement of Vice President Gore by AFL-CIO President John Sweeny, followed by excerpts from a Gore speech to labor leaders.[36] In the primaries, John McCain was a lightning rod for issue advocacy attacks in New Hampshire and South Carolina by groups critical of his stand on campaign finance reform, his support for fetal tissue research, and his support of an increased tobacco tax. The attacks in New Hampshire did not hurt McCain and may have backfired, but in South Carolina they helped George W. Bush.[37] Some groups used the primaries to launch attacks on the leading contender in the other party, and others sat out the primaries and saved their resources for the general election.[38] The political parties, in part because there was no incumbent running, chose not to invest soft money in the primaries.

COSTS OF OUTSIDE CAMPAIGNS

Just as parties and interest groups realized that they had to intervene earlier in the elections, they also realized that their money could make more of a difference depending on what media markets they invested it in. The 2000 elections saw extreme variations in media costs. Media market prices vary dramatically; competitive contests in inexpensive media markets provide an even heavier draw for soft money and election issue advocacy, because parties and groups can get more for their money in these states. Montana in 2000 and Nevada in 1998 provide good examples of this. Lisa Wade of the League of Conservation Voters has said, "Montana was a cheap media market, so you got lots of value for your money,"[39] and one Montana newspaper even editorialized on the extent of outside advertising in the Senate race: "For better or worse, Montana has become a national political battleground and always will be. The reason is simple. A Senate seat can be purchased cheap in Montana."[40] Data we collected from television stations show a substantial variation in the costs per ad across districts. On average, the least expensive broadcast spots were in Montana ($121 per spot) and the most expensive in California ($3,269 per spot). In contrast, ads never exceeded $500 per spot in Kentucky and Arkansas, and Oklahoma only saw ads exceed $500 per spot during the week of 24–30 September. But average costs per spot climbed to $2,270 in New Jersey, $1,934 in Illinois, and $1,642 in Washington.[41]

Unlike candidate campaigns, political parties and interest groups are not eligible for the lowest unit rate for broadcast advertising in a given time slot (prime time, late night, etc.). As expected, candidates in our races got lower rates. On average, candidates spent $694 per broadcast TV spot, compared to $953 for political parties and $924 for interest groups.[42] In 2000, as in 1998, some stations charged double their normal rates for soft money funded ads and issue ads, especially those purchased late in the campaign. Figure 1.2 plots cost per spot for ads in our races over time and exhibits a substantial increase in cost per spot as the election approaches, with a sharper increase in late October. During the week of 1–7 October, the cost per spot was about $700, but by the last week before the election (29 October–4 November) it had peaked to $1,200.

More typically, if groups sought to run ads late in the campaign, they were shut out entirely with no time available for purchase at any price. Deanna White of the Sierra Club reported that her organization bought time in Oregon just before the election; when they went back two days later, the cost for the same time had tripled.[43]

In 2000, however, the concern about differences in cost was eased by the relatively few competitive races overall. The parties and interest groups could invest with less concern about investment efficiency. Looking ahead to 2002, when there will be more competitive races than in 1998 or 2000, this variable may be more important in the allocation of outside money by parties and interest groups.

DATA AND METHODOLOGY

The 2000 general election research reported here builds on a 1998 project in which we monitored twelve U.S. House contests and four U.S. Senate races. A report summarizing the 1998 project is available on the Web;[44] selected cases from that report were published in *Outside Money: Soft Money and Issue Advocacy in the 1998 Congressional Elections.*[45]

Our research design is based on three assumptions confirmed in our 1998 study. First, outside money is most likely to be spent in competitive races; thus, we

Figure 1.2. Dollars per Broadcast Television Spot

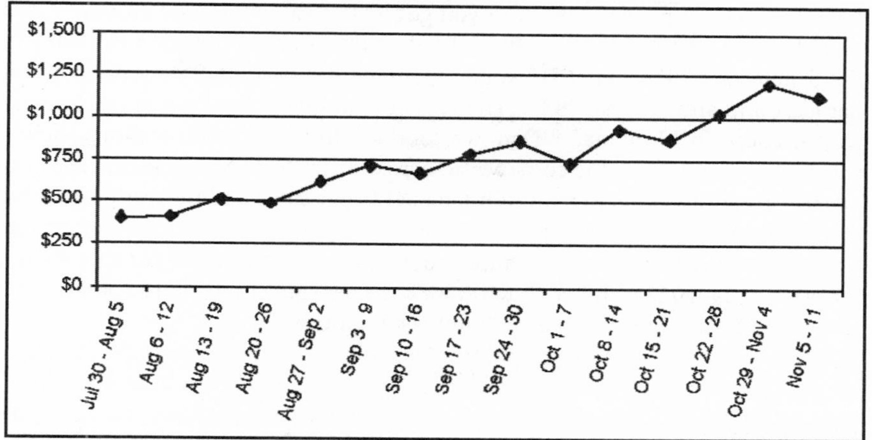

Source: Election *Advocacy* database, February 2001.
Note: See appendix B for a more detailed explanation of the data.

did not have to look at all elections to observe this activity. We observed campaign activity in seventeen of the most competitive congressional contests in 2000. Second, to understand the full impact and reach of outside money activity, we recruited academics in the competitive races, who, as knowledgeable observers, carefully monitored the campaign from the local vantage point. The academics oversaw the collection of campaign mail from the race as well as data from telephone and personal contacts by various groups and parties. The academics also gathered as much information as possible on election related advertising from the local broadcast stations.

Selection of Sample Races

The sample of races we monitored was developed based on lists of competitive races published by *The Cook Political Report*, *The Rothenberg Political Report*, and the American Enterprise Institute's *Election Watch* newsletter. This sample was circulated on a periodic basis to a panel of reporters from *Congressional Quarterly Weekly Report*, party and PAC professionals, and other political experts who helped identify the contests in which outside money was most likely to be spent and to be important.[46] Some effort was made to stratify the sample so we would have a mix of incumbent and open-seat races and a mix of Democratic and Republican contests, which would permit us to tap into a wide variety of interest group and party strategies. All but two of the contests were rated by one or more of the prognosticators as "toss-ups," meaning that the race did not lean toward one party or the other.[47] Table 1.2 presents the sample of contests we studied.

Table 1.2. Sample U.S. House and Senate Races, 2000

	Democrat	*Republican*
Senate Race		
Michigan Senate	Debbie Stabenow	*Spencer Abraham*
Missouri Senate	Mel Carnahan	*John Ashcroft*
Montana Senate	Brian Schweitzer	*Conrad Burns*
Virginia Senate	*Charles Robb*	George Allen
Delaware Senate	Tom Carper	*William Roth*
House Race		
Arkansas 4	Mike Ross	*Jay Dickey*
California 27	Adam Schiff	*Jim Rogan*
Connecticut 5	*James Maloney*	Mark Nielson
Illinois 10	Lauren Beth Gash	Mark Kirk*
Kentucky 6	Scotty Baesler	*Ernie Fletcher*
Michigan 8	Dianne Byrum*	Mike Rogers
Montana At Large	Nancy Keenan	Dennis Rehberg*
New Jersey 12	*Rush Holt*	Dick Zimmer
Oklahoma 2	Brad Carson	Andy Ewing*
Pennsylvania 4	Terry Van Horne*	Melissa Hart
Pennsylvania 13	*Joseph Hoeffel*	Stewart Greenleaf
Washington 2	Rick Larsen	John Koster*

Notes: See appendix B for a more detailed explanation of the data. Names in italics are incumbents. Seats with no incumbents are open. The party that held the seat going into the election is indicated by an asterisk.

The Academics

The academics who conducted the field research and wrote the case studies in this report were generally recruited in the summer of 2000. In the case of the Missouri Senate race, academics also monitored the Missouri presidential primary; hence, they monitored Missouri campaign activity for roughly one year. Where possible, we recruited academics who had an interest in campaign finance or electoral politics. All of the participating academics were well connected with political elites in the district or state and had reputations for sound scholarship.

All participating academics were provided with detailed training documents, including information on the intent of the study, a brief review of the literature on soft money and issue advocacy, a detailed description of the methodology of this study, detailed instructions on how to monitor the air war and ground war in their races, and a resource list.[48] Most scholars participating in the study also attended a training session. These sessions included information on data entry into a secure Web site and data collection suggestions for broadcast stations.

Interviews

We encouraged the academics studying each of the races to regularly interview political reporters, campaign staff, and party professionals to learn about party and interest group campaign activities. We sought good working relations with the campaign staff of all major party candidates; we have found that party and campaign staffs are sometimes willing to share information about what the opposition is doing in real time and what their own campaign did after Election Day. Our researchers were often placed on campaign press release fax lists. We also identified consultants for the candidates, parties, and interest groups and attempted to contact them after the election.

In both 1998 and 2000, both during and soon after the campaign, we interviewed a wide range of party and interest group professionals, who were generally forthcoming. In the weeks after the election, we conducted a series of largely in-person interviews in Washington, D.C., with the senior staff of all four congressional campaign committees, leaders of the interest groups most involved in our races, and other knowledgeable observers of the election. A list of these interviews is included as Appendix A.

Our methodology emphasized the collection of as many campaign-related communications as possible. To do this we urged the academics to build a reconnaissance team throughout the state or district to help monitor the mail, telephone, and interpersonal forms of political communication. This team could include colleagues, university or college alumni, political reporters, consultants, friends, neighbors, and a diverse set of politically connected people. In addition, we provided each academic with mailing labels of Common Cause members in their states or districts. In most of our sample contests, we also had the cooperation of members of the League of Women Voters, who either provided lists or communicated directly with their members.[49] Brigham Young University alumni in all of the contests were also asked to collect and send their political mail and to report personal or telephone contacts during the campaign.

Broadcast Data

As in our 1998 research, in 2000 we secured the cooperation of some broadcast stations that shared not only their logs of all political ads but also the times the spots ran and the amounts charged. The vast majority of stations, however, provided only the minimal information required by law in their public files on "controversial issues of public importance."[50] In a few instances stations were unwilling to provide any information, claiming that issue advocacy did not fall under the regulatory requirement of even minimal disclosure. In other cases records were unorganized or nonexistent.[51]

To gather data on broadcast issue advocacy, our research builds on the monitoring done by the Annenberg Center, which has provided summaries of groups doing television issue advocacy in the largest media markets since 1996.[52] We also incorporated data from a media monitoring service, the Campaign Media Analysis Group (CMAG),[53] which uses technology that records the full audio and every four seconds of video, producing a storyboard of every commercial run in the top seventy-five media markets in the United States. The storyboards, along with the exact time, date, location, and television station for each instance the commercial is aired, are then compiled and coded; they include estimates of the cost and gross ratings points for each ad each time it appeared.[54] Our races were in eighteen of the CMAG markets (listed in table 1.3). We use the CMAG data to help fill in the gaps where stations reported minimal information and as a point of comparison to the data we collected.

Limitations

We realize that we are attempting to study behavior that some groups and individuals want to leave undisclosed. Although we are pleased with the high level of cooperation received from all national party committees, most candidates, most state party committees, and most interest groups, some refused to cooperate or be interviewed. Noteworthy is the unwillingness of National Right to Life, Emily's List, Republican Majority Issues Committee, AFSCME, and the NAACP National Voter Fund to be interviewed. The level of cooperation from some radio and television stations was also occasionally a problem.

The campaign finance legislation enacted by Congress and signed into law by President Clinton in July helped us monitor 527 organizations more systematically. But because many of them had raised their war chests before the legislation was signed, it will probably never be known where their money came from. And while our coverage of the ground war was not perfect, based on post-election interviews we are confident that we have a great deal of it. When we combine our monitoring of television stations with the CMAG data, we have the most complete coverage of television available.[55] The research reported here is the largest

Table 1.3. Media Markets Monitored by Campaign Media Analysis Group in Our Sample Races

Race	Media Market
Arkansas 4	Little Rock
California 27	Los Angeles
Connecticut 5	Hartford, Conn. and New York, N.Y.
Delaware Senate	Philadelphia
Illinois 10	Chicago
Michigan 8	Detroit, Flint
Michigan Senate	Detroit, Flint, Grand Rapids
Missouri Senate	Kansas City, Mo. & St. Louis, Mo.
New Jersey 12	New York, N.Y. and Philadelphia
Oklahoma 2	Tulsa
Pennsylvania 4	Harrisburg & Pittsburgh
Pennsylvania 13	Philadelphia
Virginia Senate	Norfolk, Richmond, Roanoke, and Washington, D.C.
Washington 2	Seattle

Source: Campaign Media Analysis Group databases.

systematic effort to gather data on all fronts of campaign communications in modern campaigns.

Radio remains difficult to monitor, and our data are therefore spotty. This is due to the difficulty of monitoring the large number of stations within any one market and the lack of careful record keeping by some stations.

We recognize that our interpersonal and telephone contact data are also incomplete. The difficulty of gathering and analyzing all these political communications only reinforced our shared view that they are substantial and need to be understood, particularly because noncandidate campaign communications were important to the outcome of several of these races. Our interviews with political professionals also reinforced the view that the full range of communications is important in competitive races.

The task of gathering data on all forms of campaign communications is labor intensive, but recent election cycles demonstrate that in the absence of a thoroughgoing data retrieval effort, students of elections would likely miss much of the campaign going on around them. Academics participating in the 1998 and 2000 congressional projects, as well as in the contested 2000 presidential primaries, were uniformly surprised by the level of outside money activity, and often by its intensity. Field research like that reported in this volume is also of importance to policy makers, because legislation and litigation in these areas should be based on more than speculation about the nature and amount of different modes of campaigning. Hopefully this research will be of value in both the scholarly and policy worlds.

PLAN FOR THE BOOK

We begin the book by examining the most significant development in 2000 congressional elections: the surge in party soft money spending by the congressional campaign committees, especially by the Democrats. Chapter 2 explores this soft money surge in competitive races in 2000 and its implications for the candidates, for the role of congressional campaign committees, and for efforts to reform campaign finance. Eric Smith and I demonstrate that the Democrats had a substantial party money advantage in competitive Senate races in 2000, a major factor in their picking up a net gain of four seats. While House Republicans continued to raise and spend more than House Democrats, the Democrats closed the gap and raised record-setting amounts of soft money for their committee. The chapter also discusses the strategic importance of party spending in competitive races, including decisions on whether to invest in competitive primaries. Although party committees may now freely engage in independent expenditures, they have opted to invest more in a soft money strategy.

In chapter 3 Anna Nibley Baker and I explore the role of interest groups in election issue advocacy in 2000 congressional elections. We begin by reviewing the conventional role of interest groups in making hard money contributions, typically from PACs. In competitive races, interest groups now exploit the issue advocacy loophole to invest much more. How groups communicate, where they allocate their issue advocacy resources, and what impact election issue advocacy has on congressional races are major themes. In chapter 3, as in chapter 2, we discuss the ground war of mail, telephone, and personal contact, which has become such a large part of outside money campaigning.

Some interest groups have long campaigned independently in congressional races, expressly advocating the election or defeat of candidates. In chapter 4 Jason Beal and I assess which groups continue to campaign via independent expenditures in the new world of issue advocacy, permitting these groups greater anonymity. Chapter 4 also examines the often unexplored world of interest group internal communications, some of which are disclosed to the FEC.

Having provided an overview of outside money in competitive 2000 congressional races, we turn to a series of case studies of outside money spending in U.S. Senate and U.S. House elections in 2000. We begin with the Michigan Senate race, a battle between incumbent Spence Abraham and challenger Debbie Stabenow. In chapter 5, political scientist Michael Traugott concludes that "outside money made the difference in this race" and discusses why.

The most vulnerable Democratic Senate incumbent in 2000 was Virginia's Chuck Robb. Despite his incumbency, Robb fell behind early on and never caught back up to his challenger, George Allen. However, a concerted effort by interest groups and the Democratic Senatorial Campaign Committee late in the campaign made the race competitive. A team of respected Virginia political scientists, Harry Wilson, Stephen Medvic, Robert Holsworth, Scott Keeter, and Robert Dudley, summarize this race in chapter 6.

Montana was a state with heavy outside money in statewide races for the U.S. Senate and U.S. House. Craig Wilson describes both races in chapter 7 and assesses the impact of outside money as well as the cumulative impact of so much campaigning in a state with limited but inexpensive media markets.

In addition to Montana's at large contest (included in Wilson's chapter), a list of U.S. House races that had substantial outside money investments would have to begin with California's Twenty-seventh Congressional District contest, which saw candidate and outside money spending in excess of $19 million. In chapter 8 David Menefee-Libey and Drew Linzer discuss the impact of so much spending and the creative ways in which outside groups, including the parties, spent their money.

The closest House race in 2000 was in Michigan's Eighth District, decided by only 160 votes (111 after a recount).[56] This contest competed for airtime and voter attention with an intensely fought U.S. Senate race (chapter 5) and a well-funded ballot initiative in a presidential battleground state. Given all this "noise," how did the parties and outside groups compete? Journalism Professors Sue Carter and Eric Freedman provide us with an insightful case study on this race in chapter 9.

Another very close congressional contest was New Jersey Twelve. In this race, as in California Two, candidates and groups decided to run ads in their respective media markets, even though the ad was only relevant to a small fraction of the total media market audience. In New Jersey Twelve we also have an example of party ads becoming a liability to the intended beneficiary because of inaccuracies, an occurrence that was not limited to this race. Adam Berinsky and Sue Lederman observed the race and wrote chapter 10.

With Ron Klink seeking the Pennsylvania Senate seat, the Fourth Congressional District became an open seat. The Democratic Congressional Campaign Committee broke with tradition and spent money on behalf of one candidate in the primary, a strategy intended to maximize the party's chances of holding the seat. The endorsed candidate lost the primary, and the victorious candidate was immediately attacked by the Republican Congressional Campaign Committee for past racist remarks. This early involvement by the parties, as well as the extraordinary success of Republican candidate Melissa Hart in gathering outside group support, are important themes of chapter 11, written by Christopher Jan Carman and David Barker.

Our final case study in this volume describes a race in which there was extraordinary ground war activity. In the week before the election, voters in Washington's Second Congressional District received an estimated twelve pieces of mail per day.[57] Todd Donovan describes in chapter 12 how the DCCC and allied groups outperformed the NRCC and its allies, helping Democrat Rick Larsen win the race.

Chapter 13 summarizes our overall findings and the implications of our research. It contrasts the strategies of parties in 1998 and 2000, the different dynamics of a presidential and midterm year, the role of congressional campaign committee leadership, and the effects of outside money on Congress and elections.

With every branch of the federal government and some state legislatures hanging in the balance, groups, parties, and candidates shared a common objective: election victory for their team and defeat of the opposition. Soft money and issue advocacy from groups and parties, including 527 organizations, became an important means to that end.

Election issue advocacy was an important part of the 2000 congressional election story, but even more important was party soft money activity. Party activity in competitive congressional elections is the focus of the next chapter.

NOTES

1. See Martin Wattenberg, *The Rise of Candidate-Centered Politics: Presidential Elections of the 1980's* (Cambridge, Mass.: Harvard University Press, 1991) and Morris P. Fiorina, *Congress, Keystone of the Washington Establishment* (New Haven, Conn.: Yale University Press, 1989).

2. Ian Stirton et al., "PAC Activity Increases in 2000 Election Cycle," <www.fec.gov/press/053101pacfund/053101pacfund.html> 31 May 2001 [accessed 6 August 2001].

3. Common Cause, "Soft Money Donor Profiles," <www.commoncause.org/laundromat/stat/top50.htm>, 7August 2001 [accessed 13 August 2001].

4. Money not reported to the FEC, because it is spent on issue advocacy by interest groups, is sometimes called soft money. However, in this report we use the term only with respect to the political parties. See Federal Elections Commission, "National Party Nonfederal Activity through the Complete Two Year Cycle," <www.fec.gov/press/051501partyfund/tables/nonfedsumm2000.html>, 15 May 2001, [accessed 6 August 2001].

5. See John M. Broder, "Democrats Able to Circumvent Donation Limit," *New York Times,* 12 December 1999, A1; and Alexander Bolton, "Senate Races Exploit Soft Money Loopholes," *The Hill,* 27 September 2000, 6.

6. Paul S. Herrnson and Kelly D. Patterson, "Financing the 2000 Congressional Elections," in *Financing the 2000 Election,* ed. David B. Magleby (Washington, D.C.: Brookings Institute Press, forthcoming).

7. Darrell M. West, *Air Wars: Television Advertising in Election Campaigns 1952–1996,* 2d ed. (Washington, D.C.: Congressional Quarterly Inc., 1997), 189.

8. *Buckley v. Valeo,* 424 U.S. 1 (1976), n.52.

9. David B. Magleby, ed., "Dictum Without Data: The Myth of Issue Advocacy and Party Building," report presented at the National Press Club, Washington, D.C., <www.byu.edu/outsidemoney/dictum>, November 2000 [accessed 1 February 2001].

10. Dick Morris, *Behind the Oval Office: Getting Reelected Against All Odds* (Los Angeles: Renaissance Books, 1999), 141.

11. Annenberg Public Policy Center, "Issue Advertising in the 1999–2000 Election Cycle," <www.appcpenn.org/political/issueads/1999-2000issueadvocacy.pdf> [accessed 6 August 2001].

12. Marianne Holt, interview by author, Washington, D.C., 25 July 2001.

13. Compiled from FEC data. See Federal Elections Commission, "Campaign Finance Reports and Data," <www.fec.gov>, 31 July 2001 [accessed 6 August 2001].

14. Ibid.

15. FEC, "Campaign Finance Reports and Data."

16. Ibid.

17. Although the U.S. Supreme Court did not stand for election in 2000, the future composition of the court was a frequent topic of issue advocacy. People for the American Way made it a major emphasis with its "It's the Supreme Court, Stupid!" theme. Other groups that used the court as a theme in election issue ads were Christian Coalition, Citizens for Sound Economy, Human Rights Campaign, Hunting and Shooting Sports Heritage Foundation, NARAL, and Planned Parenthood.

18. See chapter 8 for more information about California's Twenty-seventh Congressional District race; Michael Nelson, ed., *The Elections of 2000* (Washington, D.C.: CQ Press, 2001), 196 ; and "Homepage of the American Political Science Association, <www.apsanet.org/PS/june01/linzer.cfm>, 1 June 2001 [accessed 7 August 2001].

19. Ian Stirton et al., "FEC Reports on Congressional Financial Activity for 2000," press release, 15 May 2001.

20. David Espo, "For Gephardt, the Goal Is a Democratic Majority in the House," *Los Angeles Times,* 4 November 2000.

21. Linda Lipson, Trial Lawyers Association, interview by author, Washington, D.C., 13 December 2000.

22. "2000 House Summary," *The Cook Political Report* (23 June 2000): 43–45.

23. Karin Johanson, Democratic Congressional Campaign Committee (DCCC), interview by author, Washington, D.C., 20 November 2000.

24. Bernadette Budde, Business-Industry Political Action Committee (BIPAC), interview by author, Washington, D.C., 10 November 2000.

25. Magleby, "Dictum Without Data."

26. See David B. Magleby, "Interest-Group Election Ads," in *Outside Money: Soft Money and Issue Advocacy in the 1998 Congressional Elections,* ed. David B. Magleby (Lanham, Md.: Rowman & Littlefield, 2000), 49; David B. Magleby, "Outside Money in the 2000 Presidential Primaries and Congressional General Elections," in "Outside Money," ed. David B. Magleby, *PS: eSymposium,* <www.apsa.com/PS/june01/magleby.cfm>, June 2001 [accessed June 2001].

27. See chapter 9.

28. David B. Magleby, ed., *Financing the 2000 Election* (Washington, D.C.: Brookings Institute Press, forthcoming).

29. Magleby, *Outside Money.*

30. *F.E.C. v. Christian Action Network,* 110 F.3d 1049, 1057 (1997). Kenneth P. Mayer, *Issue Advocacy in Wisconsin: Analysis of the 1998 Elections and a Proposal for Enhanced Disclosure* (Madison: University of Wisconsin-Madison, Department of Political Science, September 1999), 7–9; West, *Air Wars,* 189–190.

31. Diana Dwyre, "Interest Groups and Issue Advocacy in 1996," in *Financing the 1996 Election,* ed. John C. Green (Armonk, N.Y.: M.E. Sharpe, 1999).

32. West, *Air Wars,* 191.

33. Magleby, *Outside Money.* The complete set of case studies can be found at <www.byu.edu/outsidemoney/1998>. Election issue advocacy was also a part of the 2000 presidential primaries, especially in the South Carolina Republican primary. See David B. Magleby, ed., "Getting Inside the Outside Campaign: Issue Advocacy in the 2000 Presidential Primaries," report presented at the National Press Club, Washington, D.C., 7 July 2000. This report is also available on the Web at <www.byu.edu/outsidemoney>.

34. Ibid.

35. Magleby, "Getting Inside the Outside Campaign," 4; and Magleby, "Outside Money."

36. Arthur Sanders and David Redlawsk, "Money and the Iowa Caucuses," in "Outside Money," ed. Magleby.

37. Linda Fowler, Constantine Spiliotes, and Lyn Vavrek, "The Role of Issue Advocacy Groups in the New Hampshire Primary" and Bill Moore and Danielle Vinson, "The South Carolina Republican Primary," in "Outside Money," ed. Magleby.

38. The Sierra Club attacked Bush's environmental record early in the primary season, a theme that Bush supporters hiding behind an innocuous name, Republicans for Clean Air, ran during the New York, California, and Ohio primaries. National Abortion and Reproductive Rights Action League also attacked Bush early, claiming he was a threat to choice on the abortion issue. To a much lesser extent Republican-allied groups attacked Gore. See David Magleby, "Outside Money in the 2000 Congressional Elections and Presidential Primaries," in "Outside Money," ed. Magleby.

39. Lisa Wade, League of Conservation Voters (LCV), interview by author, Washington, D.C., 13 November 2000.

40. See chapter 7.

41. Average costs of spots on cable television were much lower, ranging from $12 in Oklahoma to $60 in Virginia; Illinois, California, Washington, and Connecticut. Cable also fell within that range. Information from Center for the Study of Elections and Democracy Database.

42. The Campaign Media Analysis Group (CMAG) data from our races estimate candidates in our Senate races spent the most per Gross Rating Point, as well as per spot. CMAG, instead of using actual dollars spent, estimates the cost of the spots using the average cost of spots across stations and time slots in a particular market. CMAG admits that they miss the last-minute inflation of television prices near election time. They also fail to collect data on cable and do not account for candidates getting preferred or "lowest unit" rates. See Jonathan S. Krasno and Daniel E. Seltz, *Buying Time: Television Advertising in the 1998 Congressional Elections*,(New York: Brennan Center for Justice, NYU Law School, 2000), 197.

43. Deanna White, Sierra Club, interview by author, Washington, D.C., 14 December 2000.

44. This report was presented at the National Press Club in Washington, D.C., in February 1999. See David B. Magleby and Marianne Holt, eds., "Outside Money: Soft Money and Issue Advocacy in the 1998 Congressional Elections," <www.byu.edu/outsidemoney/1998> [accessed 6 August 2001].

45. Magleby, *Outside Money.*

46. We acknowledge the assistance of Karen Ackerman, Bob Benenson, Suzanne Bogherty, Bernedette Budde, Tom Cole, Charlie Cook, Saundra Dasu, Jeff Girouix, John Guzik, Dave Hansen, Jim Jordan, Karin Johanson, Barbara Murray, Emily Pierce, Stuart Rothenberg, and Derrick Willis.

47. Different prognosticators use slightly different terms. *The Cook Political Report* rates races in one of seven different categories: "Solid Democrat," "Solid Republican," "Likely Democrat," "Likely Republican," "Leaning Democrat," "Leaning Republican," and "Toss-Up." *The Rothenberg Political Report* uses the following categories: "Democrat/Republican Favored," "Tilt Democrat/Tilt Republican," or "Toss-Up."

48. They were also provided with copies of *Outside Money*, the edited book from our 1998 project, and the reports from the 1998 and 2000 presidential primary study.

49. We acknowledge the assistance of Ed Davis and Laura Williams at Common Cause, and Lloyd Leonard and Betsy Lawson at the League of Women Voters.

50. We are grateful for the advice provided by Bobby Baker and Hope Cooper at the Federal Communications Commission.

51. In Pennsylvania Thirteen there was not a good paper trail because Congressman Hoeffel's local buyer simply called the station manager to request more spots.

52. The Annenberg Center's reports on issue advocacy are available at <www.appcpenn.org/political/issueads>.

53. Professor Ken Goldstein of the University of Wisconsin, Madison, who has overseen the coding of political commercials in the 1998 and 2000 cycles, graciously shared his codes of the CMAG 2000 data.

54. Krasno and Seltz, *Buying Time.*

55. One of the difficulties with ad buy data is determining the content of the ads. The parties or interest groups that purchased the ad buy could have run ads promoting presidential candidates, other House or Senatorial candidates within that media market, or even ballot propositions. Unless the participating academics were able to determine the exact

content of the ad buy from the limited information given by the station, our data may contain some observations that do not pertain to the relevant House or Senate races. CMAG theoretically helps combat this problem by using a basic code to categorize the commercials that are played within the monitored markets. However, some inconsistencies can arise when using a basic code, or a "cookie cutter" method, to categorize commercials across multiple markets. Commercials may have nearly identical content, changing only the candidate's name, race, or tagline. In some instances with interest group or party ads, the technology employed by CMAG will categorize near-identical commercials as the same ad, even if shown in markets in different states for different candidates. The question becomes whether the market, the candidate coded into the entry, or the sponsoring group is correct. In using the CMAG data, we assumed the market and sponsoring group were coded correctly and the name of the candidate was coded incorrectly due to the cookie cutter problem.

56. See chapter 9.

57. See chapter 12.

2

Party Soft Money in the 2000 Congressional Elections

David B. Magleby and Eric A. Smith

A frequent refrain in political science is the weakness of the party system in the United States compared to many other democracies. Proponents of the weak party argument say that voters, rather than party elites, control nominations; candidates, more than parties, dominate campaign agendas and raise and spend their own campaign money; party identification is less important to voting choice; and parties are only one of many cues to legislators when making voting decisions in Congress.[1]

Despite these arguments, U.S. parties are still important institutions because they help orient voters in general elections, help recruit candidates to run for office, provide training for candidates, and channel soft money into the fray in competitive races. Some have cited the growth in the number of Independents as a sign of weakened parties. However, two-thirds of Independents are in fact closet partisans, whose party leanings strongly predict their voting behavior.[2] Party is an important "cue" for legislators as well. In recent years, party-line voting in Congress has been high by historic standards.[3]

Although parties are important in determining legislative behavior and remain a strong predictor of voting behavior, our electoral system remains largely candidate centered. As new and more expensive campaign technologies have developed, including the broadcast media, pollsters, and the use of computers in campaigning, candidates have continued to build their own electoral organization of professional staff consultants, contributors, and advisors. Although many consultants have a background that includes work for their parties, their orientation has been much more toward candidates.[4] This professionalism has resulted in candidate campaigns that are largely independent of parties, and these candidate-centered campaigns are reinforced by the fact that a vast majority of incumbents win easily or that in many open-seat races, the district's demography makes the district a safe seat for one party.

These regularities hold for most congressional elections, but the role of political parties has expanded dramatically in the most competitive contests. This trend of greater party influence, especially in the election cycles from 1996 to 2000, has been largely driven by soft money. *Soft money* is the term frequently applied to funds raised by the parties that are not subject to the same contribution and expenditure limitations as money raised by the parties for electioneering purposes. In 1979, Congress recognized the parties' right to support their candidates and strengthen party infrastructure. The Federal Election Campaign Act (FECA) was amended to permit party committees to fund some generic party activities with hard dollars (subject to the contribution limits of FECA). These expenditures were not counted toward any candidate's party contribution or coordinated expenditure limits and were therefore labeled by the FEC as nonfederal money.[5] In a series of Federal Election Commission (FEC) advisory opinions, the ability of parties to use nonfederal or soft money was expanded. Donations to the parties for nonfederal or soft money accounts are now disclosed but unlimited. As we demonstrate in this book, soft money spending may have been the most important factor in several competitive 2000 elections.

Over the past twenty years, the growth in soft money spending has been immense. During the 1980 election cycle, Republican Party committees used soft money for the first time. Overall in 1980, the parties raised and spent an estimated $19 million in soft money.[6] But these figures pale in comparison to party soft money spending in 1996, 1998, and 2000 (see figure 2.1). A number of developments in soft money spending made the 2000 cycle particularly unique. Those developments included an open-seat race for the presidency, party control of both houses of Congress up for grabs, and the fact that the parties and interest groups and individuals had learned in 1996 and 1998 that soft money can be effectively used to campaign for and against particular candidates. Furthermore, for the first time since the advent of soft money, when all party committees' soft money receipts were combined, the Democrats achieved parity with the Republicans.

Has the dramatic increase in soft money in 2000 resulted in stronger political parties? To the extent that soft money is spent on party building—voter lists, voter registration, candidate recruitment, and generic party communication—the parties may reap a lasting benefit from soft money. If, however, the parties are merely bank accounts into which wealthy donors can deposit large checks with the intent of funding campaign communications for or against particular candidates, then soft money reinforces the candidate-centered nature of parties, or as Barbara Salmore and Stephen Salmore argue, "Party activity merely subsidizes candidate-centered campaigns."[7]

This chapter examines the development of soft money, its role in the 2000 congressional elections, and the relative amount of power it has offered to the parties. We must first examine certain questions to lay the groundwork: What is hard money, and how do partisans use it? How did soft money come about, and how is it used? To what extent has it grown? How did soft money affect the 2000 elec-

Figure 2.1. Soft Money (Nonfederal) Activity

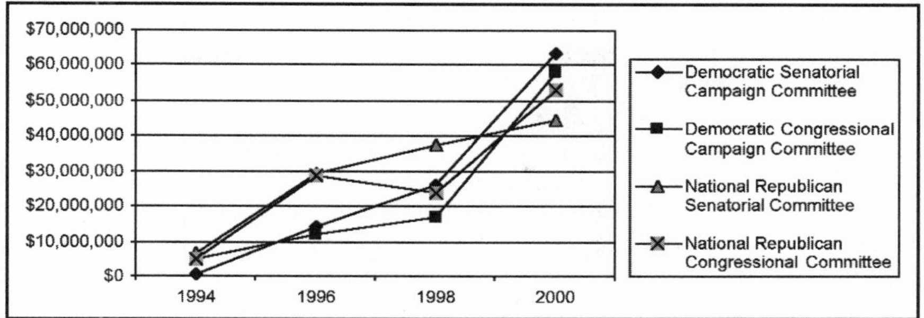

Source: Federal Election Commission, "National Party Non-federal Activity through the Complete Two Year Election Cycle," press release, <www.fec.gov/press/051501partyfund/tables/nonfedsumm2000.html>, 15 May 2001 [accessed 23 August 2001].

tions, and how did the Democrats finally emerge from under the Republicans' long soft money shadow? Why was soft money so important in 2000 that Jim Jordan, the political director of the Democratic Senatorial Campaign Committee, called it the "key" to the 1999–2000 cycle?[8] Has the soft money explosion positively or negatively affected the campaign environment and party organization? If limits on soft money are not enacted or are unconstitutional, what is the likely future of soft money in congressional elections?

HARD MONEY

The 1974 Federal Election Campaign Act (FECA) allows political parties to raise hard money, or federal funds, for limited involvement in federal campaign activity. Parties can contribute this money directly to candidates; spend it in coordination with the candidate campaigns; or, as recently interpreted by the U.S. Supreme Court, use it to engage in independent expenditures (see chapter 4 for more details).[9] Compared to other party hard money activity, independent expenditures were not as prevalent in 2000. Republicans spent $1.6 million in independent expenditures, and Democrats spent nearly $2.3 million.[10] Hard money is difficult to raise in large quantities, because contributions from individuals and political action committees (PACs) to parties for these election-related purposes are subject to static and comparatively low federal limits. Furthermore, all hard money activity must be fully disclosed to the FEC. Table 2.1 provides the hard money contribution limits for individuals, parties, and PACs.

It is important to note that for the candidate there is no aggregate hard money limit on receipts from individuals or PACs. If candidates want to raise more hard money, they can either get more contributors to give the maximum allowable or

Table 2.1. Federal (Hard Money) Contribution Limits

Donors	*Recipients*				*Special Limits*
	Candidate (or candidate committee)	Political action committee (multicandidate PAC[a])	State or local political party (party committee	National Political Party (party committee)	
Individual (or partnership)	$1,000 per election[b]	$5,000 per calendar year	$5,000 per calendar year[c] (combined limit on contributions to all state and local parties)	$20,000 per calendar year[c]	$25,000 per calendar year (combined limit on contributions to all candidates, PACs, and parties
National Political Party[c]	$5,000 per election[b]	$5,000 per calendar year	unlimited "transfers" to other party committees		$17,500 to a U.S. Senate candidate per campaign
State or Local Political Party (party committee)	$5,000 per election (combined limit on contributions to all candidates)	$5,000 per calendar year (combined limit on contributions to all PACs)	unlimited "transfers" to other party committees		—
Political Action Committee (multicandidate PAC[a])	$5,000 per election[b]	$5,000 per calendar year	$5,000 per calendar year[c] (combined limit on contributions to all state and local parties)	$15,000 per calendar year[c]	—
Corporations and Labor Unions	Prohibited	Prohibited	Unlimited by federal law provided money used or noncandidate specific activities[d] (see also footnote c below)		—

Source: Anthony Corrado, *Beyond the Basics: Campaign Finance Reform* (New York: The Century Foundation Press, 2000), 16.

[a]Most business, labor, and ideological/issue PACs are "multicandidate" committees under federal law, which means they have been registered for at least six months, have at least fifty contributors, and have made contributions to at least five federal candidates. Non-multicandidate committees are subject to the same contribution limits as individuals.

[b]Each primary and general election counts as a separate election.

[c]This limit applies only to money used to support or oppose federal candidates. There are no federal limits on money that individuals and PACs can give to political parties for noncandidate-specific "party building" activities such as issue advocacy, voter registration, and get-out-the-vote drives. Money used for these nonfederally regulated purposes is called "soft money."

[d]Some states impose their own limits on contributions to state and local parties, regardless of how the money is used.

[e]Includes U.S. Senate and House of Representative campaign committees, as well as parties' national committees, each of which may contribute $5,000 to a candidate or PAC.

get more individuals or PACs to give to their campaign. However, candidates have only one party from which to receive limited hard money contributions. Therefore, parties in the aggregate are much less important to candidate finance than individuals and PACs.

The Republicans have consistently led in hard money receipts. Their hard money advantage stems in part from their more effective small donor and direct mail fundraising efforts, dating back to the late 1970s when they embarked on their first successful direct mail fundraising campaign.[11] Table 2.2 shows the hard money receipts for the four congressional campaign committees and the state and local committees in each party.

The GOP advantage in hard money continued in the 1999–2000 election cycle as the Republicans outraised the Democrats $465.8 million to $275.2 million. Although hard money was not the most important factor in the 2000 elections, these funds continued to increase over past election cycles, and hard money remained an extremely important part of campaign finance. Both the Democratic National Committee (DNC) and the Republican National Committee (RNC) experienced growth in hard money receipts in 2000 as compared to the previous presidential election cycle: DNC receipts climbed more than $15.6 million, and RNC receipts increased by almost $20 million. And, as it has done in the past, the National Republican Congressional Committee (NRCC) led all congressional campaign committees in hard money receipts at over $97 million, up by more than $20 million over the last two election cycles. The NRCC hard money receipts were more than double those of the Democratic Congressional Campaign Committee (DCCC). But there was cause for celebrating at the DCCC, because it set new records in hard money fundraising, exceeding what it had raised in 1998 by more than $20 million. In sum, both

Table 2.2. Hard Money (Federal) Receipts by Party Committees

Committee	*1991–1992*	*1993–1994*	*1995–1996*	*1997–1998*	*1999–2000*
DNC	$ 65,790,724	$ 41,843,770	$108,372,562	$ 64,779,752	$123,997,509
DSCC	$ 25,450,835	$ 26,429,878	$ 30,798,424	$ 35,645,188	$ 40,488,666
DCCC	$ 12,815,844	$ 19,424,492	$ 26,623,493	$ 25,180,286	$ 48,394,476
D S&L	$ 73,652,909	$ 55,572,758	$ 93,194,978	$ 63,354,386	$149,341,257
Total D	**$163,279,568**	**$132,786,892**	**$221,613,028**	**$159,961,869**	**$275,230,680**
RNC	$ 85,447,469	$ 87,392,680	$193,029,129	$104,048,689	$212,798,761
NRSC	$ 73,810,640	$ 65,325,336	$ 64,541,312	$ 53,423,388	$ 51,475,156
NRCC	$ 35,272,672	$ 26,696,951	$ 74,224,879	$ 72,708,311	$ 97,314,513
R S&L	$ 72,768,188	$ 74,974,114	$128,444,139	$ 89,392,101	$176,556,202
Total R	**$264,915,932**	**$244,101,180**	**$416,513,249**	**$285,007,168**	**$465,840,139**

Source: Federal Election Commission, "National Party Financial Activity through the End of the Election Cycle," press release, <www.fec.gov/press/051501partyfund/051501partyfund.html>, 15 May 2001 [accessed 24 August 2001].
Note: Total receipts shown do not include moneys transferred among the listed committees; therefore individual columns do not equal totals shown.

House party committees raised approximately $20 million more in hard money in 1999–2000 than they did in 1997–1998.

Although the general pattern in 1999–2000 was to raise unprecedented amounts of hard money, the National Republican Senatorial Committee (NRSC) actually brought in less hard money receipts than in 1997–1998, continuing a four-cycle slide. Between 1992 and 2000, the NRSC dropped from $73.8 million in hard money receipts to $51.5 million. Reasons for the NRSC's fundraising slippage may include a perception that the more intense competition in 2000 would be for control of the White House and House of Representatives. It may also be that with several incumbents running in competitive races, the party committee was competing with its own candidates for hard money. In contrast, the Democratic Senatorial Campaign Committee (DSCC) raised over $40 million in 1999–2000, a new record high for the committee, up $5 million from 1997–1998.

As discussed in chapter 1, in *Buckley v. Valeo* the Court removed any limitation on individuals or groups spending independently of parties or candidates—what have come to be called *independent expenditures.* In 1996, the Supreme Court opened the same opportunity to the political parties to spend independently. The decision in *Colorado Republican Federal Campaign Committee v. Federal Election Commission* allowed parties to make unlimited independent expenditures for or against a candidate for federal office.[12] For parties, as for individuals and interest groups, independent expenditures have to be paid for using disclosed hard money, which, as we have shown, is more difficult to raise. An additional disadvantage of independent expenditures is that the parties cannot coordinate these expenditures with their candidates and cannot work through friendly and responsive state party committees as they can with soft money.

As Diana Dwyre and Robin Kolodny found in their study of party spending in the 2000 elections, only the DCCC made much use of independent expenditures. As in 1998, the parties instead continued to use their hard dollars to match soft dollars, because they found the requirement that they be "independent" of candidates onerous. Dwyre and Kolodny found that the DCCC independent expenditures of $1.9 million in 1999–2000 were "spent on phone banks averaging $50,000 each in thirty-eight close House races in the last few days before the election."[13] Independent expenditures are well suited for phone banks, because such activity requires no coordination with the candidate. As long as parties have the soft money option, independent expenditures are likely to play a secondary role. But if soft money is banned, independent expenditures could grow dramatically.

ORIGINS AND DEVELOPMENT OF SOFT MONEY

The development of soft money began with the 1976 presidential campaign, the first year in which the presidential elections were publicly funded under the FECA. In that election, the presidential candidate campaigns maximized their limited public allotments on media advertising and dedicated few resources to traditional party activities like grassroots campaign materials, generic party advertisements, bumper stickers, and lawn signs. But the parties did not fund these traditional activities either, because they would have been considered in-kind contributions from the parties to candidates and would have counted toward the limited contributions parties may give candidates.[14]

Party leaders from both parties asked to have the FECA modified, claiming that the new law hurt their ability to increase, inform, and activate party membership. Congress responded by amending the FECA in 1979 to change "the legal definition of contributions and expenditures to exclude 'grass-roots' activities, provided that the funds for those activities were raised in compliance with FECA limits."[15]

The 1979 amendment to the FECA did not apply to expenditures intended to assist any federal office candidates; such expenditures were limited to hard money activity in the form of direct party contributions to candidate campaigns or party/candidate-coordinated expenditures. The expenditures under the amendments were also not to be used on mail or other forms of public advertising. Under the 1979 amendment, contributions remained strictly limited, and party committees were not allowed to accept corporate or labor union treasury funds.

However, when asked to provide advisory opinions arising from FECA amendments, the FEC substantially expanded the ability of party committees to use nonfederal money, or soft money, to conduct candidate electioneering. State parties were allowed to create nonfederal accounts for state and local activities; unions and corporations were permitted to contribute unlimited amounts of money, including treasury funds, to these accounts. When party activities benefited both federal and nonfederal candidates, the states could mix federal and nonfederal moneys based on the ratio of federal and state candidates running in each election. The FEC rulings unintentionally allowed the state party committees to indiscriminately use these unlimited and unregulated nonfederal funds to pay, at least in part, for activities that benefited federal candidates.[16]

Although the FEC rulings were in response to state cases, the national parties argued that they also applied to the national party committees. National party leaders claimed that they too participated in nonfederal activities by providing assistance and contributions to leaders and officials at all party levels and by working with state and local organizations on party-building activities.[17] The FEC agreed and allowed the national party committees to create both federal (hard money) and nonfederal (soft money) accounts. This paved the way for national party committees to raise unlimited soft money from previously illegal sources: corporation and labor union treasuries and individuals who had already maximized their federally regulated contributions to candidates and/or parties.

Soft money was initially spent on nonfederal activities, such as gubernatorial and state races and generic get-out-the-vote (GOTV) drives. However, parties began using soft money in the 1980s to fund any activity they could justify as party building.[18] They used soft money to pay for part of their staff salaries, arguing that the staff spent at least a fraction of their time on nonfederal activity. Other expenses, such as overhead and mailings, were also apportioned partly federal (hard) and partly nonfederal (soft) dollars.

Many individuals and watchdog organizations, including Common Cause, believed that the party committees were using their nonfederal funds for thinly veiled federal election and candidate campaign activities. After numerous attempts at bringing their case to the Supreme Court, Common Cause succeeded in 1991 in persuading the Court to require a better-defined set of disclosure and allocation rules from the FEC. The FEC responded by developing better disclosure rules and by creating explicit formulas that defined the ratios of hard to soft dollars that parties could use in paying for certain "party-building" activities, such as voter registration and mobilization and supplies. When the party money is spent by the national committees directly, the ratios are 40 percent soft to 60 percent hard in nonpresidential election years and 35 percent soft to 65 percent hard in presidential election years.[19] However, states are still not required to report their nonfederal fund activity, and they are also permitted to develop their own hard-to-soft ratios, which generally allow more soft money to be matched with fewer hard dollars. For example, state parties in Missouri could use 30 percent hard to 70 percent soft for issue advocacy during the 1999–2000 election cycle; national parties were required to use 65 percent or more hard money for the same activity.[20] Because the soft/hard-money ratio is more favorable at the state level, national parties realize that they can spend soft money more effectively by transferring large sums of money to the state parties along with instructions about how that money should be spent.

National parties now transfer much of their money, both hard and soft dollars, to state parties. In establishing a nexus between national party committees and state party committees, the congressional campaign committees (DSCC, NRSC, NRCC, and DCCC) have sought ways to justify their nonfederal spending. For these congressional campaign committees, the nexus between them and state level races (governor and state legislature) is less clear than for the RNC or DNC. According to Anthony Corrado, the basis for their claim is that "by contributing to state legislatures and party building, a congressional campaign committee is able to build congressional candidates of the future."[21]

ADVANTAGES OF SOFT MONEY

Building future congressional candidates is not the only reason that national party committees transfer large amounts of money to their state affiliates. Soft money, especially soft money used at the state level, has a number of advantages over hard money.

Soft money is attractive to party committees because it can be raised in unlimited amounts and is therefore easier to raise. It takes one hundred hard money donors giving $1,000 each to match a single $100,000 soft money contribution. As campaign finance attorney and former NRSC general counsel William B. Canfield reports, "It's very easy for the treasurer at a national party committee to raise soft money—it comes in far greater amounts than people really ask for, or desire . . . The acquisition of it is the easy part, the expenditure, lawfully, is the tough part."[22]

Parties and the candidate beneficiaries of soft money also like soft money because it is fungible. Unlike hard-dollar party contributions to candidates and coordinated expenditures that are limited and not transferable once they are allocated, soft money can be transferred and spent in whatever amounts the party committee chooses and at whatever time in the election cycle. Hard money can also be spent as independent expenditures in unlimited amounts and at any time in the election cycle, but, as previously noted, parties have not used this option as much.

A third reason parties like soft money is that it has the advantage of freeing up hard money for other purposes. As William Timmons, Ronald Reagan's campaign political director in charge of field operations and now a Washington, D.C., lobbyist, has said, "It doesn't make much difference what you can use [soft money] for, because it frees up your other money."[23] Only hard money can be contributed to candidates, spent on coordinated campaigns, and used for independent expenditures. The more soft money that can be raised to help pay for registration, mobilization, buildings, staff, and issue ads, the more hard money can be liberated to max out all candidate contributions and coordinated expenditures.

Although soft money was initially intended to fund party-building activities such as voter registration and GOTV drives, much of the soft money in recent elections has been used to pay for candidate electioneering. In the past few election cycles, parties have primarily used soft money to pay for issue advocacy communications that promoted or attacked a particular candidate. These advertisements, even though technically paid for by the state parties, are often actually funded by money transferred from the national parties and can refer to federal elections as long as they do not expressly advocate the election or defeat of a particular candidate (express advocacy) and as long as the ad does not mention words of express advocacy outlined by the Supreme Court in *Buckley v. Valeo* ("vote for," "vote against," "elect," "defeat," etc.).[24]

Parties and the competitive candidates like being supported with soft money because the money is often spent in ways that raise doubts and concerns about the opposing party's candidates. As we observed in our sample races, there is often a division of labor between the parties and candidates, with the parties being more negative and the candidates more positive. In addition, in most cases the parties reinforce the themes and messages of the candidates they support with their soft money-funded ads. When the parties are "off-message," as the NRCC was in 1998, it puts that set of candidates at a disadvantage.[25] In 2000, the parties and the candidates they supported consistently emphasized the same themes.

In just two decades, the parties have experienced a vast swing in campaign finance freedom as they moved from strict contribution and coordinated expenditure limits under the FECA to the opportunity to raise unlimited amounts of soft money while taking advantage of the more generous hard and soft money matching formulas allowed when money is transferred to the state parties. Today soft money is raised primarily to run express ads under the guise of issue ads in the most competitive races.

THE SURGE IN SOFT MONEY

The various advantages of using unlimited soft money resources has forced political parties to reevaluate their spending strategies. The result of this reevaluation has been a surge in soft money over the past three election cycles as parties have continued to discover more effective ways to deploy this money.

1996: Soft Money Used for Candidate Promotion

As discussed in chapter 1, the *Buckley* decision and its subsequent aftershocks created an atmosphere of unlimited electioneering through issue advocacy, some of it funded with party soft money. Starting in the early 1990s and mushrooming in the 1996 election cycle, parties used greater amounts of soft money matched with hard money to create broadcast advertisements, mail pieces, and telephone calls. The parties claimed that they were promoting issues and the party, when in reality they were clearly advocating the election or defeat of a federal candidate.

This expanded use of soft money was key in the reelection campaign strategy for Bill Clinton in 1996. President Clinton's advisors wanted to spend approximately $55 million on the issue advocacy campaign during the primary; however, accepting the FECA matching funds limited the campaign to a budget of $37 million. The solution was to let the DNC run the issue advertisements with party soft money.[26] The DNC eventually spent some $44 million in the advertising blitz and disbursed over $135 million in total soft money for the whole cycle.[27] Clinton himself participated in raising large quantities of the soft money, hosting guests in the Lincoln bedroom of the White House, holding luncheons, and hosting intimate coffees in the White House.

Clinton was not alone in expanding soft money use in 1996. In response to the Democrats' media blitz, the RNC began to run ads in favor of Bob Dole, spending approximately $24 million on pro-Dole advertisements and over $114 million in total soft money.[28] A total of over $271 million was spent in soft money during the 1996 election cycle, a threefold increase from the previous cycle. Not only did the party committees learn the near limitless nature of the soft money supply, but perhaps more important, they discovered that soft money could be used for candidate-defining purposes, a lesson the congressional campaign committees applied aggressively in 1998 and all party committees applied in 2000.

1998 and the Soft Money Surge in Congressional Elections

As parties discovered the efficacy of soft money raising and spending in the presidential contest, party spending in congressional races shifted from primarily hard-dollar candidate contributions and coordinated expenditures to a combination of soft and hard money, with those expenditures targeted to fewer races. Speaking of the 1998 election cycle, former NRSC political director David Hansen said, "In the past, incumbents have kind of looked at the coordinated money as a kind of God-given right, and they expected to get it no matter what kind of race they were in. Quite frankly, that did not happen this time."[29]

Instead, soft money in 1998 poured into targeted states with the most competitive races and was divided between air (television and radio) and ground war (mail, phone calls, personal visits, e-mail, Internet) activities. The two parties combined to disburse over $220 million in soft money, approximately $69 million of which was transferred to the state and local parties. The soft money-funded ground war possibly proved to be the deciding factor in the Democrats' successful election, as they were able to mobilize African Americans and women using phone banks and direct mail.

The 1998 cycle is also noteworthy for the NRCC's unsuccessful effort to capitalize on the character problems associated with President Clinton in a strategy entitled "Operation Breakout." The NRCC focused an advertisement blitz on fifty to sixty competitive races in thirty states and sixty-two media markets, buying out the markets until saturated. The advertisements were characterized by "cookie-cutter" ads in which the same ad was used for multiple candidates with only the picture and name changed. Republicans erred in the assumption that President Clinton's personal misdeeds would be an important issue in the vote for a U.S. representative or U.S. senator. Democrats avoided the issue of Clinton, instead emphasizing health care, Social Security, and education, and sought to put Republicans on the defensive on these issues. The Democratic issues turned out to be more salient to voters. The Democrats' success on the ground and the failure of the broadcast-driven Operation Breakout prompted Representative Livingston (R-La.) to state on the day after the election that the Republicans had been "beat on the ground" and that "relying on TV was a major tactical mistake."[30]

SOFT MONEY IN THE 2000 ELECTIONS

Soft money developments were especially noteworthy in the 2000 elections because they marked a shift in major party funding trends. With the exception of soft money parity in the 1993–1994 election cycle, Republicans have long enjoyed a substantial advantage in both hard and soft money. In 2000, when all national committees are combined, the Democrats significantly narrowed the Republican's advantage in soft money disbursements for the first time since 1994. National and congressional party committees, in the aggregate, were nearly tied in soft money receipts, with $249.9 million for the Republicans (RNC, NRSC, and NRCC) and $245.2 million for the Democrats (DNC, DSCC, and DCCC) in 1999-2000.

Near Parity in Soft Money Spending by Party Committees

The use of soft money to promote or attack federal candidates grew substantially in 2000. Once again, the Republicans outspent the Democrats in soft money in this election cycle. The Republicans (RNC, NRSC, and NRCC) spent over $252 million, while the Democrats (DNC, DSCC, and DCCC) spent nearly $245 million, but the Democrats significantly narrowed the gap.

Both national party committees (DNC and RNC) were also flush with cash in 2000 and both transferred substantial sums of hard and soft money to the state parties. Overall the RNC transferred $35.8 million in hard money and $93.2 million in soft money, compared to the DNC transfers of $38.3 million in hard money and $76.4 million in soft money. Some of the money likely went to help with Senate races and may have reduced the Democratic Party soft/hard money advantage in some states. But current FEC reporting provisions do not require the parties to report the specific items on which the national party money was spent, so precise spending estimates are difficult.

One advantage of our methodology of having academics develop contacts in the state parties is that the contacts will sometimes tell us how national party hard- and soft money transfers were actually spent in races in the state. Sandra Suarez and Robin Kolodny monitored Pennsylvania's Thirteenth Congressional District race in 1998 and 2000. In 2000, one-term Democratic incumbent Joe Hoeffel faced Republican State Senator Stewart Greenleaf. The national Republican committees spent about $77,000 in hard money contributions (93 percent of the legal maximum) for Greenleaf. According to Greenleaf's campaign, the committees sent no soft money to Pennsylvania specifically earmarked for Greenleaf. The Democrat, Hoeffel, by contrast, received only about $16,000 in hard money contributions (16 percent of the maximum) from the Democratic Party. However, the DCCC reported transferring almost $1.4 million in soft money to Pennsylvania specifically for Hoeffel's campaign. This influx of soft money may have been a deciding factor, as Hoeffel received 52 percent of the vote to Greenleaf's disappointing 45 percent.[31]

The fact that the Democrats nearly pulled even in overall soft money spending is noteworthy. But even more important is the surge in party soft money spending by Democratic congressional campaign committees in the 1999–2000 election cycle, often through disbursements to the state parties. For the first time, the Democratic campaign committees' soft money spending was greater than GOP committee spending. The DSCC and DCCC spent $121 million, compared to $97.6 million for the NRSC and NRCC. This $23 million advantage exceeds the $20 million advantage the Republican congressional committees enjoyed over their Democratic counterparts in 1997–1998. Figure 2.1 shows congressional campaign committee party soft money disbursements for the 1994–2000 elections.[32]

Perhaps the greatest soft money surprise in 1999–2000 was the DSCC resurgence. The DSCC had been slow to enter the soft money arena. Looking at the period of one six-year Senate term, DSCC soft money spending rose from $417,000 in 1994 to $63.3 million in 2000, an astonishing 151-fold increase. The DSCC raised and spent more soft money than any congressional campaign committee and for the first time outspent the NRSC—by more than $18 million. The DSCC surge was central to Democrats' success in the 2000 Senate race.

In contrast, the NRSC, which had often led the congressional campaign committee money chase, spent the least of any committee in 2000. The NRSC hard money receipts were still higher than the Democrats', but, taking hard and soft money together, this was not a good year for the NRSC compared to other congressional campaign committees.

Following the DSCC's lead in soft money, the DCCC also outraised and outspent its Republican counterpart, the NRCC, for the first time. In 2000, between the parties, the two House committees raised almost $104 million in soft money, up from $44 million only two years before. In both houses, the Democrats clearly pursued an aggressive soft money strategy in 2000. Jim Jordan, political director of the DSCC, confirmed this, "Soft money was a key to this cycle . . . the DSCC was at message parity with the Republicans at the end."[33] How that strategy played out in the competitive races is a major focus of this research. The research design for this study cultivated contacts in the state and national parties, in candidate campaigns, and with political professionals. These contacts permitted us to more effectively monitor soft money activity.

Congressional Campaign Committee Strategies

In their aggressive pursuit of soft money, the congressional campaign committees used a number of methods to more effectively raise the maximum amount of money and more effectively deploy it. In 1999–2000, both parties expanded their use of "victory funds" or joint fundraising committees. In the past, joint fundraising committees were used to split proceeds from a fundraising event between two or more candidates. The 2000 election cycle saw the creation of victory funds, which would help raise money in the same method as joint fundraising committees but would share the raised funds between one candidate and his or her party campaign committee, not with other candidates.[34] The implicit assumption was that the party committee would then spend the soft money raised through the victory fund on that particular contest, usually a U.S. Senate race, or transfer it to that particular state's party. The Illinois Tenth Congressional District Victory Fund became controversial because more than $120,000 was raised for Lauren Beth Gash (D) from "two unions and a dozen individuals who had already given the maximum allowed by federal law to the Gash campaign."[35]

Party committees also try to deploy their funds in the most competitive races where it will make the biggest difference. Congressional campaign committees allocate their soft money based on perceived competitiveness of races and the funding needs of "their team." Hence, Democrat John Corzine received little soft money from the DSCC for his New Jersey Senate race, because he was able to spend $60 million of his own money.[36] Corzine's resources and the cost of a race in New Jersey discouraged the NRSC from spending in New Jersey.[37] One advantage the Democrats had in the 2000 Senate races was their supply of self-funded candidates in New Jersey, Minnesota, and Washington. This permitted them to concentrate resources more heavily in states like Virginia, Michigan, Missouri, Delaware, and Montana.

Where Soft Money Was Spent

The strategies used by both parties resulted in increased levels of both hard and soft money. But this surge in party money raises a number of questions: If the surge in hard money was not going to party contributions or coordinated expenditures, where was it going? Was the enormous amount of soft money used effectively? And where did all this money, both hard and soft, come from?

As previously noted, to maximize the impact of their soft money bonanza, the parties need to match it with hard money and transfer it to state parties. These transferred funds provide the strategic advantage of being easily targeted to where they will make the most difference in competitive races. Consequently, the amount of soft money transferred to state party committees is perhaps the best way to measure the effectiveness of soft money deployment in congressional contests. The extent to which the Democrats pursued a soft money strategy and their ability to outspend Republicans in key races is evidenced by the fact that they out-transferred the NRSC in all the races in our sample (see table 2.3).

Table 2.3. Transfers to State Parties

	DSCC			*NRSC*		
State	*Hard*	*Soft*	*Percent Soft*	*Hard*	*Soft*	*Percent Soft*
Delaware	$ 1,402,032	$ 2,954,313	68	$ —	$ 250,000	100
Michigan	$ 2,391,714	$ 4,280,606	64	$ 1,668,200	$ 2,821,560	63
Missouri	$ 1,649,107	$ 4,110,834	71	$ 1,270,800	$ 2,691,900	68
Montana	$ 824,089	$ 1,886,558	70	$ 516,700	$ 778,900	60
Virginia	$ 4,132,687	$ 4,968,600	55	$ 2,303,800	$ 3,052,100	57
Grand Total	**$10,399,629**	**$18,200,911**	**64**	**$ 5,759,500**	**$ 9,594,460**	**62**

Source: Federal Election Commission, "National Party Financial Activity through the End of the Election Cycle," press release, <www.fec.gov/press/051501partyfund/tables/cong2state2000.html>, 15 May 2001 [accessed 27 August 2001].

In our five states with contested Senate races, DSCC soft money spending was roughly double NRSC spending. However, in some competitive races outside our sample, Democrats out-transferred Republicans to an even greater degree. In New York, for example, the DSCC spent $6.9 million in hard and just under $8.7 million in soft money, compared to the NRSC's $208,000 hard and $260,000 soft.[38] More typically in competitive Senate races outside our sample, such as Nebraska and Florida, the Democrats transferred more hard and soft money by about the same ratio as in our five sample races, excluding Delaware. When all the 2000 Senate races are examined, the DSCC transferred more hard and soft money than did the NRSC.

The largest anomaly of the 2000 congressional elections was the NRSC strategy of effectively ignoring the Delaware race, while Democrats expended more than $4.3 million.[39] When David Hansen of the NRSC was asked about these surprising data, he indicated that Arthur Finkelstein, Roth's consultant, and Jo Ann Barnhart, campaign manager, told the NRSC not to "mess it up" and to "stay out." Hansen continued, "NRSC polls found it to be a close race but Roth staffers and managers said Roth was up ten points."[40] Bernadette Budde also indicated "overconfidence and apathy" in the Roth campaign.[41] When candidates refuse party help as Roth did in 2000 and Russell Feingold (D-Wis.) did in 1998, it appears that the committee honors their wishes. There are some counter-examples, however. As 2000 congressional candidate Lauren Beth Gash (D-Ill.) concluded, "It is difficult to be the candidate when there is a message going out that you don't control."[42]

Hard- and soft money spending followed similar patterns in competitive House races, but following the hard- and soft-money spending in House races is more difficult than in Senate races, because the money is transferred to the state party and may be spent on more than one House contest in any given state. For example, by some accounts there were as many as eight competitive House contests in California in 2000, but in other states, such as Arkansas, Oklahoma, and Montana, the races we monitored were the only competitive contests. By using different methods for spending, parties make it even more difficult to track what they actually spend. The additional hard money transfers to state parties are not to be earmarked for federal candidates, yet the close working relationship between the national and state parties likely leads to state parties doing what the national parties desire with the transferred money. Table 2.4 contains party transfer data for the states with House races in our sample.

Despite the difficulty of tracking transferred money, it is quite clear that the DCCC, like the DSCC, transferred more than its House Republican counterpart. Nationwide, the NRCC spent $53 million in soft money compared to the DCCC's $58 million. The DCCC transferred most of its hard and soft money to the state parties ($50 million), making use of their large reserves of soft money and the beneficial soft money ratio used by state parties. The NRCC, on the other hand, only transferred $26.8 million to state parties, opting to direct and produce more activity in-house or through transfers to other committees.

Table 2.4. Party Transfers to Sample Races

	DCCC			NRCC		
State	*Hard*	*Soft*	*Percent Soft*	*Hard*	*Soft*	*Percent Soft*
Arkansas	$ 462,922	$ 1,213,117	72	$ 329,232	$ 763,692	70
California	$3,270,856	$ 4,567,717	58	$1,163,262	$ 702,497	38
Connecticut	$ —	$ —		$ 150,000	$ —	0
Illinois	$ 933,352	$ 2,655,125	74	$ 795,185	$1,550,363	66
Kentucky	$ 640,138	$ 2,551,666	80	$ 360,368	$ 753,970	68
Michigan	$ 789,819	$ 1,673,634	68	$ 941,543	$1,209,888	56
Montana	$ 276,771	$ 601,410	68	$ 407,194	$ 317,499	44
New Jersey	$ 39,750	$ 55,250	58	$ 300,000	$ 28,500	9
Oklahoma	$ —	$ —		$ 90,513	$ 312,989	78
Pennsylvania	$1,175,150	$ 2,705,775	70	$ 864,386	$ 791,734	48
Washington	$ 833,970	$ 1,945,930	70	$ 850,560	$ 1,781,401	68

Source: Federal Election Commission, "National Party Transfers to State/Local Party Committees," press release, <www.fec.gov/press/051501partyfund/tables/cong2state2000.html>, 15 May 2001 [accessed 27 August 2001].

Along with raising as much hard and soft money as they can, the party committees have also realized that it is just as essential to make sure that their strongest candidate makes it into the general election. It has long been assumed that party committees and many PACs await the outcome of contested primaries, especially in open seats, before donating money or becoming involved in the race. But with relatively few competitive races and with the stakes so high in competitive races, that is changing.[43] As mentioned previously, during the 1999–2000 cycle the DCCC identified preferred candidates in a few contested primaries and spent money on their behalf, much to the chagrin of their fellow party candidates.

Sources of Soft Money

But where did all this money come from? The single largest surge in party soft money contributions came from labor unions. They gave a whopping 210 percent more in 1999–2000 than they had in the previous presidential election cycle. Individual donors also dramatically increased their soft money giving: Their contributions rose by 151 percent. The business sector increase was well behind individuals and labor unions: Their aggregate contributions rose by 56 percent. Business, however, still dominates soft money giving although to a lesser degree; they gave about half of all soft money in 1999–2000, down from their two-thirds share in 1995–1996.[44]

Labor unions were among the major soft money donors to the Democrats,[45] especially the Affiliated Federal, State, County, Municipal Employees (AFSCME),[46] and the Association of Trial Lawyers of America.[47] The sources of soft money in 2000 had not changed much in twenty years. Elizabeth Drew found in 1980 that

Republican soft money comes mainly from businesses and corporations, while labor supplies most of the Democratic soft money.[48]

How Soft Money Is Spent

Knowing who the major donors are as well as the amount of party committee money that is transferred to state parties allows us to make guesses about how that money was used at the state level, but it doesn't pinpoint the exact uses for the money. Reports on receipts and transfers to state parties are available from the FEC, but once the money is transferred to state parties, it becomes more difficult to monitor. However, the methodology in our study helps us monitor how money is spent from the district or state's vantage point and permits us to assess how soft money was spent in 2000. The story of how this soft money was spent is one of the major objectives of this report. Because reporting by state parties on expenditures is at best spotty, our method of monitoring actual campaign communications provides the most complete assessment of how soft money is actually spent.

Our study found that party soft money is spent on the full range of campaign mass communications, including television (broadcast and cable) and radio, the air war; and on more targeted communications, including mail, telephone calls, e-mail, and personal contact, the ground war. The party communications campaigns are highly professional, relying on media professionals, pollsters, and experienced campaign strategists.

The focus of party communication was specific candidates. In 90 percent of the party communications we monitored, the communication addressed only one contest. The messages of the party committee communications covered broad themes like Social Security, health care, and education, which meant that in any given district one or more of these themes would converge well with what the candidate and allied groups were communicating. Often the theme of the party ad was adapted to the context of a particular race. We discussed the high level of issue congruence in 2000 in greater detail in chapter 1.

AIR WAR

Parties have long run generic television ads promoting the party and since 1996 have increasingly used more specific candidate messages. In the advertising we monitored in 2000, the party-funded ads were largely indistinguishable from the candidate ads. State parties mounted television ads in all of the races in our sample. For example, in Virginia it was estimated that the state party organizations, funded by national party transfers, spent $9.2 million dollars on television ($5 million for Virginia Democrats and $4.2 million for Virginia Republicans), matching the total spent by the candidates.[49]

Soft money-funded ads generally reinforced the candidates' campaign themes but occasionally became controversial. The Republicans successfully challenged the accuracy of DCCC ads in the Kentucky Sixth and New Jersey Twelfth Congressional District races. The ads were pulled from the air, and the Republican candidates achieved public relations victories against not only the DCCC but also the Democratic candidates. A spokesperson for the Kentucky Sixth Congressional District candidate Scotty Baesler stated that having the ad pulled "hurt us in a significant way. It allowed Fletcher to raise a credibility issue."[50] Interestingly, as the race progressed the Democratic campaigns were more careful and it was the Republicans who had more controversial ads pulled. Both parties tried to make the opposing candidates take the heat for soft money ads that went too far.

The tone and nature of the soft money expenditures can pose problems for individual candidates as well. To what extent can a candidate disavow his or her own party? Will parties stay away when asked to? In the Pennsylvania Fourth District race, Republican candidate Melissa Hart claimed that if her opponent could not control ads run by his party on his behalf, he "lacked the political weight within his party to be an effective member of Congress."[51] But Hart's own party Chair, Tom Davis (R-Va.), said that Hart "doesn't have any say about what we do in her race. . . . We have to protect our candidate whether she likes it or not."[52] Other candidates who criticized their own party ads included Senator Conrad Burns (R-Mont.) and Representative James Rogan (R-Calif. 27).

GROUND WAR

Both political parties made targeted mail an important component of their campaign efforts in 1998 and 2000. The use of mail in competitive races was often funded with soft money. State parties in our races sent out at least 423 distinct pieces of mail, with other party committees sending another 187 distinct mailers. We observed a number of instances where the parties created a template in which the local candidate's name and images were inserted. These cookie-cutter ads suggest that party committees achieved some economies of scale with their ads. This was possible because of similar issue agendas across districts. Soft money was also used to contact voters by telephone and in GOTV drives in many of our districts, reminding supporters to get to the polls on Election Day

Surge in Republican Mail

Coming out of the 1998 cycle was a widespread perception that the Democrats had done better than Republicans in deploying soft money resources, primarily because Republicans nationalized the election through Operation Breakout while Democrats invested in ground war strategies.[53] In 2000, the NRCC was much more aggressive on the ground. John Guzik of the NRCC reports that his committee "did more mail and phones than in 1998. We made sure that campaigns did a significant amount of ground war."[54] This focus showed in our sample races: The NRCC sent nearly double the amount of unique mail pieces as did the DCCC. Furthermore, the Republican parties at all levels combined sent approximately thirty more unique mail pieces than the Democratic counterpart did. The Democratic phone bank activity, however, was nearly double that of the Republicans. When the efforts at voter mobilization by the interest groups (see chapter 3) are combined with the parties, it is clear that in competitive districts and states this element of campaign strategy was important to both sides.

The Impact of Soft Money on Congressional Races

Important consequences flow from these parallel party campaigns in competitive races. First, the national party committees' ability to transfer large sums of money makes them more powerful. All party committees insist that their allocation patterns are "by the numbers," meaning driven by professional polling numbers, but there is intense competition for party soft money spending, and by definition not all candidates are happy with the allocation decisions. The role of the party committee chair in these allocation decisions has been controversial.[55] Although allocation decisions do not affect all candidates, they do force candidates in tight races to rely heavily on party support, thus lending the parties a certain amount of power amid a typically candidate-centered system.

This raises the question of whether the power gained from the influx of money available to party committees actually reflects the role parties are meant to play in a democracy, or if in reality it simply means that whoever can raise and spend the most is the most important. Anthony Gierzynski decries the increased flow of money into the party system. He explains that

> political parties are a majoritarian institution in our pluralistic political system. They strive to win elections by aggregating the preferences of citizens into majority coalitions. Our elections are structured so that the party that represents the preferences of the greatest block of citizens wins. In the process the parties promote political equality in elections through the representation of those interests and by encouraging participation. Our privately financed, free-spending system contaminates the functioning of the political parties, giving the party backed by wealthier interests a financial advantage of consequence over the other, an advantage that doesn't reflect their popular support.[56]

To the extent that parties expend soft money on communications with voters, the impact of the money on the parties is transitory. Of more lasting significance may be the party investment in voter canvasses and databases, which can be used by other party candidates and build up an infrastructure for the party in the future. However, because most of the soft money in our sample of races was spent on television, radio, and mail communications, we do not see party soft money as strongly strengthening the parties.

REFORM

Soft money was a focus of Republican John McCain's 2000 presidential campaign, and early in 2001 the Senate passed legislation that effectively banned soft money. In previous congresses the House had passed a similar soft money ban. The pressure to reform soft money has long come from groups like the League of Women Voters and Common Cause. More recently, many corporations have already begun to decrease their soft money involvement. Five of eight corporations that gave more than $1 million in soft money in 1995–1996 scaled their donations back in 1999–2000: Philip Morris, RJR Nabisco, Arco, MCI, and Seagram. Others scaled back as well, including Lehman Brothers, Toyota, Xerox, Trump Organization, Dole Food, Fruit of the Loom, Kaiser Group, and Bear, Stearns. Many, like AOL, Intel, and IBM, have completely stopped contributing, and many big company executives have endorsed the ban, including people in Goldman Sachs, Hasbro, MGM Mirage, American Electric Power Co., and Siemens Energy & Automation. A lobbyist explained why so many corporations are beginning to scale back and decry soft money: "We are getting sick and tired of people calling us up for money."[57] A recent study found that 50 percent of corporate heads fear repercussions if they turn down requests for soft money.[58]

But the forces against reform are formidable, and incumbents correctly perceive that the current system benefits them. Even if reform were to pass, it is unclear how it would fare in the courts. Would a ban on soft money, for example, survive a Supreme Court challenge? If reform is not enacted or sustained by the courts, future congressional elections are likely to be much like the 1998 and 2000 election cycles. Redistricting following the 2000 elections will result in more competitive House contests. Both parties will pursue a soft money strategy and target those resources to competitive contests. In midterm years, the emphasis will be even more on voter mobilization. This scenario elevates the importance of the party committees and those who fund them. The level of soft money spending and the clear issue agenda of soft money donors will continue to be reasons reformers give to ban soft money.

NOTES

1. See William J. Crotty, *American Parties in Decline,* 2d ed. (Boston: Little, Brown, 1984).

2. David B. Magleby et al., *The Myth of the Independent Voter* (Berkeley: University of California Press, 1992).

3. Robin Toner, "The World: New Math; Going Along, But Not Getting Along," *New York Times,* 10 June 2001, 1 (section 4).

4. Paul S. Herrnson, *Party Campaigning in the 1980s* (Cambridge, Mass.: Harvard University Press, 1988); Robin Kolodny, *Pursuing Majorities: Congressional Campaign Commit-*

tees in American Politics, vol. 1 of *The Congressional Studies Series* (Oklahoma City: University of Oklahoma Press, 1998); David B. Magleby and Kelly D. Patterson, "Campaign Consultants and Direct Democracy: Politics of Citizen Control," in *Campaign Warriors: The Role of Political Consultants in Elections*, ed. James E. Thurber and Candice J. Nelson (Washington, D.C.: Brookings Institution Press, 2000), 14–16.

5. According to Frank Sorauf, Drew popularized—not coined—the term "soft money." Frank J. Sorauf, *Money in American Elections* (Glenview, Ill.: Scott Foresman, 1988), 320.

6. Anthony Corrado, "Giving, Spending, and 'Soft Money,'" *Journal of Law and Policy* 6, no. 1 (1997): 50.

7. Barbara G. Salmore and Stephen A. Salmore, *Candidates, Parties, and Campaigns: Electoral Politics in America* (Washington, D.C.: Congressional Quarterly Press, 1989), 58.

8. Jim Jordan, DSCC political director, interview by David B. Magleby, Washington, D.C., 19 November 2000.

9. In 1996 a divided Supreme Court, in *Colorado Republican Federal Campaign Committee et al. v. Federal Election Commission*, 533 U.S. 2001 (1996), ruled that parties enjoyed the same First Amendment rights as any other group or individual and could engage in independent expenditure election-express-advocacy efforts, including broadcast activities, without facing any limitations.

10. "FEC Reports Increase in Party Fundraising for 2000," FEC press release, <www.fec.gov/press/051501partyfund/051501partyfund.html>, 15 May 2001 [accessed 24 August 2001].

11. Herbert E. Alexander, *Financing Politics: Money, Elections, and Political Reform*, (Washington, D.C.: Congressional Quarterly Press, 1992), 53; Anthony Corrado, *Beyond the Basics: Campaign Finance Reform* (New York: The Century Foundation Press, 2000), 69–71; Xandra Kayden, "The Nationalizing of the Party System" in *Parties, Interest Groups, and Campaign Finance Laws*, ed. Michael J. Malbin (Washington, D.C.: American Enterprise Institute, 1980), 263; and Salmore and Salmore, *Candidates, Parties, and Campaigns*, 55.

12. *Colorado Republican Federal Campaign Committee v. Federal Election Commission*, 533 U.S. 2001 (1996).

13. Diana Dwyre and Robin Kolodny, "Throwing Out the Rule Book: Party Financing of the 2000 Elections," in *Financing the 2000 Elections*, ed. David B. Magleby (Washington, D.C.: Brookings, forthcoming).

Independent Expenditures in Dollars

DNC	0
DSCC	133,000
DCCC	1,900,000
Democrat state and local	243,929
Total Democrat	2,310,175
RNC	0
NRSC	267,600
NRCC	548,800
Republican state and local	740,402
Total Republican	1,556,802

Source: "FEC Reports Increase in Party Fundraising for 2000," FEC press release, 15 May 2001.

14. See Anthony Corrado, "Party Soft Money" in *Campaign Finance Reform: A Sourcebook*, Anthony Corrado et al. (Washington, D.C.: Brookings Institution Press, 1997), 170.

15. Ibid.

16. See Federal Election Commission, "Advisory Opinions: 1976-72, 1978-10, and 1982-5," in *Campaign Finance Reform: A Sourcebook*, Anthony Corrado et al. (Washington, D.C.: Brookings Institution Press, 1997), 187–97.

17. Corrado, *Campaign Finance Reform*, 172.

18. Anthony Corrado, "Giving, Spending, and 'Soft Money,'" *Journal of Law and Policy* 6, no. 1 (1997): 49–50.

19. See the 1991 FEC regulations, 11 C.F.R. §§ 102, 104, 106.

20. Robert Biersak, "State Party Transfers," personal e-mail to Anna N. Baker, 28 August 2001.

21. Corrado, "Giving, Spending, and 'Soft Money,'" 50.

22. Quoted in James A. Barnes, "Party Favors," *National Journal*, no. 19 (11 May 1996): 1038–41.

23. Quoted in Elizabeth Drew, *Politics and Money: The New Road to Corruption* (New York: Macmillan, 1983), 106.

24. *Buckley v. Valeo*, 424 U.S. 1 (1976).

25. David B. Magleby, ed., *Outside Money: Soft Money and Issue Advocacy in the 1998 Congressional Elections* (Lanham, Md.: Rowman & Littlefield , 2000), 30–31.

26. Dick Morris, *Behind the Oval Office* (Los Angeles: Renaissance Books, 1999), 141.

27. Ruth Marcus and Charles R. Babcock, "System Cracks Under Weight of Cash," *Washington Post*, 9 February 1997, A1.

28. Ibid.

29. NRSC executive director David Hansen at lunchtime discussion panel at the Pew Press Conference, "Outside Money: Soft Money & Issue Advocacy in Competitive 1998 Congressional Elections," report presented at the National Press Club, Washington, D.C., 5 February 1999.

30. Quoted in Ruth Marcus, "Outside Money Wasn't Everything," *Washington Post*, 5 November 1998, A39.

31. Robin Kolodny, Sandra Suarez, and Kyle Kreider, "The 2000 Pennsylvania Thirteenth Congressional District Race" in *Election Advocacy: Soft Money and Issue Advocacy in the 2000 Congressional Elections*, ed. David B. Magleby, report presented at the National Press Club, Washington, D.C., 5 February 2001.

32. The data over time for the DNC and RNC follow:

Nonfederal Disbursements, 1992–2000

Committee	*1992*	*1994*	*1996*	*1998*	*2000*
DNC	$28,388,869	$45,097,098	$100,483,977	$57,411,879	$135,332,105
RNC	$33,601,431	$42,413,166	$114,401,973	$74,325,722	$163,521,510

Source: Federal Election Commission, "National Party Nonfederal Activity through the Complete Two Year Election Cycle," press release, <www.fec.gov/press/051501partyfund/tables/nonfedsumm2000.html>, 15 May 2001 [accessed 23 August 2001].

33. Jordan, interview by Magleby.

34. Larry Makinson, "The Old Soft Money Ain't What It Used to Be," *The Capital Eye* VIII, no. 1, <www.opensecrets.org/newsletter/ce74/softmoney.asp>, 18 December 2000 [accessed 15 January 2001].

35. See Barry Rundquist et al., "The 2000 Illinois Tenth Congressional District Race" in "Outside Money," ed. David B. Magleby, *PS: eSymposium*, <www.apsa.com/PS/june01/rundquist.cfm>, June 2001 [accessed June 2001].

36. Center for Responsive Politics, <www.opensecrets.org/2000elect/dist_total/NJS1.htm>.

37. David Hansen, National Republican Senatorial Committee (NRSC), interview by David B. Magleby, Washington, D.C., 8 December 2000.

38. Hard- and soft money spending by the senatorial campaign committees for Florida, New York, and Pennsylvania. Federal Election Commission, "Party Fundraising Escalates"; Robert Biersak, "Clarification on FEC Soft Money Rules," personal e-mail to Anna N. Baker, 28 August 2001.

39.

Transfers to Delaware

Committee	*Hard*	*Soft*	*Total Transferred*	*Percent Hard*
DSCC	$1,402,032	$2,954,313	$4,356,345	32
DNC	$ 183,138	$ 444,295	$ 627,433	29
Democrat Total	$1,585,170	$3,398,608	$4,983,778	32
NRSC	—	$ 250,000	$ 250,000	0
RNC	$ 17,685	$ 574,269	$ 591,954	3
Republican Total	$ 17,685	$ 824,269	$ 841,954	2

Source: Federal Election Commission, "FEC Reports Increase in Party Fundraising for 2000," press release, <www.fec.gov/press/051501partyfund/051501partyfund.html>, 15 May 2001 [accessed 27 August 2001].

40. Hansen, interview by Magleby.

41. Bernadette Budde, Business-Industry Political Action Committee (BIPAC), interview by David B. Magleby, Washington, D.C., 10 November 2000.

42. Lauren Beth Gash, interview by Barry Rundquist, 9 January 2001. See Rundquist, "2000 Illinois Tenth Congressional District Race."

43. Budde, interview by Magleby.

44. Charlie Mitchell and Brody Mullins, "Saying 'No' to Soft Money," *National Journal*, no. 12 (24 March 2001): 870–75. This citation is the source for all numbers in this paragraph.

45. Ruth Marcus and Mike Allen, "Democrats' Donations from Labor Up Sharply," *Washington Post*, 18 July 2000, final edition.

46. Susan Schmidt, "Last-Minute Donations a Boon for Both Parties," *Washington Post*, 19 December 2000, final edition.

47. Ibid.

48. Drew, *Politics and Money*, 16.

49. CMAG database.

50. Penny Miller and Don A. Gross, "The 2000 Kentucky Sixth Congressional District Race," in "Outside Money," ed. Magleby.

51. Quoted in Rachel Van Dongen, "The Reform Network: McCain on the Air," *Roll Call Online*, <www.rollcall.com/pages/politics/00/09/pol0928a.html>, 28 September 2000 [accessed 29 September 2000].

52. Ibid.

53. Magleby, *Outside Money*, 215.

54. John Guzik, NRCC executive deputy director, interview by David Magleby, Washington, D.C., 13 November 2000.

55. Magleby, *Outside Money*, 218.

56. Anthony Gierzynski, *Money Rules: Financing Elections in America* (Boulder, Colo.: Westview Press, 2000), 76.

57. Mitchell and Mullins, "Saying 'No' to Soft Money," 871.

58. Karen Masterson, "Businesses Feel Strains of Political 'Shakedown,'" *The Houston Chronicle*, 19 October 2000, A1.

3

Interest Groups in the 2000 Congressional Elections

Anna Nibley Baker and David B. Magleby

The quest for influence and power drives politics. As James Madison so eloquently articulated, "the latent causes of factions [interest groups and parties] are thus sown in the nature of man."[1] Life is associational, and Americans have long been known to organize in groups with common interests.[2] The most enduring cause of factions or interest group politics, Madison argued, was the unequal distribution of property.[3] Economic commerce continues to drive interest group politics today, but ideological and other forces also motivate individuals to form groups and attempt to influence elections and government more generally.

Madison and every generation of political scientists thereafter have been concerned about interest group behavior threatening fundamental rights and liberties or destabilizing government, what Madison labeled the "mischiefs of faction."[4] Interest groups could follow momentary passions at the expense of long-term stability; they would likely have little regard for other points of view. The cure for the mischiefs of faction has been an enduring debate. Madison hoped his design of checks and balances, staggered terms of office, and limited direct voting for public officials would be effective in changing interest groups. The most noted modern scholar of Madison and interest groups has argued that the competition between interest groups, or interest group pluralism, is the means to limit the mischiefs Madison warned about.[5]

Interest groups are more prevalent today then ever before. We studied interest group activity in the 2000 election and found, in many instances, that interest group spending approached party committee spending and influence in competitive contests. We watched interest group strategies evolve to suit specific races and segments of the population. By dividing interest group activity into two categories—air war and ground war—and by interviewing interest group operatives, we were able to capture activities that fall below the radar screen of the media and academic assessments of campaigns.

Madison did not envision the extent of interest group power and influence today, nor did he envision the extent to which electoral democracy would be open to their influence. Madison assumed that checks and balances and competition among groups would limit the adverse impact of factions. What do soft money and issue advocacy do to the power of interest groups? Are interest groups effectively balanced by each other? These Madisonian-type questions helped guide our research.

This chapter provides a short history of interest group activity—focusing on issue advocacy—and then chronicles interest group activity in the 2000 election in that context. We use data collected from the seventeen races we studied and interviews with interest group operatives to illustrate general trends in interest group behavior. Our purpose is to reveal the growing influence of these groups in a system in which disclosure is absent.

INTEREST GROUPS

With the advent of modern telecommunications and a much-expanded electorate with the chance to vote directly for senators and representatives, interest groups compete for votes from a mass audience. As discussed in chapter 1, the FECA was intended to limit the influence of moneyed interests (individuals and groups) in elections. As the provisions and enforcement of FECA have broken down, interest groups have been free to pursue a much more aggressive strategy. In both soft money contributions to the parties and interest group issue advocacy, groups play a much larger role in congressional elections than they have for a quarter century or more.

There are several ways in which interest groups may influence elections, beyond what Madison envisioned. In the 1999–2000 election cycle, interest groups sought to influence the campaign through disclosed and limited political action committee (PAC) contributions to candidates. Interest groups, parties, corporations, unions, clubs, associations, and individuals form PACs. An interest group PAC is essentially a segregated fund containing money raised according to FECA regulations to be spent on politics, including campaign contributions. Individual-formed or association PACs are a means to collect donations from fifty or more individuals to contribute to five or more federal candidates or party committees. The FEC prohibits unions and corporations from donating treasury funds to federal candidates.[6] Political action committee contributions are limited to $10,000 per candidate per election cycle.[7] Institutions or groups may form several PACs, thus multiplying their contribution limit by the number of PACs they have created. Political action committees may donate directly to candidates and parties or use indirect means: independent expenditures, internal communications, and issue advocacy. We discuss independent expenditures and internal communications in chapter 4.

Interest groups in 2000 gave a total of $259.8 million in direct PAC contributions to candidates.[8] Consistent with past behavior, three-quarters of PAC money went to incumbents in 2000; challengers only received 11 percent. The PACs are pragmatic: They give to incumbents with legislative responsibilities relating to their interests to enhance the access of the interest groups to candidates and influence.[9]

Interest groups can also influence electoral politics by contributing to the parties. They do this through hard money PAC contributions that are limited and disclosed. Multicandidate PACs can give $15,000 per year to a national party committee and a total of $5,000 per year to local and state party committees.[10] In 1999–2000, PACs gave a total of $16.1 million to the Democratic Party and $11.1 million to the Republican Party in hard money contributions.[11]

Interest groups also participate in elections through *indirect* means: independent expenditures (express advocacy spending for or against a candidate where there is no coordination or collusion; see chapter 4) and internal communications (communications with an organization's restricted class such as voter registration drives, GOTV phone banks, and candidate endorsements; see chapter 4), soft money donations to parties (nonfederal money, see chapter 2), issue advocacy, and voter guides. Although direct contributions and independent expenditures are fully disclosed, it is much more difficult to track issue advocacy, soft money, and internal communications. In this study we attempted to track these "outside" communications.

Outside activities are unlimited because the Supreme Court ruled in *Buckley v. Valeo*[12] that legal limits could not be placed on independent campaign expenditures, but independent expenditures and spending on certain categories of internal communications with group membership must be disclosed because they contain express advocacy.[13] Chapter 4 examines interest group internal communications and independent expenditures.

As discussed in chapter 2, interest groups can contribute soft money to the parties. Soft money contributions are disclosed but unlimited. Corporations and trade associations may give treasury money to the parties as soft money, something they cannot do with candidates.[14]

Issue advocacy is the latest powerful tool in the election influence arsenal. As discussed in chapter 1, interest groups in the 1990s discovered that they could effectively campaign for or against a candidate without using the magic words of express advocacy: "vote for," "vote against," "elect," "defeat," "Smith for Congress," "reject," "cast your ballot for," etc. Some issue advocacy is devoid of any reference to candidates or an election, something we call pure issue advocacy. In the 2000 election few issue ads fit this description. Most issue ads typically show the image or likeness of one or both candidates or mention a candidate by name, and often in an unflattering or critical way. According to the Annenberg Public Policy Center, University of Pennsylvania, 94 percent of broadcast issue ads in the top seventy-five media markets "made a case for or against a candidate" in the two months before the election.[15] "Election issue advocacy," as we call these types of ads, often masks the identity of the group funding the ad and need not disclose it. The innocuous sounding group, Citizens for Better Medicare (CBM), for example, was not primarily funded by citizen donations but by the pharmaceutical industry.[16]

ISSUE ADVOCACY

Groups like CBM advocate the election or defeat of a candidate using means other than the magic words: They use candidate name, image or likeness, candidate contact information, etc. In doing this, groups stay within the limits of the law while skirting the law's intent. Although the communication fails to meet the Supreme Court's "magic words" test for electioneering, voters have a more realistic assessment of what constitutes campaign communications.

In October 2000 we tested how voters view election issue advocacy compared to pure issue advocacy through a national survey and two focus groups. Respondents from the two focus groups and the national survey saw distinct differences between election issue advocacy and pure issue advocacy. Four of five respondents believed that election issue ads urged them to vote for or against a candidate, despite the absence of the magic words.[17]

In every election since 1996, election issue advocacy has been substantial—in the tens of millions of dollars. In 2000 it climbed to an estimated $509 million.[18] This spending by interest groups is all the more impressive, because these funds are aimed at a comparatively small number of races. According to prognosticator Charlie Cook, only seventeen of the 435 House races and nine of the thirty-four Senate races were seen as toss-ups.[19] It was in these contests that the majority of issue ad spending occurred.

Issue advocacy was a little-noticed phenomenon before 1996. Groups like the Christian Coalition distributed voter guides, and some interest groups mounted pure issue advocacy efforts linked to major legislation. The best example of this type of communication effort is the 1993 "Harry and Louise" ads run by the Health Insurance Association of America (HIAA) against President Clinton's proposed health care reform package. Election issue advocacy on a large scale began in 1996 with the American Federation of Labor-Congress of Industrial Organization's (AFL-CIO) $35 million advertising blitz, much of it aimed at first-term Republicans. The campaign was largely run on television and, not surprisingly, engendered a response from Republican allies like the Chamber of Commerce.

Interest groups run a risk of activating an opponent's supporters when they broadcast a negative message about that candidate. Some observers think this may have happened in 1996 with the AFL-CIO broadcast blitz against freshman Republicans. Business countered labor by forming The Coalition: Americans Working for Real Change, a coalition of thirty-two business groups formed by the Chamber. The Coalition spent $7.1 million on issue ads in their counterattack.[20]

Interest groups expanded their election advocacy in 1998, again targeting resources to competitive races. But in 1998 the groups gave substantial emphasis to more targeted or direct forms of communications like telephone, mail, and personal contacts: the "ground war." Again, organized labor took the lead. Labor spent about $18 million on the ground war in the Labor '98 campaign, $13 million of which went toward member canvassing, rides to the polls, and GOTV calls.[21] Because of labor's intense ground war activities, more Democrats made it to the polls in 1998. Business, on the other hand, concentrated its resources on television and radio, the "air war." The Republican-allied business groups actually did do some groundwork but not enough to counter labor's efforts. To make matters worse, business efforts were overshadowed by the Clinton/Lewinsky scandal and the Republican "Operation Breakout" campaign. In the end, Bob Livingston, who succeeded Newt Gingrich, admitted, "Relying on TV was a major tactical mistake. We got beat on the ground."[22]

The interest group ground war was also an important feature of election advocacy in the 2000 presidential primaries. Labor, building on its 1998 successes, again deployed its person-to-person campaign in Iowa and New Hampshire in 2000. More than 25,000 union households in Iowa received AFL-CIO President John Sweeny's videotaped endorsements of Al Gore.[23] Other groups used 1998 strategies in Iowa and South Carolina to target messages to voters and also motivate them to turn out in a low-turnout context. Candidates also focused on the ground war; McCain's campaign mounted a telephone campaign in the Michigan primary that was made to appear as if it were issue advocacy, the "Catholic Voter Alert."[24]

Election issue advocacy ads are generally more negative than express ads.[25] The communications from interest groups in our races were categorized broadly into two categories: support and oppose.[26] An ad could support one or more candidates while opposing others. Interest group communications intended to help the Democratic candidate by supporting the Democrat and/or opposing the Republican were 56 percent of the communications coded. Upon disaggregating the communications, we found that two-thirds of those that opposed a candidate opposed the Republican, and 59 percent of those that supported a candidate supported the Democrat. Interest groups allied with Republicans were more likely to support the Republican and not attack the Democrat.

This negativity was observed in the groups attacking Arizona Senator John McCain in New Hampshire, South Carolina, California, New York, and Ohio. The attacks were especially personal and negative in South Carolina, where McCain was attacked by Right to Life Groups for his support of fetal tissue research, by the National Smokers Alliance for his support of increasing taxes on tobacco, and by a group called Keep it Flying for his lack of support of flying the Confederate flag over the South Carolina Statehouse.[27] In the end, Bush campaign resources and the allied attack against McCain secured the nomination for Bush, and the efforts by organized labor and the teachers' unions helped push Gore over the top.

MOST ACTIVE GROUPS

Interest groups took the 2000 election seriously; they spent hundreds of millions in direct hard money contributions to candidates, hard and soft money contributions to parties, and election issue advocacy, independent expenditures, and internal communication costs in federal races at all levels. The biggest interest group players were Citizens for Better Medicare (CBM) at $65 million,[28] the AFL-CIO ($21.5–46 million), the NRA ($20–25 million), the U.S. Chamber of Commerce ($15–25.5 million), Planned Parenthood ($14 million), and the NAACP National Voter Fund ($10.5 million). Bill Miller of the Chamber of Commerce told us that their effort in 2000 was a "ten-fold increase over any previous year."[29] Democratic groups like Planned Parenthood and the AFL-CIO spent in the same range as in 1998.

The second tier of groups includes the NEA ($2–10.2 million), Emily's List ($10 million), the Sierra Club ($9.5 million), NARAL ($8 million), the Business Roundtable ($6 million), Handgun Control ($4.5–5 million), and the League of Conservation Voters ($4–6.5 million). This is not intended to be a comprehensive list; for example, the Christian Coalition reportedly sent out 75 million voter guides, and the Alliance for Quality Nursing Home Care spent over $1 million in the Delaware Senate race alone. Many smaller groups were also active in specific races. Because groups employ several methods of activity, some activity is reported to the FEC, while other actions are not. Absent disclosure, we gathered data ourselves, conducted post-election interviews, and used studies like those conducted by Annenberg Public Policy Center of the University of Pennsylvania to assemble as complete a description of group election advocacy as possible.

Because of the competitive tenor of the 2000 election, these groups believed they could have an impact on competitive contests. The Annenberg Public Policy Center counted 130 groups active in the 2000 air war, nearly a hundred more than in 1996.[30] In our seventeen competitive contests alone, we counted 237 active groups in the air and on the ground. Groups expanded the scope of their activities in 2000 to include phone, mail, Internet, e-mail, and personal contacts. These methods helped groups better target their message to the desired segment of the population.

ISSUE ADVOCACY THEMES

The parties and interest groups raised strikingly similar themes in competitive 2000 congressional elections. Abortion and health care were themes common to both parties and groups; both parties and their allies ran television spots on health care. Recurrent mail themes included education, gun control, and Social Security.

Despite general similarities, themes differed among groups, and groups took up the causes of the parties they supported. Education was a Democratic and Democratic-allied interest group theme. Taxes were the most prominent GOP theme. The economy and taxes together were common themes for both parties and Republican-allied interest groups. Taxes were not a theme of Democratic allies and were ranked fifth behind jobs, gun control, health care, and abortion. Neither Republicans nor their interest group allies emphasized the environment, but it was a major concern for interest groups supporting Democrats. Interest groups on both sides, more than parties, emphasized gun control. Listed in table 3.1 are the top seven themes and messages of party-funded and interest group television ads and mail pieces.

INTEREST GROUP STRATEGY

Madison could not have imagined the influence his factions would have outside their own membership through tools including phones, Internet, television, radio, and personal contacts. Interest groups in their election advocacy campaigns have shifted from a heavy, sometimes exclusive, reliance on broadcast advertising to a more mixed strategy that includes more direct forms of communication with

Table 3.1. Most Frequent Themes of Activity Observed in Sample Races

Democratic Parties	*Democratic Interest Groups*	*Republican Parties*	*Republican Interest Groups*
Mail Pieces			
Health Care	Education	Taxes	Jobs
Education	Environment	Health Care	Gun Control
Senior Citizens	Abortion	Education	Health Care
Social Security	Union	Social Security	Abortion
Gun Control	Health Care	Senior Citizens	Taxes
Taxes	Gun Control	Abortion	Senior Citizens
Abortion	Social Security	Gun Control	Drugs
Television Ads			
Health Care	Environment	Taxes	Health Care
Education	Health Care	Health Care	Senior Citizens
Social Security	Abortion	Education	Gun Control
Senior Citizens	Drugs	Social Security	Economy
Taxes	Gay/Lesbian Rights	Senior Citizens	Drugs
Economy	(6 Issues Tied for Sixth)	Economy	Education
Jobs		Jobs	Taxes

Source: Election Advocacy database.

Notes: See appendix B for a more detailed explanation of the data. Medicare and prescription drugs were classified under the "Health Care" theme. Every list contained the "General/Unspecified" theme, which encompassed four main issues: candidates' character, candidates' experience, fundraising appeals, and straight ticket voting. In determining whether an interest group was a Democratic or Republican ally, we considered which candidates the organization's ads supported or attacked or whether the organization was anti- or pro- conservative or liberal; we used the same methodology for those interest groups that maintained neutrality.

voters. Our research methodology is uniquely well suited to monitoring these ground war activities. In the races we monitored in 2000, we detected substantial direct mail and telephone activity and picked up a fraction of what went on via the Internet.

Although many groups took an innovative Internet approach to campaigning, others simply shifted established strategies to suit their needs in specific contests. Not only did groups shift their ground/air war strategies, but they also timed their ads more effectively. Timing of communications is crucial to electoral success. In some instances, like the Michigan Senate race, groups went in early to keep Debbie Stabenow (D) competitive while she raised money for the fight ahead. After Governor Carnahan's death in Missouri, Democratic-allied groups capitalized on the tragedy, and Republican-allied groups toned down their attacks. After hearing about the death, the NFIB, for example, stopped the presses on a mailer that attacked Carnahan.[31]

Some groups tried a strategy that allowed them to influence campaigns from the inside out. These groups provided in-kind staff services to campaigns. These staffers were employed/paid by the interest group in Washington, D.C., or a regional office, but worked for a candidates' campaign. Groups using this tactic included the Human Rights Campaign, NARAL, League of Conservation Voters, Friends of the Earth, and the Sierra Club. Candidate campaigns with staff assisting them from one or more of these organizations were found in Pennsylvania Thirteen, Michigan Senate, California Twenty-seven, Oklahoma Two, and Michigan Eight. Some groups, such as the NFIB and the Chamber of Commerce, had staff that volunteered their time to campaigns in the evenings and did not declare their wages as in-kind donations.[32]

As in the past, groups continued to use innocuous names to hide their identities. In Arkansas Four, the Committee for Good Common Sense aired pro-Dickey (R) ads.[33] According to the Annenberg Public Policy Center, the Committee for Good Common Sense is an advocacy group formed in 1998 "to promote Libertarian causes."[34]The group, run mostly by Republicans with insurance and business ties, promotes privatization of Social Security. The group calls itself bipartisan.[35]

Republican-Allied Group Strategies

Republican-allied interest groups usually took either an air or ground war approach, not both. For example, Citizens for Better Medicare, Americans for Job Security, Business Roundtable, and Alliance for Quality Nursing Home Care all spent substantial sums of money on television advertising in our sample races but sent ten or fewer mailers. In contrast, the National Federation of Independent Business (NFIB) did no television advertising but was the most active Republican ally on the ground, with over fifty separate mailers in our races.

After the NFIB, the NRA was the second most active Republican-allied group in our races.[36] The NRA was the most potent Republican-allied group because of its large membership and extensive mobilization effort. Of all the Republican-allied groups, the NRA's strategy most closely mimicked labor's traditional strategy.

Republican-allied groups generally tried to diffuse the impact of issues like Social Security, prescription drug benefits, and expanded support for education. According to Dawn Laguens, Democrat Debbie Stabenow's media consultant in the Michigan Senate race, "Chamber activity was significant in the Michigan Senate race, helping muddy the water on prescription drugs. Pharmaceuticals also played a major role in muddying the water."[37] Heavy party soft money spending and interest group election issue advocacy by Citizens for Better Medicare, the Chamber of Commerce, and others largely achieved this objective.

Democratic-Allied Group Strategies

Democratic interest group allies were more inclined to pursue both an air and ground war strategy. The AFL-CIO, Sierra Club, Planned Parenthood, Handgun Control, NARAL, and the League of Conservation Voters all spent over $450,000 on television advertising in our races. Each of these groups also sent nineteen or more mail pieces. The NEA sent more mail than any other Democratic ally in our races, but spent little on television or radio.[38] On both the environment and abortion issues Democratic allies were substantially more active than Republican allies. On the abortion issue, the groups included NARAL, Planned Parenthood, People for the American Way, and Emily's List. We observed some activity from National Right to Life, but not nearly on the scale as the more Democratically-inclined groups. The battle over the environment was also one-sided, with groups like the League of Conservation Voters and the Sierra Club largely backing Democrats. No observable interest groups came to the aid of Republican candidates.

The Ground War

Democratic allies substantially outperformed the Republican allies on the ground, mainly because of labor's traditional efforts. Labor unions were the most active on the ground, with eighty-seven observed forms of ground war communications. Labor announced its plans to contact "22 percent of its membership personally," double what it did in 1998.[39] Karen Ackerman of the AFL-CIO reports that "2000 was our biggest effort ever, involving more locals, more unions, more mail, and more phones."[40]

The National Education Association was the second most active group on the ground, with seventy-two unique mail pieces in our races.[41] Also active on the Democratic side were the AFL-CIO (fifty), other labor organizations (fourteen), and AFSCME (eight). Pro-choice groups like NARAL (forty), Planned Parenthood (nineteen), and Emily's List (twelve) were generally far more active than Republican groups like National Right to Life (fourteen) and Christian Coalition (seven). NARAL confirmed that 2000 was their biggest effort since 1992; they spent $8 million on the ground with events and door-to-door visits.[42]

These observations do not account for the magnitude of the telephone campaign or the volume of pieces mailed. In that sense the data are imprecise. However, the range and level of group activity we collected is evidence that Democrats benefited from the ground war.

Republican allies were also visible and important. Glen Caroline of the NRA indicated that in 2000 they did more and spent more than in 1996 and 1998 combined; the number being "thrown around" was $20 million.[43] Chuck Cunningham, NRA acting director of federal affairs, adds that the NRA sent tens of thousands of mail pieces and made phone calls wherever there was mail.[44] The NFIB spent $8 million, mostly on internal communication mailings,[45] resulting in a much-enlarged effort in 2000. It is important to note that not all of these observed communications carry equal weight.

The Democrats traditionally spend more time and resources on the ground war. The 2000 election cycle was no exception. Although these types of communications are difficult to track, figure 3.1 shows that Democrats and their allies sent almost a third more mail and produced slightly more ground war communications than did the Republicans and their allies.

Mail

Interest groups employed direct mail as an important part of their 2000 strategy. Following the lead of labor unions, groups have diversified their communications strategies from a heavy reliance on broadcast advertising to a strategy that makes greater use of personal contacts, telephone calls, and mail. After the failure of the

Figure 3.1. Advertising Strategies for the Two Parties

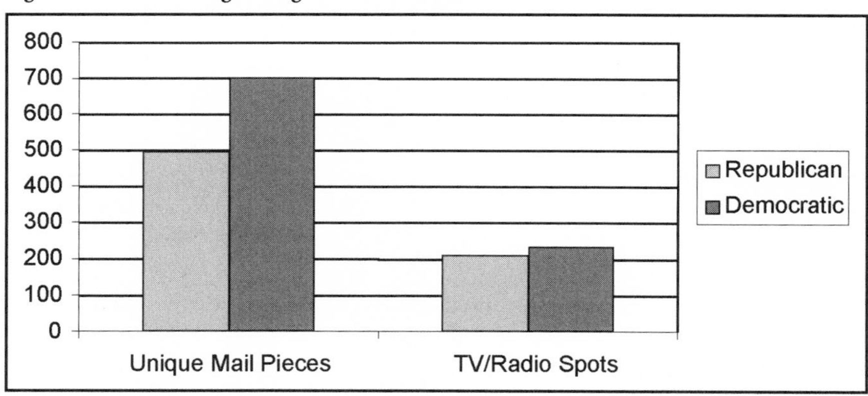

Source: Election Advocacy and *Campaign Media Analysis Group* database.
Note: See appendix B for a more detailed explanation of the data.

Republican "Operation Breakout" in 1998, more Republican-allied groups decided to focus more attention on the ground war. As Bernadette Budde of BIPAC observed, "You don't see the need for the ground unless you see TV fail."[46] Among the groups that said they either used or even increased their mail and phone this cycle and did more than ever before are the NEA, U.S. Chamber of Commerce, NRA, BIPAC, AFL-CIO, NFIB, and NARAL. All told, we collected 513 unique pieces of interest group general election mail, some of which we obtained in our post-election interviews with interest groups and campaign consultants. We collected from six to seventy-three pieces of interest group mail per race in the general election.[47] Overall, the average interest group mail in our races was thirty-three unique pieces per race.[48] In the aggregate, we observed approximately equal numbers of party and interest group mail. However, interest groups focused a larger percentage of their activity on mail than did parties. Perhaps interest groups focus a larger percentage of their own efforts on mail and phone because they already have large targeted databases to use for this form of electioneering.

Our research teams were struck by the large volume of mail in many of our sample races. In Washington Two, for example, some households received over twelve pieces of mail per day.[49] Groups often sent out four or more separate mail pieces aimed at a core audience, with focused pieces to voters based on their profile. The National Education Association was the most active, with seventy-two different mail pieces in our races.[50]

Because of the tremendous volume of mail in competitive 2000 races, interest groups sent scores of attention-getting mail, including several oversized, colorful pieces. The typical interest group mail piece was full color and multi-page (postcards were also popular). The NFIB used a gold-and-black color scheme to distinguish its mail from the hordes of colorful pieces sent out.[51] Other organizations also sought to differentiate their mail from other mail voters were receiving. Following are examples of how they did that:

> League of Conservation Voters sent a 17" by 5" color on heavy paper folded mailer with the words "Purple Haze" printed over a smoggy landscape to voters in California's Twenty-seventh Congressional District. When the recipient unfolded the mail initially, the piece opened up to 17" by 10" with the words: "Purple Haze All Across the Sky. What's Jim Rogan Doing About Our Purple Haze?" The mailer then opens to 17" by 20" and says: "Nothing: Jim Rogan Voted to Weaken Our Smog Laws." The mailer, which now more closely resembles a poster, highlights three examples of Rogan's environmental record on air pollution standards, the clean air act, and the public's right to know. The bottom quarter of the large mailer reads: "Lift the Haze and Protect Our Health. Vote No on Jim Rogan." There is a grainy photo of Rogan on this side of the poster as well.
>
> The Campaign for a Progressive Future mailed a glossy 10.5" by 4.25" folded mailer with gun cutout on the cover. Children's faces are superimposed on the gun. Next to the gun is the phrase: "Why would anyone support a law that increases gun violence in Virginia?" The mailer unfolds to a 10.5" by 17" picture of a jumble of currency (in several denominations) and the words, "Ask George Allen—He Did!" The mailer then

details, on the front and back, how much the NRA spent to elect Allen and how Allen has sided with the NRA.

Mail, like other media in our data, supports the idea that candidates try to stay positive and allow the outside money to take the negative route. The higher level of personalization and higher frequency of letters (often viewed as more personal than a large brochure or sensational and colorful fold-out) also support this idea: Only 17.2 percent of group mailers were letters.[52] Although nearly 25 percent of all non-candidate mail solely opposed a candidate, only 7 percent of candidate mail was intended solely to attack a candidate. In our sample, interest group and candidate mail were equally negative; however, interest group mail is generally more negative.

Voter guides were a common mailer. These guides usually include candidate names and photos along with a check, grade, or thumbs up/thumbs down for each candidate. Although this type of mail is meant as an educational guide to voters, not as an endorsement, it is usually clear which candidates the groups support and which they oppose. As long as these mailers do not expressly advocate the election or defeat of a candidate, the amount spent on them need not be disclosed. Voter guides are usually paid for with union or corporation treasury funds and are sent only to members of these unions or corporations.[53]

Figure 3.2 shows how Democratic efforts, more than Republican efforts, were focused on mail.

Telephone

Many groups used telephones in their voter identification and persuasion efforts. Interest groups were especially likely to use phone banks. Although it is

Figure 3.2. Unique Mail Pieces

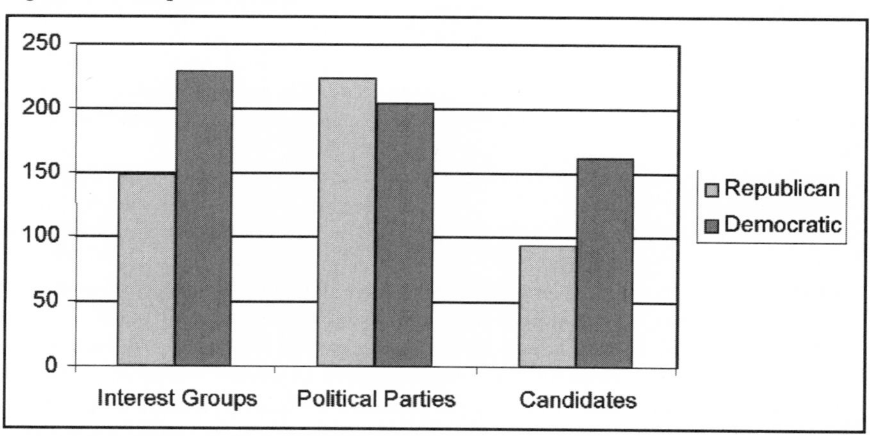

Source: Election Advocacy and *Campaign Media Analysis Group* databases.
Note: See appendix B for a more detailed explanation of the data.

harder to monitor telephone communications than mail, we learned of 148 different telephone communications in our races. Our interviews indicate that this estimate is very low.

NARAL, for example, spent close to $22,000 in the Michigan Eighth Congressional District. Most of these calls were in-house, but in some instances NARAL contracted with out-of-state political firms to call undecided Republicans and Independents to try to sway votes.[54]

BIPAC recruited small business owners to set up phone trees. Using these phone trees, NFIB and other groups "blitz[ed] small business owners with direct mail and phone calls in the weeks leading up to the Nov. 7 election."[55]

In the Missouri Senate race, a purple traveling truck, nicknamed "Barney," facilitated "hundreds of thousands" of member calls. Local volunteers used the truck, equipped with predictive dialing equipment, to make calls to local members.[56]

Other groups who told us that they used the telephone for millions of calls are National Right to Life, Christian Coalition, and the NRA.

Phone calls often came from out-of-state agencies that seem out of touch with local issues and candidates. Eric Freedman, who studied the Michigan Eighth House race, received one such call. The caller was from a New Jersey polling firm and had trouble pronouncing the candidates' names. The caller did not know who paid for the call.[57] One recorded call in the Michigan Senate race did not mention the group name or affiliation. The caller simply asked for the senior citizen in the house and stated that Spencer Abraham (R) would be "good for you."[58]

Person-to-Person Contacts

An AFL-CIO poll found that person-to-person contacts are far more effective than television commercials or mailers. By August 2000, the 13-million-member AFL-CIO announced that it would personally contact 22 percent of its membership. Labor was able to spend minimal amounts on this mobilization because of the masses of members they recruited for door-to-door visits.[59]

On the Republican-allied side, the NRA also mounted a major grassroots mobilization effort. The NRA talked about spending much of its $15 million campaign fund on voter mobilization.[60]

Where this mobilization money was actually spent is hard to track, although our researchers discovered a handful of these personal contacts. In the Washington Second Congressional District, for example, the NRA volunteers circulated voter guides at a local gun show. Bush and the Republican candidate John Koster were endorsed.

The Christian Coalition was also active in Washington Two. Volunteers distributed boilerplate voter guides that compared the Democrat and Republican U.S. Senate candidates, First Congressional District candidates, and Second Congressional District candidates. Koster responded to the survey and supports their issues; Democrat Rick Larsen did not respond.

In the Illinois Tenth District, paid volunteers from Emily's List visited local residents, characterizing Republican Kirk's views on Social Security. The Kirk team later claimed his views were misrepresented. The American Association of Retired People (AARP) passed out door hangers and distributed bookmarks at local public libraries encouraging voters to go to the polls on Election Day. These handouts highlighted issues important to seniors, including Social Security, long-term health care, and Medicare.

Internet

The Internet has great fundraising potential in politics. John McCain demonstrated this following his New Hampshire primary, raising $2 million in just a few days.[61] Groups also got in on the action; in this cycle, the U.S. Chamber of Commerce ran one of the "most sophisticated and complete get-out-the-vote programs the Internet has ever seen."[62] The Chamber sent an online survey to Juno (an Internet provider) subscribers who were likely business supporters. They then asked for contact information from survey respondents. They used this contact information, along with survey results, to tailor follow-up e-mails that talked about local candidates, voter registration information, absentee ballot information, etc. Brian Wilde, executive director of the Office of Grassroots Programs, U.S. Chamber, said, "The Internet gave us the opportunity to have a true dialogue with our audience, it also allowed our message to spread virally to others."[63]

Several business organizations in 2000, including the U.S. Chamber of Commerce, the National Association of Manufacturers, the Business Roundtable, the American Chemistry Council, and the National Association of Wholesales, joined in an effort to take a page out of labor's book to communicate more effectively and mobilize business at the grassroots. Part of this strategy included a Web-based resource designed by BIPAC called "Project 2000," at <www.Politikit.com>. This Web site enabled organizations to quickly produce information about candidates' stands on business issues. They also distributed in-depth instructions on all parts of federal campaigns, from online distribution of voter registration forms and absentee ballot requests to running independent expenditures and issue advocacy to giving and raising money.

Labor also used the Internet to its advantage. At its Web site, local union leaders could customize a number of flier templates to suit their local affiliate needs. Local unions could print the fliers themselves, or they could order printing online. In the Missouri Senate race, the AFL-CIO used this toolkit to work through local unions to send out professional messages tailored to those members.[64] And the AFL-CIO continually used Web sites and e-mails to rally members.[65] NARAL also used the Internet to get its message out. We received an e-mail message with several links to broadcast ads.

Table 3.2 shows the different ground war tactics employed by candidates, party committees, and allied groups.

Table 3.2. The Ground War: Most Active Organizations' Observed Activity in All Sample Races

Type	*Organization*	*Mail*	*News*	*Person*	*Phone*	*E-mail*	*Banner*	*Total Unique Ads*
Democratic Allies								
Candidates	Democratic Candidates	162	5	3	9	4	—	183
Political Parties	State Democratic Parties	163	11	2	11	1	—	188
	DCCC	24	—	—	—	—	—	24
	Local Democratic Parties	14	3	1	2	—	—	20
	DNC	7	2	—	—	2	—	11
	DSCC	4	—	—	—	—	—	4
Interest Groups	NEA	67	—	—	3	—	—	70
	AFL-CIO	42	4	—	3	—	—	49
	NARAL	28	—	—	8	—	—	36
	LCV	33	—	—	—	—	—	33
	Sierra Club	21	1	1	1	—	—	24
	Planned Parenthood	18	1	—	2	—	—	21
	Labor	18	2	—	—	—	—	20
	Emily's List	12	—	1	—	1	—	14
	Handgun Control	13	—	—	1	—	—	14
	NAACP	3	3	—	—	—	—	6

Table 3.2. (*Continued*)

Type	*Organization*	*Mail*	*News*	*Person*	*Phone*	*E-mail*	*Banner*	*Total Unique Ads*
Republican Allies								
Candidates	Republican Candidates	92	6	—	3	2	—	**103**
Political Parties	State Republican Parties	141	—	1	4	—	—	**146**
	NRCC	67	—	—	—	—	—	**67**
	Local Republican Parties	17	—	1	2	—	—	**20**
	RNC	11	—	—	—	1	—	**12**
Interest Groups	NFIB	48	4	—	1	—	—	**53**
	NRA	24	1	1	2	—	1	**29**
	National Right to Life	14	—	—	3	—	—	**17**
	Christian Coalition	7	—	1	1	3	—	**12**
	Citizens for Better Medicare	8	—	1	—	—	—	**9**
	Chamber of Commerce	7	1	—	—	—	—	**8**
Nonpartisan								
Interest Groups	AARP	12	3	4	2	—	—	**21**

Source: Election Advocacy database.

Notes: See appendix B for a more detailed explanation of the data. Data represent the number of unique ads/pieces by the group and do not represent a count of total items sent or made. This table is not intended to represent comprehensive organization activity within the sample races. A more complete picture can be obtained by examining this table together with table 3.3.

The Air War

Several of our studies report extraordinarily high levels of political advertising on television, a finding that is reinforced in some states by highly competitive races for more than one major office. In some cases television and radio expenditures of parties or interest groups exceeded candidate spending. This happened in congressional contests in Arkansas Four, California Twenty-seven, Illinois Ten, Kentucky Six, Michigan Eight, Pennsylvania Four and Thirteen, and Washington Two, and in the Missouri Senate race.

We estimate that at least $99.7 million was spent on radio, television, and cable television in our seventeen sample races.[66] Interest groups, as expected, spent the least on television and radio at approximately $20.5 million. Interestingly, candidates were outspent by political parties, $43.5 million to $35.7 million, in the air war.[67] In terms of the party breakdown, our estimates show the Republican Party outspending the Democrats $22.2 million to $21.3 million. The Republican-allied interest groups also outspent their Democratic counterparts $11.8 million to $8.4 million in the air war. The large soft money war chests both parties amassed for the relatively few competitive races may account for the difference in spending between parties and interest groups.

Television

The rising cost of airtime and the fact that some stations ran out of airtime forced groups to advertise via cable television in 2000. Paul Taylor and the Alliance for Better Campaigns found that stations in the top seventy-five media markets earned at least $771 million from the sale of more than 1.2 million political ads from 1 January to 7 November 2000—almost twice as much as they earned in 1996. This surge in earnings was partially a result of the numerous issue ads produced by parties and groups.[68] These ads filled up spots and allowed stations to drive up prices because demand was so high. As a result, we found that some groups turned to the cheaper and more targeted cable stations.

Our ad buy data from the seventeen races document that Democratic Party committees and allied groups used cable television much more than Republican Party committees and GOP allies. The Democratic-allied interest groups purchased nearly three times as many cable spots as Republican-allied interest groups (a difference of 3,000 spots). This difference in strategy greatly reduced the average cost per spot for Democrats and their allies. These differences are reflected in figure 3.3.

Cable was not, however, the sole possession of the Democrats and their allies. Citizens for Better Medicare, a Republican ally, spent over $70,000 in the California Twenty-seventh District alone via cable television.[69]

With cable television removed, Democratic Party committees and Democratic interest groups do not enjoy nearly the same cost advantage. Once we remove the

Figure 3.3. Average Cost per Television Spot

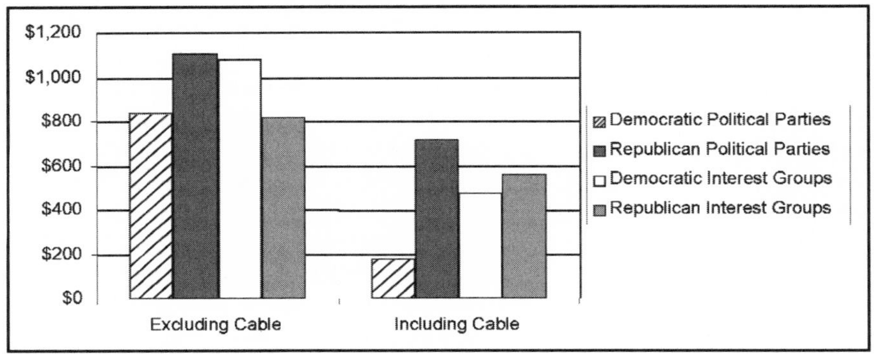

Source: Election Advocacy and *Campaign Media Analysis Group* databases.

substantial cable television buy, Democratic interest groups and the Republican Party paid the most per ad. In the four Senate races in which CMAG broadcast advertising data were available (Montana does not have a top seventy-five media market), the CMAG cost estimate indicates that the Democratic Party paid $816 and the Republican interest groups $815 on average per spot.

There was more controversy in 2000 about the accuracy and content of soft money and election issue advocacy ads, and stations pulled some ads. More typically, however, broadcasters ran the ads, often at rates well above prevailing rates.

Estimates of how much was spent on television in our races are imprecise, whether relying on the ad buy data retrieved from the stations or the CMAG data. Table 3.3 presents a summary of the amounts spent in our sample races by candidates, parties, and groups, and it tallies the estimated costs for both the ad buy data and CMAG data. Overall, when we combine the two methodologies and tally whichever estimate is higher, we arrive at an estimated $99.7 million in spending on the air war in these contests.[70]

Radio

In an NPR report by Don Gonyea, Michigan pollster Ed Sarpolus said radio was the "secret weapon of campaigning."[71] Al Gore used the radio in much the same way the NAACP National Voter Fund used cable television to broadcast the controversial hate crimes ad about the murder of African American James Byrd and George W. Bush's failure to sign hate crimes legislation in Texas. Gore's camp ran hate crime ads on local radio stations in black neighborhoods in California. Gonyea said that placement on urban radio stations was a good way to reach a very specific audience while keeping out those who might be offended by such ads.[72]

Because there are so many urban radio stations, it was difficult to track this medium. We found, however, that the NRA, Americans for Limited Terms, U.S.

Table 3.3. The Air War: Most Active Organizations' Collected Ad Buy Data in All Sample Races

Type	*Organization*	*TV*	*Radio*	*Total Ad Buy $*	*CMAG TV*
Democratic Allies					
Candidates	Democratic Candidates	$12,934,111	$177,731	**$13,111,842**	$15,315,120
Political Parties State	Democratic Parties	$13,858,164	$70,031	**$13,928,194**	$7,011,315
	DCCC	$2,156,191	$6,140	**$2,162,331**	$2,827,782
	Democratic Victory Funds	$111,687	$2,166	**$113,853**	$0
	DNC	$17,700	$0	**$17,700**	$0
	Others	$129,387	$2,166	**$131,553**	$0
Interest Groups	Planned Parenthood	$1,524,412	$0	**$1,524,412**	$0
	AFL-CIO	$1,425,866	$0	**$1,425,866**	$1,195,062
	Sierra Club	$657,587	$44,535	**$702,122**	$0
	Handgun Control	$549,676	$0	**$549,676**	$0
	Emily's List	$526,220	$0	**$526,220**	$443,120
	LCV	$491,835	N/A	**$491,835**	$263,595
	NARAL	$473,090	$0	**$473,090**	$0
	CFAW	$0	$259,500	**$259,500**	$363,786
	Voters for Choice	$113,674	N/A	**$113,674**	$678,634
	NAACP	$79,740	$29,508	**$109,248**	$0
	NEA	$23,456	$32,210	**$55,666**	$50,635
	Others	$553,711	$1,120	**$554,831**	$746,778

Table 3.3. (*Continued*)

Type	*Organization*	*TV*	*Radio*	*Total Ad Buy $*	*CMAG TV*
Republican Allies					
Candidates	Republican Candidates	$13,020,689	$359,426	**$13,380,115**	$19,852,395
Political Parties	State Republican Parties	$11,508,837	$197,318	**$11,706,154**	$5,579,985
	RNC	$2,452,425	$6,566	**$2,458,991**	$0
	NRSC	$724,503	$0	**$724,503**	$0
	NRCC	$599,125	$12,946	**$612,071**	$2,252,647
	Others	$51,725	$1,000	**$52,725**	$0
Interest Groups	Chamber of Commerce	$1,785,270	$524,100	**$2,309,370**	$2,599,697
	Citizens for Better Medicare	$1,644,191	$0	**$1,644,191**	$2,878,813
	AQNHC	$1,230,966	$0	**$1,230,966**	$1,943,608
	Americans for Job Security	$1,188,965	$9,580	**$1,198,545**	$0
	Business Roundtable	$938,545	N/A	**$938,545**	$2,020,974
	NRA	$49,880	$63,938	**$113,818**	$23,487
	Rep Leadership Council	$108,225	$0	**$108,225**	$93,721
	AMA	$105,345	$0	**$105,345**	$172,118
	Others	$318,698	$60,684	**$379,382**	$8,995
Nonpartisan					
Interest Groups	Others	$271,487	$13,560	$285,047	**$0**

Source: Election Advocacy and *Campaign Media Analysis Group* databases.

Notes: Please see appendix B for a more detailed explanation of the data. The "Others" organization combines the data of all other organizations that bought ad buys but are not listed in the table within that category (i.e., Democratic or Republican allies). This table is not intended to represent comprehensive organization spending or activity within the sample races. A more complete picture can be obtained by examining this table with table 3.2.

Chamber of Commerce, NFIB, NEA, LCV, Million Mom March PAC, Planned Parenthood, and the National Right to Life PAC, among others, aired radio ads.

Of the 105 radio ads we recorded, 97 were election issue advocacy. One typical radio issue ad is a sixty-second spot from the Missouri Senate race. The spot begins with Don Wainwright, owner of Wainwright Industries in St. Peters, talking about his employees' health insurance. Wainwright says he's depending on John Ashcroft to get a real patient bill of rights. The announcer then discusses Ashcroft's record. Wainright says that Trial Lawyers and their friends in Congress are blocking reforms. The announcer then says, "Senator Ashcroft is fighting for you, call him . . . to say 'keep on fighting.'" The tag line is different for various airings of the commercial. The ad sponsor is the Health Benefits Coalition. The five tags in the St. Louis area are Business Roundtable, U.S. Chamber of Commerce, NFIB, National Association of Wholesalers-Distributors, and the National Association of Manufacturers.

A similar thirty-second ad ran in the Delaware Senate race. In this spot a local businessman from southern Delaware voices his concern about health care for his workers and the ways in which Senator Roth has worked to make this a reality. The business owner says that Trial Lawyers are blocking progress in Washington. An announcer then takes over to explain that Roth has been working on this and encourages voters to call him to say, "Keep on fighting." Business Roundtable paid for the ad.

IMPACT OF INTEREST GROUP ACTIVITY IN 2000

With substantial GOTV efforts, interest groups in 2000 increased voter turnout, especially among minorities.[73] In Michigan and Missouri, labor unions even gave employees the day off so they could take time to vote. Interest groups also help to educate the electorate on certain issues. In some instances, interest groups forced candidates to address important issues the candidates would rather not have discussed. In the Montana Senate race, for example, the Trial Lawyers forced incumbent Senator Conrad Burns (R) to address his cosponsored legislation dealing with asbestos. This legislation limited corporate liability for asbestos-caused illness. At that time, 192 miners in Libbey, Montana had died of asbestos poisoning, and 375 were fatally ill due to asbestos in the Montana mine. The negative attention Burns received from the Trial Lawyers and the media focused attention on Schweitzer, Burns's opponent, who mentioned that corporations that would benefit from the legislation donated to Burns's campaign.[74] Interest groups also helped challenger Debbie Stabenow (D) stay afloat at the beginning of her campaign when she did not have the funds to do so.[75]

Election issue advocacy had both positive and negative effects. Candidates appreciated and even relied on interest group help, but at the same time candidates were forced to answer to the public regarding negative ads. Examples include the asbestos issue in Montana Senate and prescription drugs in Michigan and Montana. In other cases the effects of issue ads were so great that candidates were forced to focus funds on these issues to answer their attacks. In Montana, for example, Democratic challenger Brian Schweitzer was forced to spend almost two-thirds of his coffer to answer attack ads aired by Citizens for Better Medicare.

In instances like Montana, issue ads essentially set part of the campaign agenda. The ads bring an issue to the forefront of the campaign and force the candidate to spend money on the issue. Citizens for Better Medicare also helped set the agenda in California Twenty-seven and Arkansas Four. In California, CBM and the U.S. Chamber of Commerce spent $750,000 trying to get Democratic challenger Jim Schiff to talk more about Medicare and prescription drugs. Eventually Schiff responded, spending more than he planned on the issue.[76] Tim Ryan, CBM's executive director, said that these "attack" ads were simply ads aimed at an issue. Ryan said the ads were not meant to influence the election.[77] Whether or not the ads were meant to affect the election, they forced Schiff to respond. California researchers David Menefee-Libey and Drew Linzer said that whether the groups intended to or not, CBM's and the Chamber's efforts damaged Schiff's integrity and forced him to follow their agenda.

Because the tone and message of election advocacy is more negative and attention getting than candidate ads, these ads can offend voters and make them more likely to vote for the candidate attacked in the ad. In the 2000 cycle, ads of this type included the NAACP National Voter Fund hate crimes ad against George W. Bush and some of the NRA ads that featured Charlton Heston attacking Bill Clinton and Al Gore. These types of ads, however, are usually so well targeted that they are not likely to be seen by someone who would be offended by them. When groups target their message to an audience of likely supporters, they run less of a risk of activating the opposition, while being freer to attack the less-preferred candidate. These targeted modes of communication include mail, telephone, Internet, personal contact, and voter guides.

CONCLUSION

Interest groups today have an expanded array of means to communicate with the public about candidates and elections. Issue advocacy is the most recent and among the most important means of communication, at least in competitive races. Unlike other PAC contributions from interest groups, election issue advocacy is unpopular with many elected officials because it injects uncertainty into the electoral process. Although these outside communications often help a candidate, they also weaken a candidate's control of the campaign. And candidates and the public object to the anonymous speech components of issue advocacy and the predominantly negative tone of most of these ads.

Efforts to reform or limit election issue advocacy quickly encounter First Amendment concerns about the need to protect freedom of speech. Political speech and the rights of individuals and groups to express themselves about issues are fundamental rights. When does a group's expression of opposition to a politician's vote or issue position stop being about a legislative issue and start being about electing or defeating that candidate? Would Madison have been satisfied that interest groups' competition was enough to "cure the mischiefs of faction?" Meaningful elections require individuals and groups to express themselves, but election-related speech, the Supreme Court has repeatedly ruled, can be more subject to regulation than issue-related speech. Here, what distinguishes election speech from issue speech is crucial, and often confusing.

The most compelling arguments by those who want to require greater disclosure of issue advocacy and a broader definition of what constitutes electioneering than the present "magic words" test are that the large infusion of unlimited and undisclosed money into elections reduces electoral accountability for candidates, permits anonymous groups to affect the agenda of elections, drives up the cost of campaigns, and alienates voters from the democratic process. The most compelling arguments of defenders of unregulated issue advocacy are that such regulation will limit speech by groups and individuals and that regulation of this expanded definition of issue advocacy will be difficult.

In 1998 the Shays-Meehan Bipartisan Campaign Reform Act passed the House but not the Senate. Included in it was a soft money ban and an expanded express advocacy definition. The definition said that communications run in the last sixty days before an election that feature the name or likeness of a federal candidate are campaign communications and so should be subject to FECA regulations and reporting.[78]

Issue advocacy was an important element of the 2001 congressional debate over campaign finance reform. In February 2001, Senators Olympia Snowe (R-Maine) and James Jeffords (R-Vt.), along with Paul Wellstone (D-Minn.), revived the 1998 amendment to the McCain-Feingold/Shays-Meehan bill first debated in February 1998. The amendment restricted outside group issue ads intended to influence the election or defeat of a candidate. Snowe-Jeffords also banned the use of union dues and corporate funds for this type of electioneering within sixty days of an election and required disclosure of contributions over $200 meant for such ads. The 2001 version of the McCain-Feingold bill passed the House, but its counterpart in the Senate, Shays-Meehan, did not make it to a vote.

In theory, issue ads are strictly about issues. In practice, groups skirt the intention of *Buckley v. Valeo*, the case that defined issue ads, to produce ads that fit the issue ad criteria because they avoid words like "vote for" or "elect" but that aim to influence the election or defeat of a candidate using the candidate's name or image. The Snowe-Jeffords amendment essentially redefined "issue ad" to include these "electioneering communications."[79]

With the varied tools of influence available to interest groups and with their sights set on more than just the good of the individuals or corporations they represent, the factions Madison said were inevitable have become dominant. As recent elections have demonstrated, interest groups see issue advocacy as another means to influence the outcome of elections. Campaign finance reform that ignores this reality will likely mean that groups simply shift from soft money contributions to the parties to issue advocacy on their own. Such a shift would actually reduce disclosure, should Congress not at the same time alter the disclosure requirements for issue advocacy.

NOTES

1. James Madison, "The Federalist No. 10," in *The Federalist Papers*, ed. Roy P. Fairfield (Baltimore: Johns Hopkins University Press, 1981), 18.
2. Alexis de Tocqueville, "Of the Use Which the Americans Make of Public Associations in Civil Life," in *Democracy in America 1835–1839*, <xroads.virginia.edu/~HYPER/DETOC/ch2_05.htm> [accessed August 2001].
3. Madison, "The Federalist No. 10," 18.
4. Madison, "The Federalist No. 10," 17.
5. Robert A. Dahl, *A Preface to Democratic Theory* (Chicago: University of Chicago Press, 1956), 22.
6. Diana Dwyre, "Interest Groups and Issue Advocacy in 1996," in *Financing the 1996 Election*, ed. John C. Green (New York: M. E. Sharpe, 1999), 190.
7. Ibid., 191.
8. Federal Election Commission, "PAC Activity Increases in 2000 Election Cycle," news release, <www.fec.gov/press/053101pacfund/053101pacfund.html>, 31 May 2001, [accessed 30 July 2001].
9. Marke J. Rozell and Clyde Wilcox, *Interest Groups in American Campaigns: The New Face of Electioneering* (Washington, D.C.: CQ Press, 1999); Dwyre, "Interest Groups and Issue Advocacy in 1996."
10. Anthony Corrado et al., *Campaign Finance Reform: A Sourcebook* (Washington, D.C.: Brookings Institution Press, 1997), 7. Non-multicandidate PACs may contribute up to $20,000 per year to national party committees and can give $5,000 per year to local and state party committees.
11. Sheila Krumholz, "PACs to Parties '00 Cycle," personal e-mail to Anna Nibley Baker, 24 August 2001.
12. *Buckley v. Valeo*, 424 U.S. 1 (1976).
13. Groups may avoid disclosure through internal communications. These communications are restricted to members, stockholders, executive or administrative personnel, and their families. These communications include GOTV drives, phone banks, and registration drives. Internal communications over $2,000 that expressly advocate election or defeat of a particular candidate must be reported. See Corrado, *Campaign Finance Reform*, 11.
14. Corporate and union treasuries contain mostly dues, but other sources also fill the treasuries. Unions and corporations may spend these moneys on exempt activities aimed at their restricted class or on issue advocacy and voter education aimed at the public. See

Joseph E. Cantor, "Political Spending by Organized Labor: Background and Current Issues," Congressional Research Service report for Congress, <www.opensecrets.org/regulation/s96-484.htm>, 29 May 1996 [accessed June 2001].

15. Erika Falk, "Content and Tenor of Issue Ads," in *Issue-Advertising in the 1999–2000 Election Cycle* (unpublished report by the Annenberg Public Policy Center), <www.appcpenn.org/political/issueads/1999-2000issueadvocacy.pdf> [accessed June 2001].

16. Tim Ryan, executive director, Citizens for Better Medicare, telephone interview by David B. Magleby and Anna Nibley Baker, 14 May 2001.

17. David B. Magleby, "Dictum without Data," report presented at the National Press Club, Washington, D.C., November 2000, 7.

18. This number is an estimate by the Annenberg Public Policy Center of the University of Pennsylvania. The figures come specifically from *Issue-Advertising in the 1999–2000 Election Cycle.* The estimate includes broadcast (television and radio) ads only.

19. Cook and Company, *The Cook Political Report,* 14 April 2000, 1 and 73.

20. Dwyre, "Interest Groups and Issue Advocacy in 1996," 204.

21. David B. Magleby, *Outside Money: Soft Money and Issue Advocacy in the 1998 Congressional Elections* (Lanham, Md.: Rowman & Littlefield), 50.

22. Magleby, *Outside Money,* 73.

23. Art Sanders and David Redlawsk, "Money in the Iowa Caucuses," in *Getting Inside the Outside Campaign: Issue Advocacy in the 2000 Presidential Primaries,* Report presented at the National Press Club, Washington, D.C., <www.byu.edu/outsidemoney>, 7 July 2000, 23 [accessed 5 April 2001].

24. Roy Fletcher, McCain 2000, telephone interview by authors, 6 June 2000.

25. Most respondents (85–86 percent) in a national Web TV survey saw these ads as intending to hurt a particular candidate. See table 2 in Magleby, "Dictum without Data."

26. Academic researchers were asked to code communications as either supporting or attacking a candidate. Because "oppose" is the more common phrase used to describe communications that attack or oppose a candidate, we use it in the text.

27. Bill Moore and Danielle Vinson, "The South Carolina Republican Primary," in *Getting Inside the Outside Campaign.*

28. These estimates come from a combination of sources: (1) interviews we conducted with interest group leaders; (2) the Annenberg Public Policy Center of the University of Pennsylvania. *Issue Advertising in the 1999–2000 Election Cycle* (The estimates include only broadcast (television and radio) ads); (3) an internal NARAL memo (Clyde Henderson III to Kate Michelman and Gloria Totten, memorandum, 7 November 2000) given to us by Will Lutz of NARAL. The following table shows from where we obtained these estimates.

Interest Group Spending Estimates

Interest Group	*Memo*	*Annenberg*	*Interview*
CBM	—	65 million	—
AFL-CIO	46 million	21.1 million	—
NRA	25 million	20 million	20 million
Emily's List	10 million	—	—
Chamber	—	25.5 million	15 million overall
Planned Parenthood	14 million	—	2 TV/radio only
NAACP Nat'l Voter Fund	—	—	10.5 million*
Sierra	9.5 million	—	—

Interest Group Spending Estimates (*Continued*)

Interest Group	*Memo*	*Annenberg*	*Interview*
NEA	2 million	—	10.2 million
NARAL	—	—	8 million on the ground
Business Roundtable	—	6 million	—
Handgun Control	5 million	—	4.5 million
LCV	4 million	—	6.4 million

Sources: Glen Caroline, National Rifle Association (NRA), interview by David B. Magleby, Washington, D.C., 15 November 2000; Bill Miller, U.S. Chamber of Commerce, telephone interview by David B. Magleby, 18 November 2000; Rachel Lyons, PAC director, Planned Parenthood, interview by David B. Magleby, Washington, D.C., 13 December 2000; Will Lutz, deputy communications director, and Gloria Totten, political director, National Abortion Rights Action League (NARAL), interview by David B. Magleby, Washington, D.C., 14 December 2000; Naomi Piass, communications director, Handgun Control, interview by Eric A. Smith and Anna N. Baker, Washington, D.C., 15 November 2000; and Lisa Wade, League of Conservation Voters (LCV), interview by David B. Magleby, Washington, D.C., 13 November 2000. The NAACP estimate came from a presentation by Heather Booth, NAACP, at the Finance and Nonprofit Advocacy Seminar, <www.urban.org/advocacyresearch/heather%20booth.html>, 8 December 2001.

29. Miller, interview by Magleby.

30. Annenberg Public Policy Center, *Issue Advertising in the 1999–2000 Election Cycle*, 1.

31. Sharon Wolff, National Federation of Independent Business (NFIB), interview by authors, Washington, D.C., 14 November 2000.

32. Ibid.

33. Harold F. Bass, Kathryn A. Kirkpatrick, and Amber E. Wilson, "The 2000 Arkansas Fourth Congressional District Race," in "Outside Money," ed. David B. Magleby, *PS: eSymposium*, <www.apsanet.org/PS/june01/outsidemoney.cfm>, June 2001 [accessed August 2001].

34. Annenberg Public Policy Center, "Issue Ads Group Index," <www.appcpenn.org/issueads/Committe%20for%20Good%20Common%20Sense.htm> [accessed May 2001].

35. Julie Kosterlitz, "A Blast from Clinton's Past," *National Journal* (12 June 1999): 1600.

36. "Most active" means most communications on the air and ground combined. In our seventeen races we counted fifty-six NFIB communications and thirty-eight NRA communications.

37. Dawn Laguens, Stabenow chief media strategist, interview by David B. Magleby, Washington, D.C., 15 November 2000.

38. Seventy-two pieces in our sample, but the group only spent $55,666 on television or radio.

39. Jerry Zremski, "Labor Is Working Overtime for Gore," *The Buffalo News*, 19 August 2000, 1A.

40. Karen Ackerman, AFL-CIO, interview by David B. Magleby, Washington, D.C., 9 November 2000.

41. In the samplewide data we have combined state and local affiliates into the national group tally.

42. Will Lutz, deputy communications director, and Gloria Totten, political director, National Abortion Rights Action League (NARAL), interview by David B. Magleby, Washington, D.C., 14 December 2000.

43. Caroline, interview by Magleby.

44. Chuck Cunningham, National Rifle Association (NRA), interview by David B. Magleby, Washington, D.C., 12 November 2000.

45. Wolff, interview by authors.

46. Bernadette Budde, Business-Industry Political Action Committee (BIPAC), interview by David B. Magleby, Washington, D.C., 10 November 2000.

47. With party mail included, we collected between twenty-five and one hundred pieces of mail per race.

48. The average, including party mail, is sixty-one pieces of mail per race.

49. Todd Donovan and Charles Morrow, "The 2000 Washington Second Congressional District Race," in "Outside Money," ed. Magleby.

50. In the samplewide data we have combined state and local affiliates into the national group tally.

51. Wolff, interview by authors.

52. Over 30 percent of candidate mail in our sample races was letters, and nearly 38 percent of candidate mail was personalized to the recipient (compared to 27 percent by political parties and interest groups).

53. Dwyre, "Interest Groups and Issue Advocacy in 1996," 206.

54. Chris Mather, telephone interview by Jonathan Ladd, 5 December 2000.

55. Susan Schmidt, "Businesses Ante up $30 Million," *Washington Post*, 26 October 2000, A26.

56. Martha Kropf et al., "The 2000 Missouri Senate Race," in "Outside Money," ed. Magleby.

57. Eric Freedman, telephone conversation with Anna N. Baker, September 2000.

58. Marcia W. Marshall, e-mail to authors, 8 November 2000.

59. Nancy Cleeland, "Revitalized Unions Pour Money, Labor Into Democratic Campaigns," *Los Angeles Times*, 14 August 2000, 1. This effort saved Democrats millions. Democrats budgeted only $50 million for voter mobilization, one-half of what the Republicans budgeted.

60. Eric Bailey, "Foot Soldiers Fight to Boost Turnout," *Los Angeles Times*, 29 October 2000, 1.

61. David B. Magleby, ed., "Getting Inside the Outside Campaign: Issue Advocacy in the 2000 Presidential Primaries," report presented at the National Press Club, Washington, D.C., <www.byu.edu/outsidemoney>, 7 July 2000, 14 [accessed June 2001].

62. Roger Stone, "Case Studies: Using the Internet to Build Citizen Armies," *Campaigns & Elections* (April 2001): 44.

63. In a follow-up interview with Roger Stone, the author of the article cited in note 62, we asked if the word "virtually" was misprinted as "virally;" this is his response: "The word is 'virally' and it is reference to what has become known in the Internet as 'viral marketing.' Basically that is the phenomenon we have all witnessed as one e-mail message is forwarded and then re-forwarded to first hundreds and then thousands and then tens of thousands of people. In politics the classic example is <move-on.org>."

64. Kropf, "The 2000 Missouri Senate Race."

65. Nancy Cleeland, "Revitalized Unions Pour Money, Labor Into Democratic Campaigns," *Los Angeles Times*, 14 August 2000, 1.

66. These figures were derived after careful comparison between CMAG data and the ad buy data collected by the academics. In instances in which the CMAG television figure for a group was higher than the ad buy figure from the *Election Advocacy* database, the CMAG figure was combined with the radio ad buys to create a more accurate estimate for that group. Also note that these data are low estimates.

67. Ibid.

68. Alliance for Better Campaigns, "Gouging Democracy: How the Television Industry Profiteered on Campaign 2000," unpublished report, 3, 11.

69. Patrick McGreevy, "California Elections U.S. House; High-Profile Contest Is Awash in Soft Money," *Los Angeles Times*, 22 October 2000, home edition.

70. Adding up the higher expenditure is defensible because the data collected from stations more accurately reflect actual costs of advertising, but since not all stations provided data, this is not a complete estimate. In some instances, perhaps because stations were unwilling to provide ad cost data, the CMAG estimate is higher. In instances where CMAG failed to identify spots that we learned about by gathering ad buy data from stations, those data are included.

71. Don Gonyea, "Special Report," *Morning Edition: National Public Radio*, 1 November 2000.

72. Ibid.

73. Robert Dreyfuss, "Till Earth and Heaven Ring: The NAACP Is Back and Plans on Being Heard," *The Nation* 4, no. 273 (23 July 2001): 11.

74. Craig Wilson, "The 2000 Montana Senate Race," in "Outside Money," ed. Magleby.

75. See Michael Traugott, "Soft Money and Challenger Viability: The 2000 Michigan Senate Race," in "Outside Money," ed. Magleby.

76. Drew Linzer and David Menefee-Libey, "The 2000 California Twenty-seventh Congressional District Race," in "Outside Money," ed. Magleby.

77. Ryan, interview by Magleby and Baker.

78. Dwyre, "Interest Groups and Issue Advocacy in 1996," 212.

79. According to Senator Feingold, in this amendment, these "electioneering communications" are made through the broadcast media (radio and television, including satellite and cable), they refer to a clearly identified official candidate (they use the candidate's name or image), and they appear within sixty days of a general election or thirty days of a primary in which the candidate is running. See *Congressional Record*, 105th Cong., 2d sess., 25 February 1998, no. 15.

4

Independent Expenditures and Internal Communications in the 2000 Congressional Elections

David B. Magleby and Jason Richard Beal

The dramatic growth in noncandidate campaigning came in the 1996 election cycle with the growth in party soft money used for candidate promotions by the Democrats for the Clinton/Gore ticket and in issue advocacy by the AFL-CIO against House Republicans. The 1996 issue advocacy by labor was largely waged on television. Since 1996, the AFL-CIO has diversified its tactics to give much greater emphasis to its internal communication efforts. Building on the person-to-person campaigning against the California anti-union paycheck protection initiative (Proposition 226 of June 1998), the unions have applied the same personal contact, direct mail, and telephone contact tools with their membership in key congressional races in 1998, like the Nevada Senate race,[1] the Iowa caucuses in the 2000 presidential nomination contest,[2] and in several states in the closely contested 2000 general elections. Omitting internal communications such as member-to-member contacts, direct mail, and phone banks would have caused them to miss important elements of the 1998 and 2000 elections.

Campaign communications outside the control of the candidates include party soft money spending, discussed in chapter 2, and issue advocacy by interest groups, examined in chapter 3. Clearly soft money and issue advocacy have been the more visible and predominant modes of outside money spending. This chapter discusses the less high profile but growing means of electioneering: internal communications and independent expenditures.

An independent expenditure, as defined by the Federal Election Commission (FEC), is:

> [A]n expenditure by a person expressly advocating the election or defeat of a clearly identified candidate which is made without cooperation or consultation with any candidate, or any authorized agency of such candidate, and which is not made in concert with, or at the request or suggestion of, any such candidate.[3]

The Supreme Court, in *Buckley v. Valeo,* "established that the First Amendment protects the right of individuals and political committees to spend unlimited amounts of their own money on an independent basis to participate in the election process."[4] Because of this and subsequent Supreme Court decisions, there is no limit on what individuals, party committees, and groups can spend on independent expenditures. Independent expenditures must, however, be reported to the FEC.[5] Independent expenditures can be targeted at any sector of the population. Also, unlike soft money, independent expenditures give the contributor complete control over the content and tone of the communication.

Internal communications occur between an organization (such as a union or club) and its membership or a corporation and its stockholders, executive or administrative personnel, and their families, referred to in the law as a "restricted class."[6] Federal statutes, although banning unions and corporations from using treasury funds to make direct campaign contributions, allow those funds to be used on certain exempt activities, including internal communications on any subject.[7] These communications may be completely partisan but must be made only to a union's membership or a corporation's restricted class; the general public may not be the intended audience of these communications. Internal communications range from direct mail and phone calls, to videotaped endorsements of candidates, to voter registration drives, get-out-the-vote (GOTV) telephone banks, and candidate scorecards.[8] Internal communications that do not use the "magic words" (as defined in chapter 1) of express advocacy are not disclosed to the FEC. However, *express* internal communications over $2,000 per election, with some exceptions, must be reported to the FEC.[9]

Unions and corporations usually avoid disclosure by using issue advocacy, but disclosure can be avoided even in the case of internal communications that contain express advocacy as long as that advocacy is not the "primary" focus of the communication. For example, an interest group might include two pages in a twenty-page membership monthly to expressly promote a federal candidate and not report the activity to the FEC. Because of such exemptions, it is virtually impossible to determine the full scope of internal communications spending. This chapter uses the data on internal communications reported to the FEC as well as interviews with interest groups to assess the extent of this activity.

Internal communications have a number of advantages. First, because individuals may view official information from the group they belong to as more credible, its message about a candidate may be better received than a message from an unaffiliated source.[10] Second, unlike issue advocacy and independent expenditures, internal communications permit corporations and unions to "coordinate their internal communications with candidates in order to better tailor the message to the candidate's needs" and to "solicit contributions for a candidate or political party."[11] Finally, because only members of an organization receive them, internal communications are more likely to go unnoticed by opposition candidates and groups, thus reducing any counterattacks to the information they convey.

Independent expenditures and internal communications have important similarities and differences. Both can expressly advocate the election or defeat of a candidate, but each targets a different audience, uses funding from different sources, and is subject to different disclosure regulations. With independent expenditures, communications can be broadcast or distributed to the general public, expenses cannot come from union dues or corporation treasuries, and contributions must be disclosed. Internal communications, on the other hand, are limited to a group's membership, can be paid for with union dues or corporation or organization treasury funds without limitation, and more easily escape disclosure requirements.

A group's choice of issue advocacy, independent expenditure, or internal communication depends on the nature of the group and its political strategy. If a person or group prefers anonymity, then issue advocacy, where disclosure is not required, may be preferred. Groups that want to communicate with the general public and that are not concerned about anonymity will likely pursue independent expenditures. If a group wants to mobilize its membership, it can use internal communications and may pay for them with treasury funds. Groups with substantial membership in a particular state or congressional district will be more likely to deploy internal communications. Finally, some groups will deploy all three strategies, tailoring their message to each audience.

INDEPENDENT EXPENDITURES AND INTERNAL COMMUNICATIONS IN HISTORICAL CONTEXT

As already noted, in the 1976 *Buckley v. Valeo* decision, the U.S. Supreme Court ruled that individuals and groups could spend unlimited amounts of money advocating the election or defeat of candidates as long as they did not coordinate their efforts with the candidate. According to the Supreme Court, to limit such contributions "heavily burdens core First Amendment expression."[12]

After 1976, independent expenditures played a small but sometimes important role, with conservative groups initially accounting for most of the activity. When individuals or groups report independent expenditures to the FEC, they indicate whether their spending was in favor of the candidate or against the candidate. We have aggregated these categories into spending intended to help the Republican (spending in favor of the Republican or against the Democrat) and spending intended to help the Democrat (spending in favor of the Democrat or against the Republican). Figure 4.1 plots independent expenditures and internal communications for congressional races in inflation-adjusted dollars in terms of the intended party beneficiaries from 1978 to 2000.

Republican congressional candidates have generally been the intended beneficiaries of independent expenditures more often than have Democrats. Early efforts by groups like NCPAC helped orient Republican-leaning groups to their

Figure 4.1. Independent Expenditures and Internal Communications 1978–2000 (in 2000 Dollars)

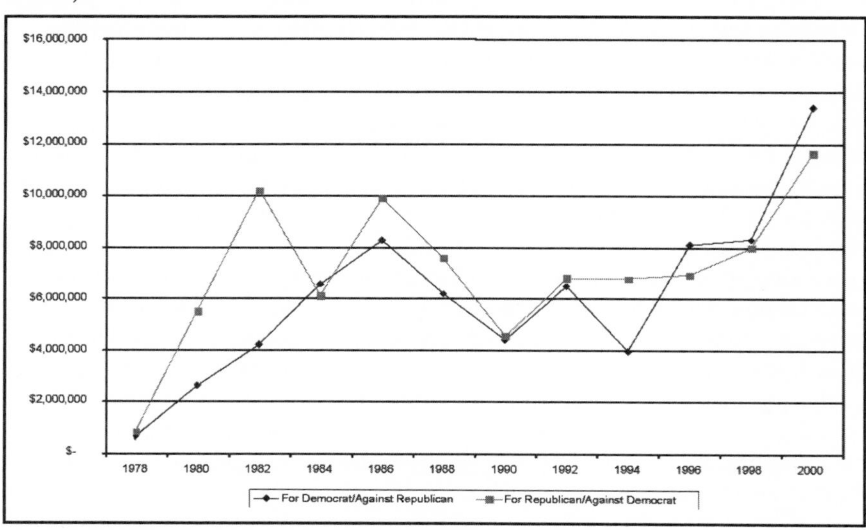

Source: FEC, "Disclosure Database," <ftp.fec.gov> [accessed 26 September 2001].

mode of campaigning. However, Democratic congressional candidates more often benefit from internal communication spending than do Republicans. This stems in part from the Democratic leanings of large membership organizations such as labor unions.

A group that used independent expenditures in hopes of helping Republicans is the National Conservative Political Action Committee (NCPAC). This group used independent expenditures on an unprecedented scale. It accounted for 46 percent of all independent expenditure spending in 1980 congressional races. In that seminal year NCPAC spent $1.1 million on independent expenditures against six Democratic U.S. Senate incumbents; four of those senators were narrowly defeated. The total combined itemized contributions from individuals to the four defeated candidates alone (without considering party, PAC, or any other donations) were more than double what NCPAC spent against all six candidates, a fact that did not alter NCPAC's claim to have influenced the outcome.[13] In 2000 dollars, the 1980 NCPAC spending would have been $2.6 million.

In 1982, NCPAC expanded its activities, targeting House as well as Senate races, with a total expenditure of $2.85 million (58 percent of total independent expenditure spending) for that year, but still only a small proportion of all spending. This time, eleven of the twelve NCPAC-opposed Democratic candidates were reelected. By the late 1980s, the prevalence of independent expenditure spending by NCPAC and all other groups had dwindled significantly. In fact, by 1990 NCPAC contributions totaled just $366,600.[14] Although no group has been able to fill the role NCPAC did in the 1980 election, the important legacy of the independent expenditure groups is found in issue advocacy in 1996 and later elections. The tendencies to target particular races, tailor messages, operate independently, and work to advance an issue or ideology are all common to both issue advocacy and independent expenditures. Indeed, many of the tactics of issue advocacy flow from the earlier independent expenditure campaigns. Similarly, politicians use much the same rhetoric to disavow any connection to issue advocacy that was used by candidates to distance themselves from independent expenditures in the early 1980s.

Individuals can also make independent expenditures. In the 1984 Illinois Senate campaign, Michael Goland, a wealthy Californian, spent more than $1 million ($1.6 million in 2000 dollars) to defeat Republican incumbent Charles Percy.[15] In the 2000 presidential election, Stephen Adams, owner of an outdoor advertising firm, spent $2 million in support of Governor George W. Bush.[16] But in general, independent expenditures by individuals are rare.

Although *Buckley v. Valeo* allowed individuals and interest groups to make unlimited independent expenditures, political parties were presumed to be not independent of candidates and therefore could not spend independently. However, in the *Colorado Republican Federal Campaign Committee v. Federal Election Commission* decision in 1996,[17] the Supreme Court ruled that political parties could make unlimited independent expenditures in federal campaigns. In the senatorial elections of that year, the Republican Party spent $10 million on independent expenditures; the Democratic Party spent $1.45 million. In the House race, independent expenditures for both parties totaled less than $68,000.[18]

The 1996 elections were the high water mark for party independent expenditures. Since then, the Democrats have increased their activity slightly while Republicans have dropped dramatically. In the 2000 congressional races, the Democratic Congressional Campaign Committee (DCCC) was the biggest independent expenditure spender, with only $1.9 million. The Republican state and local committees spent $740,402, and the National Republican Congressional Committee (NRCC) spent $548,800.[19] Independent expenditures have not grown because parties consider soft money spending and issue advocacy to be more effective than independent expenditure spending.

The history of internal communications is more difficult to track. One of the earliest Supreme Court cases to address the issue (long before the *Buckley* ruling) was *United States v. Congress of Industrial Organizations* (CIO), which concerned the legality of a statement published in *The CIO News* encouraging CIO members to vote for a specific congressional candidate. The Supreme Court ruled that if campaign finance laws prohibited publication "by corporations and unions in the regular course of conducting their affairs, of periodicals advising their members, stockholders or customers of danger or advantage to their interests from the adoption of measures, or the election to office of men espousing such measures, the gravest doubt would arise in our minds as to its constitutionality."[20]

More recently, in *FEC v. Machinists Non-Partisan Political League*, the District of Columbia circuit court echoed Supreme Court jurisprudence in its decision that intra-office communications "represent the very heart of the organism which the First Amendment was intended to nurture and protect: political expression and association concerning federal elections and office holding."[21]

Democratic allies, particularly labor unions, have traditionally used internal communications as a campaign tool more often than have Republican allies. Labor is responsible for about one-quarter of reported internal communications.[22] However, in recent elections Republican allies have increased the volume of internal communications to better compete with labor. Examples in 2000 include the National Federation of Independent Businesses (NFIB) and the U.S. Chamber of Commerce, which, in an attempt to counter labor's membership strength, increased circulation of its internal communications by 3 million new businesses.[23]

Because much internal communication goes unreported, data on internal communications spending are incomplete; they do however suggest certain trends in group activity. Since 1978, total internal communications spending in congressional elections has risen eight-fold, from $318,023 ($872,545 in 2000 dollars) to $6.5 million in 2000.

While significant, independent expenditures and internal communications spending constitute a small proportion of all congressional campaign contributions. This is one reason they receive less attention in discussions of campaign finance than do more high-profile issues like soft money. However, independent expenditures and internal communications remain important because of their potential to expand if other avenues of spending are closed by reform.[24] For example, in states like Oregon, New Hampshire, and Wisconsin that have attempted to regulate campaign finance, independent expenditures have increased dramatically.[25] After losing his 1996 bid for a New Hampshire Senate seat in an election in which the National Republican Senatorial Committee (NRSC) spent close to $1 million in independent expenditures, Democrat Dick Swett remarked, "I think that the capping of spending is a good idea only if you don't have all kinds of back doors through which a flood of independent expenditures can be allowed to come into play."[26] Clearly, any analysis of our current campaign finance system and the prospects for reform would be incomplete without a discussion of how individuals, parties, and interest groups seek to influence elections through independent expenditures and internal communications and how they might exploit these modes of spending in the future.

INDEPENDENT EXPENDITURES AND INTERNAL COMMUNICATIONS IN THE 2000 CONGRESSIONAL ELECTIONS

As did campaign spending generally, independent expenditure and internal communication spending grew in 1999–2000. Our research agenda in the area of independent expenditures includes not only assessing the relative role of this form of electioneering but also investigating which groups continue to engage in this activity when the issue advocacy option is readily available. Why do some groups use independent expenditures and not issue advocacy? Why do some use both? We also explore interest groups' use of internal communications, a phenomenon that has not been systematically documented in previous research.[27] Political practitioners speculate on the impact of these communications, generally without being able to provide substantiation. One assumption is that internal communications are more important to unions than to corporations. Republicans would agree, asserting that unions conduct substantial internal communications efforts that go unreported. As we document in this chapter, some groups clearly make internal communications a part of their overall strategy.

In the 1999–2000 congressional races, interest groups spent $22 million on independent expenditures. In 1978, they had spent just over $280,000 ($770,000 in 2000 dollars). As figure 4.1 demonstrates, independent expenditures by interest groups are more frequently made in support of Republican candidates or against Democratic ones. In 2000, for the first time, independent expenditure spending by interest groups for Democrats or against Republicans accounted for more than half of total independent expenditure spending. Clearly Democratic supporting groups have expanded their efforts in this form of electioneering.

This pro-Democratic increase in congressional election spending can be attributed to a concerted effort by interest groups allied with the Democrats. The League of Conservation Voters (LCV) led the pack with $3.2 million, followed by the National Education Association (NEA) at $2.4 million and the National Abortion and Reproduction Rights Action League (NARAL) at $2.2 million.[28] For these groups, the 2000 election provided an opportunity to capture the House and possibly gain seats in the Senate.

Of the pro-Republican groups, only the National Rifle Association (NRA) matched or exceeded the LCV, NEA, or NARAL. Spending $4.2 million in 1999–2000, the NRA made the most independent expenditures of any interest group. The NRA's independent expenditures in 2000 were more than three times greater than its largest previous total. The second most active pro-Republican group, the National Right to Life Committee (NRLC), spent $749,771, which is only a third of what the pro-Democratic and pro-choice group NARAL spent on independent expenditures.

Lack of required reporting to the FEC results in a skewed picture of how much groups are actually spending on internal communications with their membership. For example, in the 2000 election the U.S. Chamber of Commerce, in attempt to counter labor's spending, increased its internal communications base by 3 million businesses and reportedly spent $15 million on election activities. Despite this enormous increase, only $2,155 of that was reported to the FEC in internal communications expenditures.[29] Like the Chamber, most groups use the legal loopholes with exempt activities to underreport the extent of their activities within their membership.

Although internal communication spending reported to the FEC is incomplete, it demonstrates some important trends in group activity. Total internal communications in congressional elections have risen from $318,023 in 1978 ($872,545 in 2000 dollars) to $6.5 million in 2000. This growth was magnified in the 2000 election when pro-Democratic groups spent a significant amount more than in any previous year. This growth was almost entirely from unions. The NEA led the effort, spending $921,995 on internal communications. The American Federation of Labor and Congress of Industrial Organizations (AFL-CIO) spent only $456,707 on congressional races.[30] Reported internal communications by unions in 1999–2000 were much more concentrated in the presidential race, probably on the assumption that activating voters for Gore/Lieberman would assist other Democrats also on the ballot. Spending by unions combined for congressional Democrats was surpassed by pro-Republican spending from the National Rifle Association ($1.7 million). Other GOP allies included the National Association of Realtors ($492,735) and the National Federation of Independent Business ($421,737).

Looking at just congressional races and combining independent expenditures and internal communications, we find that pro-Republican groups spent slightly more than pro-Democratic groups throughout the 1980s. In the 1990s pro-Democratic groups began to match and then exceed pro-Republican groups in independent expenditures and internal communications in congressional races.

INDEPENDENT EXPENDITURES AND INTERNAL COMMUNICATIONS IN OUR SAMPLE RACES

We detected independent expenditures and internal communications in all of the seventeen races we monitored in 2000. Over $28.5 million in independent expenditures and internal communications was spent on all congressional races in 2000. The seventeen races we monitored had almost $9,833,319 in independent expenditure and internal communication spending, or 35 percent of all such spending in congressional races.[31] This demonstrates that this form of spending is concentrated in competitive races. Although this amount is much smaller than the amount of party soft money or interest group election issue advocacy, it remained important in several of our races.

The Washington Second Congressional District race (WA 2) provides an example of the way in which independent expenditures and internal communications can affect an election. In that race Democrat Richard Larsen spent $1.6 million and Republican John Koster spent $1.1 million.[32] However, Koster was disadvantaged by outside group spending. Groups like the NEA spent $248,348 for Larsen or against Koster. The teachers' union paid for direct mail ads contrasting Larsen's positions on education with Koster's.[33] In terms of total independent expenditures and internal communications, over $617,210 was spent, most of it intended to benefit Larsen. When all the independent expenditures and internal communications are combined with candidate spending totals, Koster was outspent 2/1.

In total, independent expenditures and internal communications exceeded $200,000 in nine of our twelve House races and exceeded $150,000 in all but one of our House races. Clearly in competitive races candidates must be prepared to face hundreds of thousands in independent expenditures and internal communications, not to mention issue advocacy and party activity.

Independent expenditures and internal communications exceeded $1 million in three of our five Senate races and $500,000 in four of our five races. In the Michigan race, over $2.4 million was spent on independent expenditures and internal communications, compared to just over $95,000 spent in the Delaware contest. Spending in the Virginia, Missouri, and Montana races was in the middle, with amounts over $1.2 million, $1.1 million, and $550,000, respectively.

TONE OF INDEPENDENT EXPENDITURES AND COMMUNICATIONS

Most independent expenditures in our sample races were spent in favor of a candidate ($5.6 million) rather than against a candidate ($2.6 million). Independent expenditures in our sample races were somewhat more likely to be against a candidate than independent expenditures in 2000 congressional races generally (32 percent compared to 27 percent). Virtually all (99 percent) of the reported internal communications in our races were in favor of a candidate.

As with outside money, independent expenditures and internal communications often have a partisan slant. Some interest groups allocate PAC money to both parties and especially to incumbents from both parties in hopes of advancing their legislative agenda.[34]As our sample races indicate, independent expenditures and internal communications by interest groups are much more consistently partisan. Of the top ten spenders in our seventeen races, the NRA and the NRLC spent almost 100 percent favoring Republicans, and the other eight groups spent almost 100 percent supporting Democrats. There were, however, a few instances in which a group helped both parties. For example, the NRA spent $9,000 helping Democrat Brad Carson in Oklahoma's Second District and also helped the Democratic candidates in Michigan's Eighth District and in Montana at large (see chapter 7 and chapter 9).

The Democrats in our races were the overwhelming beneficiaries of independent expenditures and internal communications. Table 4.1 shows that in the seventeen races, $6.6 million was spent in independent expenditures and internal communications in favor of Democrats and against Republicans, compared to only $3.2 million favoring Republicans and against Democrats.

Democratic allies using independent expenditures or internal communications opposed the Republican candidate more often than Republican allies opposed the

Table 4.1. Overall Total Independent Expenditures and Internal Communications in Our Seventeen Races

	Supporting Democrats			*Supporting Republicans*			
	IE/IC for Democrat	*IE/IC against Republican*	*Total*	*IE/IC for Republican*	*IE/IC against Democrat*	*Total*	*Percent Aiding Democrat*
Grand Total	**$4,053,051**	**$2,558,685**	**$6,611,736**	**$3,197,819**	**$50,764**	**$3,248,583**	**67**

Source: FEC, "Disclosure Database."
Note: IE = Independent Expenditures and IC = Internal Communications.

Democratic candidate. In all congressional races more than four-fifths (83 percent) of all internal communications and independent expenditures against candidates were against Republicans; in our sample races, this jumps to 98 percent.

Table 4.2 lists our Senate and House races in order of total independent and internal communication expenditures. It also provides the money spent favoring one candidate and opposing the other, the proportion of money intended to benefit each candidate (includes support candidate and oppose opponent), and the percent of the total express expenditures in the race attacking that candidate.

House Democratic candidates benefited the most from internal communications and independent expenditures in 2000. With the exception of the Pennsylvania Fourth district race, the majority of attack communications were against Republican candidates, actually exceeding the amount spent by groups for them. For example, in the California 27 District race, $455,848 was spent on independent expenditures and internal communications against James E. Rogan or for Adam Schiff, as compared to only $25,633 spent for James Rogan and against Adam Schiff.

The partisan advantage in independent expenditures and internal communications is largely absent in our sample Senate races, where only Montana Democrat Brian Schweitzer enjoyed a substantial overall advantage over Republican Conrad Burns: $404,000 compared to $69,211. In Missouri, Michigan, and Virginia, candidates were close to even in independent expenditures and internal communications spent for them or against their opponent. Democrat Debbie Stabenow had a slight advantage in Michigan; Republicans John Ashcroft and George Allen had slight advantages in Missouri and Virginia. In Delaware, William Roth had a slight advantage, but more noteworthy was the small amount spent by any individual or groups in independent expenditures and internal communications in that state.

WHO ENGAGES IN INDEPENDENT EXPENDITURES AND INTERNAL COMMUNICATIONS

When groups select campaign tools they consider their membership base, financial resources, and the extent to which they want to disclose their activity.

Table 4.2. Independent Expenditures and Internal Communications for/against Candidates in Sample Races

Race	*Candidate*	*Total for Candidate*	*Total against Opponent*	*Total Benefiting Candidate*
MI Sen	Abraham–R	$1,114,554	$ 8,568	$1,123,122
	Stabenow–D	$ 563,643	$773,095	$1,336,738
VA Sen	Allen–R	$ 713,208	$ 20,790	$ 733,998
	Robb–D	$ 162,021	$363,943	$ 525,964
MO Sen	Ashcroft–R	$ 664,756	$ 434	$ 665,190
	Carnahan–D	$ 369,501	$130,316	$ 499,817
WA 2	Koster–R	$ 90,876	$ 1,364	$ 92,240
	Larsen–D	$ 444,461	$ 80,509	$ 524,970
CA 27	Rogan–R	$ 25,219	$ 2,194	$ 27,413
	Schiff–D	$ 246,343	$280,605	$ 526,948
MT Sen	Burns–R	$ 107,901	$ 714	$ 108,615
	Schweitzer–D	$ 121,931	$324,518	$ 446,449
MT AL	Keenan–D	$ 437,351	$ 61,698	$ 499,049
	Rehberg–R	$ 83,229	$ 3	$ 83,232
MI 8	Byrum–D	$ 313,533	$116,172	$ 429,705
	Rogers–R	$ 59,201	$ 3	$ 59,204
KY 6	Baesler–D	$ 127,660	$195,443	$ 323,103
	Fletcher–R	$ 51,866	$ 467	$ 52,333
AR 4	Dickey–R	$ 73,002	$ 3	$ 73,005
	Ross–D	$ 160,301	$139,870	$ 300,171
CT 5	Maloney–D	$ 297,957	$ 290	$ 298,247
	Nielsen–R	$ 11,727	$ 346	$ 12,073
IL 10	Gash–D	$ 254,950	$ 18,951	$ 273,901
	Kirk–R	$ 631	$ 331	$ 962
NJ 12	Holt–D	$ 220,104	$ 28,902	$ 249,006
	Zimmer–R	$ 1,819	$ 3,742	$ 5,561
OK 2	Carson–D	$ 151,681	$ 28,688	$ 180,369
	Ewing–R	$ 11,574	$ 3	$ 11,577
PA 13	Greenleaf–R	$ 3,001	$ 8,851	$ 11,852
	Hoeffel–D	$ 153,436	$ —	$ 153,436
PA 4	Hart–R	$ 70,941	$ 566	$ 71,507
	Van horne–D	$ 22,731	$ 15,238	$ 37,969
DE Sen	Carper–D	$ 5,447	$ 447	$ 5,894
	Roth–R	$ 87,314	$ 2,385	$ 89,699

Source: FEC, "Disclosure Database."

Some groups invest in one or two forms of electioneering—candidate contributions, soft money, issue advocacy, internal communications, and independent expenditures—others invest in most or all of these. Some groups focus on statewide Senate races while others prefer cheaper House races. Those with limited resources typically focus on a few races; those with more money spend more broadly. The presence or absence of a presidential race also alters strategy, as some groups coordinate their presidential and congressional election efforts.

The NRA and NEA are excellent case studies of how groups use these different strategies with their resources. In 2000, the NRA, as noted, was the largest overall independent spender and focused heavily on Senate races and broadly on House races. In 2000, the NRA spent $3.9 million on independent expenditures and internal communications in all Senate races, almost $530,000 of which was spent in support of John Ashcroft in Missouri. The NRA spending in House races was much lower per race but spread out over almost every race. The NRA spent more than $100,000 in only one House race, but invested in 405 races.

The NEA, on the other hand, spent more than $100,000 in fifteen different House races compared to spending $177,000 in five different Senate races combined. Altogether the NEA spent over $3.3 million on internal communications and independent expenditures in House and Senate races. As the NEA told us, they avoided the more expensive Senate races to try to make an impact in targeted House races.[35]

An example of how the NEA strategy operated on the district rather than the national level is the New Jersey Twelfth District race, in which the NEA spent a total of $165,078 on independent expenditures and internal communications. Taking into account its large membership base, the NEA spent its treasury funds heavily on internal communications, investing in direct mail, e-mail, and personal contacts. To reach the general public, the NEA spent PAC money on independent expenditures. In the Washington Second District, the NEA spent significantly less on its membership but invested PAC money heavily in independent expenditures, utilizing its positive public name recognition to build support for Richard Larsen through radio ads.[36] In short, the NEA altered its strategy to fit its perceived opportunity. In all cases, as noted, the groups that used independent expenditures and internal communications did so with a strong partisan bias.

THE AGENDA IN OUR RACES

Aside from labor organization (including the National Education Association), independent expenditures and internal communications are most evident in gun control and gun rights, environmental protection, and abortion. There are active interest groups on both sides of the gun and abortion issues, while the pro-environment groups have virtually no opposition. Table 4.3 provides a list of the interest groups active in our sample races and the nature of their spending.

On the gun control issue, both sides targeted our races with independent expenditures, but the NRA spent substantially more. The NRA was especially active in the Virginia, Missouri, and Michigan Senate races. For example, the NRA invested $606,000 in independent expenditures to support George Allen in Virginia

Table 4.3. Top Groups in Independent Expenditure and Internal Communications in Our Sample Races (1999–2000)

	Supporting Democrats			Supporting Republicans			
Organization	*IE/IC for Demcrat*	*IE/IC against Republican*	*Total*	*IE/IC for Republican*	*IE/IC against Democrat*	*Total*	*Percent Aiding Democrat*
NRA Political Victory Fund	$ 11,235	$ 256	$ 11,491	$2,340,099	$13,465	$2,353,564	0
LCV	$ 87,772	$1,551,442	$1,639,214	$ 5,335	$ 20	$ 5,355	100
NEA	$1,462,640	$ 104,123	$1,566,763	$ —	$ —	$ —	100
NARAL	$1,211,851	$ —	$1,211,851	$ —	$ —	$ —	100
DCCC–Expenditures	$ 348,768	$ 254,638	$ 603,406	$ —	$ —	$ —	100
Handgun Control Voter Education Fund	$	$ 421,764	$ 421,764	$ —	$ —	$ —	100
National Right to Life PAC	$ 719	$	$ 719	$ 202,424	$20,137	$ 222,561	0
American Medical Association PAC	$ 200,559	$ —	$ 200,559	$ 414	$ —	$ 414	100
AFL-CIO Cope Political Contributions Committee	$ 187,548	$ —	$ 187,548	$ —	$ —	$ —	100
Sierra Club Political Committee	$ 90,465	$ 79,796	$ 170,261	$ 3,902	$ 865	$ 4,767	97
National Association of Realtors	$ —	$ —	$ —	$ 147,933	$ —	$ 147,933	0
Grand Total	**$3,601,557**	**$2,412,019**	**$6,013,576**	**$2,700,107**	**$34,487**	**$2,734,594**	**69**

Source: FEC, "Disclosure Database."
Note: IE = Independent Expenditures and IC = Internal Communications.

and $480,000 in support of John Ashcroft in Missouri. On the other side, Handgun Control countered the NRA in the Michigan Senate, Missouri Senate, and Kentucky Sixth House races. In Missouri, Handgun Control spent $130,000 against Ashcroft.[37] Handgun Control had committed $255,000 to this race, but after Mel Carnahan's tragic death in an airplane accident, subtracted $125,000 from that figure.[38] Handgun Control outspent the NRA on independent expenditures only in the Kentucky Sixth District race ($170,000 to $30,000).

Environmental groups spent the next largest sum on independent expenditures/internal communications in our races, with the League of Conservation Voters (LCV) spending $1.6 million. The level of independent expenditures and internal communications used by the LCV in Michigan was unusually high. For example, the LCV singled out Spence Abraham, spending over $550,000 against him. The LCV also spent $265,000 against James E. Rogan in the California Twenty-seventh Congressional District and $74,000 against Michael J. Rogers in Michigan Eight. The Sierra Club made more modest expenditures, supporting Democrats with $65,000 in the Montana At-large House race and $98,000 in the Washington Second Congressional District.[39]

Third in spending after gun control and environmental groups were education groups, specifically the NEA. The NEA spent $3,337,062 on independent expenditures and internal communications on congressional elections nationwide, $1.5 million of which went to fourteen of our races. The NEA's largest independent expenditure and internal communications allocation among our races—$220,000—went to the Washington Second Congressional District race. Its second largest allocation went to the Arkansas Fourth Congressional District race, in which the NEA accounted for 52.8 percent of total independent expenditures and internal communications, spending $197,000. In Senate races, the NEA contributed to just three (Montana, Virginia, and Michigan) of the five we monitored, spending a total of $128,693 in independent expenditures and internal communications.

Abortion was another issue that attracted a great deal of outside money in our sample races. There was a tremendous imbalance, with NARAL spending almost $1 million more than the NRLC (approximately $1,210,000 to $223,000). The NARAL made its biggest expenditures in the Michigan and Missouri Senate races ($388,000 and $357,000 respectively); the NRLC reported a total of only $106,815 in those two races.[40]

CONCLUSION

In the 2000 election $28.4 million was spent on internal communications and independent expenditures in congressional races. This was mainly due to an increase in the use of independent expenditures and internal communications as a campaign tool by pro-Democratic groups. This growth in spending for Democratic and against Republican candidates came from a wide range of labor, environmental, pro-choice, and other groups. Their efforts far exceeded those by the NRA and the NRLC, the only major supporters of Republican candidates in independent expenditures and internal communications. In House and Senate races, multiple single-issue interest groups generally allied with the Democrats, plus the NEA, were the biggest spenders using both independent expenditures and internal communications. Meanwhile, the other major supporter of Democratic candidates—the labor unions—focused the bulk of their efforts on helping Al Gore capture the presidency.

The surge in activity by interest groups allied with the Democrats was not found among pro-GOP interest groups except for the NRA. Independent expenditures and internal communications in organizations are part of the complex campaign environment in competitive congressional elections. Although smaller than party soft money and interest group election issue advocacy, internal communications and independent expenditures can be important to campaigns, totaling in the millions of dollars. Participants in the campaign process now exploit all the means of communication open to them. This in turn requires examination of independent expenditures and internal communications along with the other tools of campaigning. The case studies that follow assess the impact of independent expenditures and internal communications in particular congressional races.

NOTES

1. David B. Magleby. "Outside Money and the Ground War in 1998," in *Outside Money: Soft Money and Issue Advocacy in the 1998 Congressional Elections*, ed. David B. Magleby (New York: Rowman & Littlefield, 2000), 71.

2. Arthur Sanders and David Redlawsk, "Money and the Iowa Caucuses," in *Getting Inside the Outside Campaign*, ed. David B. Magleby, <www.byu.edu/outsidemoney/2000primary/iowa.htm>, 7 August 2001 [accessed 26 September 2001].

3. Michael J. Malbin, ed., *Money and Politics in the United States: Financing Elections in the 1980s* (Washington, D.C.: American Enterprise Institute for Public Policy Research, 1984), 149.

4. Anthony Corrado et al., *Campaign Finance Reform: A Sourcebook* (Washington, D.C.: Brookings Institution Press, 1997), 9.

5. Ibid.

6. Corrado, *Campaign Finance Reform,* 11.

7. 2 U.S.C. § 441b(b)(2)

8. Corrado, *Campaign Finance Reform,* 11.

9. Ibid.

10. Jack Polidori and Jack Pacheco of the NEA, interview by David B. Magleby and Jason Beal, Washington, D.C., 7 December 2000.

11. Derek Willis, "Business Groups Gear Up to Counter Unions' Spending Clout," *Campaigns and Elections* (May 2000): 8.

12. *Buckley v. Valeo,* 424 U.S. 1 (1976).

13. PoliticalMoneyLine. "FECInfo," <www.tray.com/fecinfo> [accessed 27 September 2001].

14. Frank J. Sorauf, *Inside Campaign Finance: Myths and Realities* (New Haven, Conn.: Yale University Press, 1992), 40.

15. Frank J. Sorauf, *Money in American Elections* (Glenview, Ill.: Scott, Foresman, 1998), 64–65.

16. Federal Election Commission (FEC), "Disclosure Database: PAS200.ZIP," <ftp.fec.gov/fec>, 2001 [accessed 26 September 2001].

17. *Colorado Republican Federal Campaign Committee v. Federal Election Commission,* 533 U.S. 2001 (1996).

18. Paul S. Herrnson, "Financing the 1996 Congressional Elections," in *Financing the 1996 Election,* ed. John C. Green (Armonk, N.Y.: M. E. Sharpe, 1999), 121–22.

19. Federal Election Commission (FEC), "FEC Reports Increase in Party Fundraising for 2000," <www.fec.gove/press/051501partyfund/051501partyfund.html>, 2001 [accessed 27 August 2001].

20. *United States v. Congress of Industrial Organizations,* 355 U.S. 106 (1948).

21. *FEC v. Machinists Non-Partisan Political League,* 655 F. 2d 380, 388 D.C. Cir. 1981

22. Willis, "Business Groups Gear Up to Counter Unions' Spending Clout," 8.

23. Bill Miller, U.S. Chamber of Commerce, telephone interview by David B. Magleby, 18 November 2000.

24. This concern, at least in the case of independent expenditures, dates at least as far back as the late 1980s, but has been muted in the wake of the soft money and issue advocacy surges of the 1990s. See Candice J. Nelson, "Loose Cannons: Independent Expenditures," in *Money, Elections, and Democracy: Reforming Congressional Campaign Finance,* ed. Margaret Latus Nugent and John R. Johannes (Boulder, Colo.: Westview Press, 1990), 47–68.

25. Eliza Newlin Carney, "Taking on the Fat Cats," *National Journal* (18 January 1997): 110–14.

26. Carney, "Taking on the Fat Cats," 113.

27. Our research in 1998 and 2000 is the first to include internal communications within the scope of noncandidate electioneering. We express appreciation to Bob Biersack, Supervisor Statistician at the Federal Election Commission, for his assistance in compiling these data.

28. FEC, "Disclosure Database."

29. Miller, interview by Magleby; FEC, "Disclosure Database."

30. Karen Ackerman of the AFL-CIO, interview by David B. Magleby, Washington, D.C., 9 November 2000.

31. FEC, "Disclosure Database."

32. Federal Election Commission (FEC), "Campaign Finance Reports and Data," <herndon1.sdrdc.com/cgi-bin/cancomsrs/c>, 2001, [accessed 27 August 2001].

33. David Postman, "Campaign Notebook," *The Seattle Times,* 31 October 2000, B2.

34. Public Campaign, "Press Release: Who's Warming Whom? Corporations Soften US Global Warming Position After Warming Party Coffers with Over $8 Million in Soft Money," <www.publicampaign.org/press_releases/pr10_24_97.html>, 2001 [accessed 26 September 2001].

35. Polidori and Pacheco, interview by Magleby and Beal.

36. Ibid.

37. FEC, "Disclosure Database."

38. Naomi Piass, communications director, Handgun Control, interview by Eric A. Smith and Anna N. Baker, Washington, D.C., 15 November 2000.

39. FEC, "Disclosure Database."

40. Ibid.

5

The 2000 Michigan Senate Race

Michael W. Traugott

Historically, Michigan has been a very competitive state politically, and the 2000 U.S. Senate race between Republican first-term incumbent Edmund S. (Spence) Abraham and his Democratic challenger Deborah (Debbie) Ann Stabenow was targeted early as a key contest. Poll data suggested on a number of accounts that Abraham was vulnerable, and Stabenow emerged early as the single, strong challenger around whom the Democratic Party could unite. Both parties and many interest groups focused on the contest, and money poured into both campaign coffers and the state's media markets. In all, the candidates and interest groups spent an estimated $40 million on the race, almost equally divided among them.[1]

In Michigan, the 2000 Senate election was an unusual one for a number of reasons. Any first-term senator is highly vulnerable when seeking reelection, and Spence Abraham was even more so because he chose to make a consistent voting record one of the cornerstones of his tenure. By the time he completed his service in the late 2000 special session, he had cast 2,002 consecutive votes on the floor of the Senate, never missing a vote. But he accomplished this at the cost of infrequent visits to Michigan, which resulted in low levels of visibility and popularity among his constituents. At the beginning of the 2000 Senate campaign, one-quarter of the Michigan electorate could not recognize Abraham, and half said they would not vote for him.[2] This lack of identity proved to be an issue in the race.

Stabenow was a skilled campaigner with relatively limited resources. She devised a carefully controlled strategy that hoarded resources until the late stages of the campaign. She was then able to overtake Abraham with a carefully orchestrated sprint to the finish line. At several crucial stages of the campaign, when she did not have resources of her own, various interest groups advertised in support of her or in opposition to Abraham in ways that kept her in the race.

Throughout the campaign, Abraham led consistently in the polls (see figure 5.1). But he could not crack the crucial 50 percent mark—a sign that an incumbent's campaign is in trouble—and after he finally debated Stabenow with two weeks to go, she began to close the gap. In the end, a constellation of factors, including interest group mobilization and Democratic party money, worked against Abraham and for Stabenow, as she captured the seat with 50 percent of the vote compared to Abraham's 49 percent. The gap between the two was only 43,000 votes out of 4 million cast.

Figure 5.1. Poll Results in the 2000 Michigan Senate Race

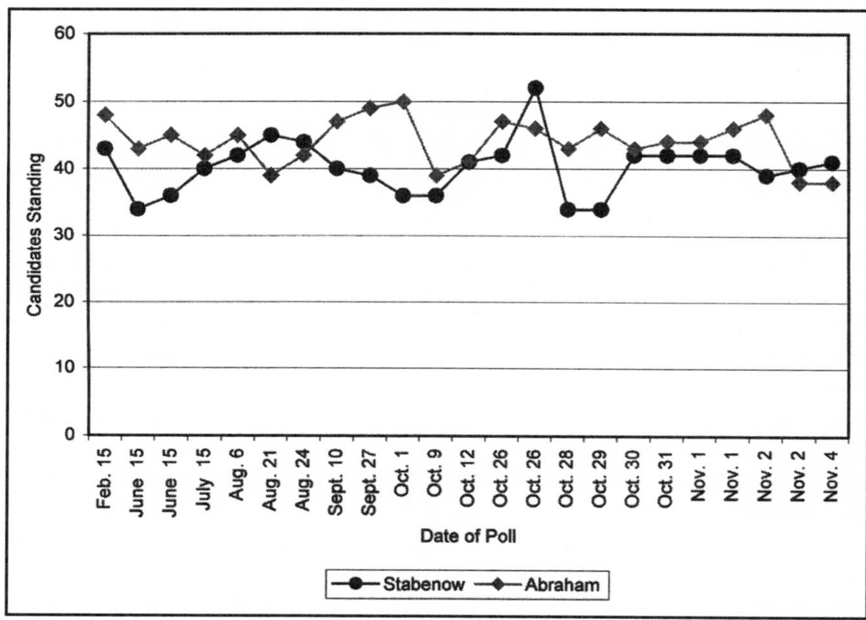

Source: EPIC/MRA polls conducted for the *Detroit Free Press*, February 15–November 4, 2001.

MICHIGAN'S BACKGROUND AND HISTORY

Data from the 2000 Census show that population growth in Michigan has lagged behind the rest of the country. The current population stands just shy of 10 million, reflecting a growth of 6.9 percent across the decade. This is only about half the national growth rate of 13.2 percent, and it will cost Michigan one congressional seat when redistricting takes place. Michigan's urban population continues to decline, especially in Detroit, but population is growing in the suburban and rural areas.

The majority of Michigan's population is white (80.8 percent), and one-seventh is African American (14.1 percent). Most African American residents live in urban areas, especially in Detroit. The Michigan economy still relies heavily on a manufacturing base, and the labor force is relatively unionized; about one in eight households (13 percent) contains a union member.[3] The state's economy tends to suffer downturns prior to the national economy and to recover more slowly. But the unionized labor force also means that median household income is slightly higher than the rest of the nation ($41,821 compared to $38,885 in 1998).

The state has regionalized politics, reflecting geographical differences in the location of its unionized labor force and its conservative, religious population. The main Democratic strongholds are in southeastern Michigan—in Detroit and Wayne County—as well as in a Democratic corridor running north along I-75, where there are substantial manufacturing facilities, including cities like Flint, Saginaw, Bay City, and Midland. Democrats have to run up large margins to offset Republican advantages in two suburban counties surrounding Detroit—Oakland and Macomb (the home of the "Reagan Democrats")—as well as in the rural areas of the state and in the western cities of Grand Rapids, Kalamazoo, and Battle Creek. The state capital, Lansing, lies in an area becoming more Republican, although for four years Debbie Stabenow represented the Eighth Congressional District, which included Lansing and parts of Flint.

Like many of the Great Lakes states, Michigan has been a key to recent presidential campaigns because of its swing voters, who have a propensity to split their votes. And like a number of other states, Michigan experienced a drift toward Republican control of state politics in recent elections, despite returning large margins for Bill Clinton and Al Gore. At the state level, there have been long periods when one party or the other has controlled state politics. With the results of the most recent election, the Republicans will be in full control of redistricting congressional seats for the next decade.

In national politics, the state is often viewed as a Democratic stronghold, especially because of the large unionized segment of the electorate, but between 1972 and 1988, they voted for six successive Republican presidential candidates. Since the redistricting after the 1970 Census, the state's congressional delegation has had a slight Democratic majority, currently at ten Democrats and six Republicans, and a split delegation to the U.S. Senate.

THE CANDIDATES AND THEIR CAMPAIGNS

Spence Abraham was elected to the U.S. Senate in 1994 after a career as an "insider" Republican. Born and raised in East Lansing, Michigan, and a graduate of Michigan State University and Harvard Law School, Abraham got his start in politics as chairman of the Michigan Republican Party from 1983 to 1989.[4] He served briefly as deputy chief of staff to Vice President Dan Quayle in 1990 and then became co-chair of the National Republican Congressional Committee (NRCC) from 1990 to 1992. He returned to Michigan after Bill Clinton was inaugurated in 1993 and was elected in 1994 as the first Republican senator from Michigan since 1979.

Throughout his term, Abraham had relatively little contact with his constituents, particularly because he pledged to never miss a floor vote. Republican Governor John Engler tried to remedy Abraham's visibility problem, in conjunction with a "Clean Michigan" bonding issue, which had little serious opposition. The issue involved a $3.5 million advertising campaign, and Engler named Abraham as chief spokesman, despite Abram's low environmental ratings from the Sierra Club and the League of Conservation Voters. Americans for Tax Reform also tried to increase Abraham's visibility by spending $1 million in ads touting Abraham's support for tax cut legislation in 1999.

Despite his lack of identity within the state, Abraham had some built-in organizational advantages in the contest thanks to the recent shifts in the parties' fortunes in Michigan. Most important, the Republican Party and Governor John Engler had a ready-made statewide apparatus to support his campaign, while there was no equivalent Democratic statewide campaign organization. Abraham also had incumbency advantages in raising money from individuals and organized interests.

Stabenow, the incumbent member of the U.S. House of Representatives from the Eighth Congressional District, was raised in a middle-class family in the small, central Michigan city of Clare.[5] Her political activity began when she attended Michigan State University. Shortly after graduating, she became interested in a local political issue surrounding the closing of a nursing home, and she continued her political activity when she was elected Ingham County commissioner at age twenty-four. She moved on to become a state representative and senator with sixteen years of service, and during this period she returned to school to earn a master's degree in social work. Her primary legislative focus was education, health care, and children's issues. Stabenow was an unsuccessful candidate for lieutenant governor in 1994, but in 1996 she won a seat in the U.S. House of Representatives. In addition to continuing her work on education and health care, she also became a strong advocate for women's issues.

Stabenow is known as an experienced candidate and good campaigner, skilled at making effective contact with voters. Although Abraham refused to debate with her until late October, they finally appeared together on two successive days, with only one debate televised. Stabenow's performance was very effective, and the direct comparison voters got from the event stimulated her campaign at a crucial point.

The direct comparison between the candidates was also captured in one Stabenow ad that included several of the key issues in the campaign. It involved an interview with a parent who claimed that she had made twelve calls to Abraham's office with a request for help with an HMO problem but had never received a response.[6] The ad also suggested that during this same period, Abraham had responded to a request from a major donor to help a convicted embezzler. This single ad not only highlighted Stabenow's concerns about regular citizens in the context of health care but also suggested Abraham's disengagement from his constituents and his responsiveness to big contributors and special interests.

The senatorial campaigns by Abraham and Stabenow were the most expensive ever conducted in Michigan, especially when the contributions and expenditures of others are taken into account. The two campaigns totaled almost $40 million. About half that amount consisted of direct expenditures by the candidates, and the other half came from soft money. Abraham reported receipts of $11.8 million, while Stabenow had $8.3 million, placing both of them among the top fifty campaigns in terms of individual contributions, according to the Federal Election Commission (FEC).[7] Although most of their money came from individuals ($8.8 million for Abraham and $6.6 million for Stabenow), Abraham's total also included $2.5 million from other committees, and Stabenow's included almost $1 million of such funds.

POLITICAL PARTY ACTIVITY

The FEC records also show that the national committees transferred millions of dollars to the state and local parties in Michigan, most of it in nonfederal soft money.[8] These funds were available for a number of offices, including the U.S. Senate race. The Democratic National Committee (DNC) actually sent more ($12.7 million total, of which $8.1 million was nonfederal) than the Republican National Committee (RNC) ($11.1 million, of which $6.3 million was nonfederal). The Democratic Senatorial Campaign Committee (DSCC) itself transferred $6.7 million to Michigan, including $4.3 million in nonfederal funds; the Republican Senatorial Campaign Committee transferred $4.5 million, of which $2.8 million was nonfederal funds. The DSCC also made independent expenditures to support a phone bank to assist Stabenow's campaign.[9] The Michigan Republican Party spent $1 million to support Abraham.[10] Overall, the Democratic Party enjoyed about a $3.7 million advantage over the Republican Party when both sources of funding are taken into account.

Although both candidates had ample funds, the two spent their money in quite different ways. Abraham and the Republican Party spent more money initially. This strategy was dictated partly by his low recognition levels but also as a needed response to attacks during the spring and summer from groups like the Federation for American Immigration Reform (FAIR). The Michigan Republican Party and the Michigan Republican State Committee spent $2.5 million on ads between February and October, although Abraham had no primary opposition. Even the NRCC spent $92,300 to help Abraham, although he was running for the Senate. John McCain did a commercial for Abraham, and his media adviser, Mike Murphy, signed on with the Abraham campaign. Murphy created a spoof Stabenow Web site—the "Liberal Debbie" site—which referred to "Deborah Rodham Stabenow."

As mentioned previously, Stabenow could not raise as much as Abraham, so Carol Butler, her campaign manager, developed a deliberate strategy of hoarding resources until the end of the campaign.[11] She had little advertising in the ten-week period between the August primary and October. Knowing that Abraham's media adviser was also Rick Lazio's (the Republican candidate in the New York Senate race), the Stabenow campaign often timed their attacks for periods when they thought that Murphy would be preoccupied in New York.[12] Although as a typical incumbent Abraham initially raised and spent more money than Stabenow, in October the two candidates were fairly evenly matched in how much they had left to spend for the remainder of the campaign.

THE AIR WARS

Given Michigan's centrality to the presidential campaign and the importance of the U.S. Senate race and several congressional races, Michigan airwaves were saturated with political ads.[13] Across the entire campaign, three Michigan markets (Detroit, Grand Rapids, and Flint-Saginaw) consistently appeared among the "Top Ten" in the country.[14] By the end of the campaign, eight political ads were appearing each hour in the Detroit market, and the Flint and Lansing markets were completely sold out.[15]

Two other factors contributed to the crowded airwaves and affected the senatorial race. A statewide proposal to create a system of school vouchers divided the Republicans and stimulated turnout among Democratic-leaning groups. Proposal A, as it was known, was supported and bankrolled by conservative Republicans in the western part of the state, but was opposed by Governor John Engler. Republicans feared that the referendum would attract money and other resources from the National Education Association (NEA) to the campaign, thereby drawing members of the Michigan Education Association to the polls and increasing turnout among likely Democratic voters. At the same time, an unusually contested set of slates for the state supreme court involved very heavy advertising expenditures that emphasized crime as an issue. Although nominally nonpartisan, the slates of judicial candidates are nominated at the state party conventions, and the Republican-backed nonpartisan slate spent heavily. As a result, a total amount of more than $25 million in campaign advertising was spent in the Detroit market alone,[16] which had the second highest total number of political ads of any media market in the country.[17] In fact, three of the top ten markets for political advertising across the country were in Michigan.

INTEREST GROUP ACTIVITY

Because the Senate race was a toss-up and so much was at stake in Michigan, interest groups were heavily involved. Abraham had the support of a number of groups, due in part to his incumbency and his partisanship. Health care and business groups donated generously to the Abraham effort. The pharmaceutical companies organized as Americans for Job Security and Citizens for Better Medicare to oppose the Gore-Stabenow prescription drug benefit plan. In fact, drug companies added another $2 million of anti-Stabenow ads through the U.S. Chamber of Commerce; these ads so distorted Stabenow's platform and record that two television stations pulled them. Michigan was the focus of the Chamber's effort across the country.[18] Americans for Quality Nursing Home Care, which represented nursing home operators, also ran pro-Abraham ads, making Michigan their fifth most active senatorial campaign. The Health Benefits Coalition, a combination of the National Federation of Independent Business (NFIB) and the National Association of Manufacturers (NAM), also ran ads supporting Abraham.

On Abraham's behalf, the Business Roundtable spent $400,000 in independent expenditures. Microsoft alone spent $250,000 on anti-Stabenow ads through the Michigan Chamber of Commerce (see table 5.1). The National Rifle Association (NRA) made $621,000 in independent expenditures on behalf of Abraham, and Michigan was included in a sixteen-city, NRA-sponsored tour that featured Charlton Heston.[19] The NRA also sponsored three rallies in the state. At a rally late in the campaign, Heston appeared with Wayne LaPierre and James Baker in Flint, a city near the Eighth Congressional District, where they endorsed Abraham, Mike Rogers, and George W. Bush.

However, a strong mobilization and communication effort by certain key interest groups for Stabenow may have made the difference in such a close race. Stabenow's experience in politics also provided her with contacts and support from Washington, and in lieu of an existing statewide campaign organization, she was strongly supported by three key constituencies that provided valuable organizational resources: women, union members, and African American voters.

One of the main resources of the Stabenow campaign was Michigan unions. Most important, the United Auto Workers (UAW) had negotiated Election Day as a paid holiday in their current contract, and this made a difference. Governor Engler described this as "the largest soft money contribution in American political history."[20] In the 1998 election, the UAW had 350 poll workers in Oakland and Macomb counties; in 2000 they had 2,000 workers. Other unions were at work as well. The AFL-CIO set up a worker-to-worker network for telephone contacts, and each member received between four and seven pieces of literature. Union contact with membership picked up as Election Day approached, including the use of phone banks for get-out-the-vote (GOTV) efforts.

The National Abortion and Reproductive Rights Action League (NARAL) assigned two paid staffers to the Michigan campaign, partly because Stabenow had voted "correctly" on fifty-four of fifty-four key votes for them and partly to oppose Abraham's reelection effort.[21] NARAL recruited over five hundred volunteers for literature drops and for organizing a letter writing campaign to key newspapers across the state. Supplementing NARAL's efforts, Emily's List, another pro-choice group, spent money in the Detroit, Grand Rapids, and Flint media markets in support of Stabenow and in opposition to Abraham.[22]

Table 5.1. The Air War: Most Active Organizations' Collected Ad Buy Data in the Michigan Senate Race

Type	*Organization*	*TV*	*Radio*	*Total Ad Buy $*	*CMAG TV*
Democratic Allies					
Candidates	Stabenow for Senate	$1,249,605	$0	**$1,249,605**	$3,781,198
Political Parties	Michigan Democratic Party	$1,196,730	$0	**$1,196,730**	$ 418,674
	Michigan Democratic State Committee	$ 277,490	$0	**$ 277,490**	$ 0
	Democratic Victory 2000	$ 24,500	$0	**$ 24,500**	$ 0
	DSCC	N/A	$0	**$ 0**	$2,260,290
Interest Groups	AFL-CIO	$ 769,240	$0	**$ 769,240**	$ 271,696
	Michigan Democrats	$ 533,200	$0	**$ 533,200**	$ 0
	Emily's List	$ 526,220	$0	**$ 526,220**	$ 443,120
	Planned Parenthood	$ 461,245	$0	**$ 461,245**	$ 0
	Sierra Club	$ 119,675	$0	**$ 119,675**	$ 0
	League of Conservation Voters	$ 104,250	$0	**$ 104,250**	$ 86,845
	Coalition for the Future Am Worker	$ 259,500	$0	**$ 259,500**	$ 122,785
	Michigan Women Voters	N/A	$0	**$ 0**	$ 360,647

Republican Allies					
Candidates	Abraham Senate 2000	$2,612,141	$0	**$2,612,141**	$5,034,886
Political Parties	Michigan Republican State Committee	$1,682,425	$0	**$1,682,425**	$ 0
	Republican Party of Michigan	$ 185,800	$0	**$ 185,800**	$ 0
	National Rep State Central Committee	$ 70,485	$0	**$ 70,485**	$ 0
	2000 GOP	$ 51,725	$0	**$ 51,725**	$ 0
	Republican National Committee	$ 33,025	$0	**$ 33,025**	$ 599,044
Interest Groups	U.S. Chamber of Commerce	$ 921,335	$0	**$ 921,335**	$1,232,132
	Business Roundtable	$ 415,680	$0	**$ 415,680**	$1,152,761
	Michigan Chamber of Commerce	$ 323,175	$0	**$ 323,175**	$ 0
	Citizens for Better Medicare	$ 302,325	$0	**$ 302,325**	$ 0
	Alliance for Quality Nursing Home Care	$ 88,850	$0	**$ 88,850**	$ 0
	Americans for Job Security	$ 67,900	$0	**$ 67,900**	$ 0
	National Rifle Association	$ 5,000	$0	**$ 5,000**	$ 12,850

Source: Election Advocacy and the *Campaign Media Analysis Group* databases.

Notes: See appendix B for a more detailed explanation of the data. This table is not intended to portray comprehensive organization spending in the Michigan Senate race. A more complete picture can be obtained by examining this table together with table 5.2. Because ad buy content was often nondescriptive, a portion of this data was possibly bought for the MI 8 race. Unfortunately, it was not possible to parse the MI 8 data from the MI Senate data; the addition of the CMAG data helps allay this problem. Active organizations not listed include (Democratic Parties) DNC; (Democratic Allies) NARAL, Handgun Control, and NAACP National Voter Fund; (Republican Allies) Republicans for Good Common Sense; (Nonpartisan) American Society of Anesthesiologists.

Like NARAL, the League of Conservation Voters (LCV) supported Stabenow not only for her record as an "environmental champion" but also to oppose Abraham. The League spent $700,000 in the Michigan race and assigned a full-time staff member to the state.[23] They also provided polling information to the Stabenow campaign.

The National Education Association (NEA) devoted considerable resources to Michigan because of its opposition to the Proposal A voucher system.[24] The NEA made an estimated 1,000,000 phone calls as part of its GOTV effort regarding Proposal A.[25] In addition to efforts to derail Proposal A, the NEA also heavily endorsed Stabenow and stimulated a greater Democratic turnout on election day. Table 5.2 lists the number of unique mail and phone ads that the most active organizations distributed in the Michigan Senate race.

EXIT POLL RESULTS

Exit poll data collected by Voter News Service (VNS) show that the alliance of union members, women, and African Americans helped Stabenow forge her victory.[26] Almost half of the voters (43 percent) came from union households, and they preferred Stabenow 63 percent to 35 percent; her plurality among union members (28 percentage points) was just as large. However, voters from nonunion households preferred Abraham 59 percent to 39 percent. Women were a majority in the electorate, and they gave Stabenow a ten-percentage point plurality, while men gave Abraham an eight-point margin. Abraham had that same lead among whites; however, African Americans (11 percent of the electorate) preferred Stabenow 89 percent to 10 percent. Stabenow also enjoyed the overwhelming support of the large city population making up a quarter of the voters, garnering 63 percent of their vote to Abraham's 34 percent.

Furthermore, a majority (56 percent) of those who went to the polls supported stricter gun control laws, and these voters preferred Stabenow to Abraham 66 percent to 32 percent. (Among those who opposed stricter gun control laws, Abraham was preferred 68 percent to 29 percent.) Although the support for Abraham among gun control opponents was slightly stronger than Stabenow's among union members, the relative strength of these groups canceled each other out. Stabenow was able to hold support among union members who opposed gun control, suggesting that union efforts trumped those of the NRA. A final factor that helped contribute to Stabenow's victory was the defeat of Proposal A by 61 percent to 39 percent. Opponents of Proposal A favored Stabenow by 59 percent to 38 percent.

Table 5.2. The Ground War: Most Active Organizations' Observed Activity in the Michigan Senate Race

Type	*Organization*	*Mail*	*Phone*	*Total Unique Ads*
Democratic Allies				
Candidates	Stabenow for Senate	4	1	5
Political Parties	MI Democratic State Committee	16	—	16
	DSCC	4	–	4
	Michigan Victory 2000	4	—	4
	Democratic National Committee	2	—	2
	Michigan Democratic Party	—	2	2
	Interest Groups Sierra Club	4	—	4
	AFL-CIO	2	1	3
	Handgun Control	3	—	3
	NARAL	2	1	3
	NARAL-PAC (MI)	2	1	3
	League of Conservation Voters	2	—	2
	Planned Parenthood	1	1	2
Republican Allies				
Candidates	Abraham Senate 2000	3	—	3
Political Parties	MI Republican State Committee	11	—	11
	Republican Party of Michigan	—	2	2
Interest Groups	National Federation of Independent Business	5	1	6
	Right to Life of Michigan	3	—	3
	Citizens for a Sound Economy	2	—	2
Nonpartisan				
Interest Groups	Alliance for Better Campaigns	3	—	3

Source: Election Advocacy database.

Notes: See appendix B for a more detailed explanation of the data. Totals exclude all presidential data. Data include all ad campaigns that mentioned any MI Senate candidate, including those ads that simultaneously mentioned any Presidential or MI 8 candidate. Therefore, this table and the table for MI 8 are not mutually exclusive. This table is not intended to represent comprehensive organization activity in the MI Senate race. A more complete picture can be obtained by examining this table and table 5.1 together. Active organizations not listed above include: (Democratic Parties) Democrats 2000, Washtenaw County Democratic Committee, and Washtenaw County Democratic Party; (Democratic Allies) American Federation of Government Employees, Emily's List, English Language Political Action Committee, Michigan State AFL-CIO, National Association of Social Workers, National Committee for an Effective Congress, NEA, NOW, People For The American Way, PIRGIM, Planned Parenthood of Northern Michigan, Public Citizen, Inc., UAW Michigan CAP, Voter Education Fund; (Republican Parties) Ottawa County Republican Party, Posthumus Leadership Fund; (Republican Allies) Arab American and Chaldean Leadership Council of Michigan, Engler Hunting and Shooting Sports Heritage Foundation, National Association of Health Underwriters, NRA - Political Victory Fund, U.S. Chamber of Commerce; (Nonpartisan) 2020 Vision, Capital Eye, Center for Environmental Citizenship, Lawyers Political Action Committee, League of Women Voters, Peace Voter 2000, Save Our Environment Coalition, Women's Action for New Directions.

CONCLUSION

Michigan was a battleground state for the presidential campaigns in 2000, and the U.S. Senate race in Michigan involved a vulnerable incumbent running against a strong challenger. Therefore, it attracted a lot of money and activity from outside groups. Michigan residents were inundated by ads and phone calls, and the race became the most expensive in Michigan history. In the end, Stabenow probably could not have succeeded in the very competitive race without the support of soft money expenditures.

The role of outside money was critical to both candidates in the Michigan Senate race. Abraham, the first-term incumbent, had advantages in raising money but was forced to spend it early and often on advertising to develop name recognition and to counteract attacks from anti-immigration groups. A number of organizations used soft money to support these early campaign efforts, as well as spending large amounts during the general election campaign. Stabenow, the challenger, had her advertising campaign propped up by soft money expenditures and interest groups during periods when she was reserving her resources. Furthermore, Michigan turnout was higher in 2000 than in 1996 by about 350,000 votes, with more Democrats at the polls than Republicans. The relative turnout of Democratic partisans arguably helped Stabenow overcome the Republican incumbent, as each set of partisans supported their own candidate by six or seven to one.

Outside group support was also critical for mobilization and GOTV efforts on Stabenow's behalf. This was especially important because the Michigan Democratic Party did not control the main political institutions in the state. Unions supplied money, paid for extensive mailings, and organized GOTV drives. The National Association for the Advancement of Colored People (NAACP) and African American churches in the Detroit area also mobilized voter turnout in Detroit and other urban areas in southeastern Michigan. Women's and pro-choice groups like Emily's List and NARAL supported Stabenow's campaign with advertising, professional staff located to the state, and extensive mailings. They provided her with the critical margin in a race decided by 1 percent of the votes cast.

NOTES

I want to thank Adam Redstone, Heather Schaar, and Donald Schaefer for their research assistance.

1. "Debbie Stabenow (D-Mich.)," *Political Finance & Lobby Reporter*, 15 November 2000.
2. Ellyn Ferguson, "Expect Stabenow Back Home—A Lot," *Gannett News Service*, 8 December 2000, final edition.
3. Joseph Serwack, "Day Off Helps UAW Flex Muscle; Union Turnout Boosts Democrats," *Crain's Detroit Business*, 13 November 2000, 1.

4. This biographical summary is based on information from Nicholas Confessore, "Saving Private Abraham: How Senator Abraham, Loyal Republic Soldier, Got by with a Little Help from His Friends," *The American Prospect,* 20 November 2000, 19; and Christopher Marquis, "Edmund Spencer Abraham," *New York Times,* 3 January 2001, A9.

5. This biographical summary is based on information from Eric Schmitt, "Debbie Stabenow," *New York Times,* 13 November 2000, A14.

6. Chris Christoff, "Stabenow Joins Ranks of Women in the Senate," *Detroit Free Press,* 9 November 2000, A1.

7. Federal Election Commission (FEC), "Top 50 Senate Contributions from Individuals," <www.fec.gov/press/top50senindoo.htm>, 15 May 2001 [accessed 6 June 2001].

8. Federal Election Commission (FEC), "National Party Transfers to State/Local Party Committees," <www.fec.gov/press/congtostate00.htm>, 18 October 2000 [accessed 6 June 2001].

9. Jim Jordan, DSCC, interview by David Magleby, Washington, D.C., 19 November 2000.

10. Rusty Hills, chair, Michigan Republican Party, interview by author, Lansing, Michigan, 13 November 2000.

11. Darci McConnell, "Tide Turned for Stabenow in October," *The Detroit News,* 9 November 2000, A7.

12. Dawn Laguens, interview by David Magleby, Washington, D.C., 15 November 2000.

13. Jodi Wilgoren, "Ad-Weary Tossup City Has a Question: Is It Next Wednesday Yet?" *New York Times,* 3 November 2000, A13.

14. "Democrats Are 'Soft Money' Kings in House and Senate Races," *Brennan Center Press Center,* <www.brennancenter.org/presscenter/pressrelease_2000_1019cmag.html>, 19 October 2000 [accessed 1 January 2001].

15. Laguens, interview by Magleby.

16. "Greedy TV: Detroit," *Alliance for Better Campaigns 2000,* <wysiwig://43/greedytv.org/stations/?market=9>, 7 January 2000 [accessed 1 January 2001].

17. "2000 Presidential Race First in Modern History Where Political Parties Spent More on TV Ads than Candidates," *Brennan Center Press Center,* table 12, <www.brennancenter.org/presscenter/pressrelease_2000_1211cmag.html>, 11 December 2000 [accessed 1 January 2001].

18. "2000 Presidential Race First."

19. Karen MacPherson, "NRA's Election Spending Has Mixed Results: '[Pennsylvania] Certainly Wasn't a Total Loss for the NRA, but It Also Wasn't a Total Victory Either'," *Pittsburgh Post Gazette,* 10 November 2000, A13.

20. Serwack, "Day Off Helps UAW Flex Muscle."

21. "Stabenow Defeats Anti-Choice Incumbent Abraham," *U.S. Newswire,* 8 November 2000.

22. "2000 Presidential Race First," table 12.

23. Glen Close, interview by David Magleby, Washington, D.C., 13 November 2000.

24. "Election Results Spotlight Education, Says National Education Association," *U.S. Newswire,* 8 November 2000.

25. Jack Polidori, political affairs specialist, and Jack Pacheco, National Education Association (NEA), interview by David B. Magleby, Washington, D.C., 7 December 2000.

26. This analysis is based on VNS exit poll results, <a388.g.akamai.net/f/388/21/15m/www.cnn.com/ELECTION/2000/epolls/MI/S000.html> [accessed 1 January 2001].

6

The 2000 Virginia Senate Race

Robert Holsworth, Stephen K. Medvic, Harry L. Wilson, Robert Dudley, and Scott Keeter

The Virginia U.S. Senate election between incumbent Democrat Charles Robb and Republican challenger George Allen pitted against each other candidates with different ideological stances who had played similar roles for their parties in the 1980s and 1990s. Chuck Robb's election as governor in 1981 ended twelve years of Republican control of that office. Robb reached out to suburban voters by combining fiscal conservatism with a progressive approach to social issues.

Similarly, George Allen's 1993 election as governor turned the tides, ending twelve years of Democratic control of the governorship. Once in office, Allen promoted a vigorous conservative agenda, passing welfare reform, eliminating parole, and developing standards-based educational policies. He ushered in the most successful period of Republican leadership in Virginia history; this leadership continues today. Allen's antigovernment, tax-cutting populism generated considerable affection among party loyalists and many Independents, which helped Allen defeat Robb by a margin of 52 to 48 percent.

THE CANDIDATES AND THEIR CAMPAIGNS

Despite his status as a twelve-year Senate incumbent, Robb entered the 2000 election as an underdog in the eyes of most observers. He was generally described as the most endangered Democrat up for reelection in the Senate for a number of reasons. First, only one Democrat had received more than 50 percent of the vote in any statewide Virginia race since 1990. Robb himself obtained slightly less than 46 percent of the vote in his victory over Oliver North in 1994. Robb's victory that year was partially due to the fact that Republican Senator John Wallace refused to endorse North and instead advanced the candidacy of an independent Republican, who received 11 percent of the vote. By 2000, Robb was the last Democrat with a statewide constituency left standing in the state, and he faced the task of reenergizing a party that had been left dispirited by GOP victories in recent years.

Second, the composition of the Virginia electorate favored Allen. Although polls of adult Virginians showed a relatively even split between Democrats and Republicans, surveys of likely voters indicated that more Republicans would turn out to vote. A plurality of Virginians see themselves as moderates, but self-identified conservatives outnumbered liberals by about 2 to 1, again favoring Allen. The Gore campaign's decision to pass up Virginia meant Robb had to convince moderates who intended to vote for Bush that George Allen was unacceptable.

Third, Robb's political record and personal background led many observers, including Roll Call, to categorize the race as a "toss-up."[1] In the Senate, Robb was generally considered to be a moderate on fiscal and defense issues, but his progressive stance on some social issues meant Allen could claim Robb was out of touch with "Virginia values." For example, Robb was one of fourteen senators, and the only southerner, to vote against the "Defense of Marriage Act," legislation intended to ensure that states would not have to recognize gay and lesbian marriage if it was legalized in other states. Robb also opposed the flag-burning amendment on free speech grounds, damaging his relationship with veterans' groups that had supported him in the past because of his stellar military record. In addition, Robb had not developed a record of individual legislative accomplishment that could be easily presented and that might have given voters a reason to overlook some of his votes.

Finally, some voters still remembered revelations in the early 1990s that, as governor, Robb had attended parties where cocaine had been used and that he had engaged in extramarital relations. Although his personal indiscretions were unlikely to be directly raised in the 2000 campaign, it was part of the context of the race. Democrats mobilized behind Robb in 1994 to defeat Ollie North, but Robb's career had never regained the luster it had in Virginia during the 1980s.

By contrast, Allen was almost an icon to many Republican activists. Affection for him ran deep among the foot soldiers of the Virginia Republican Party, and there was little doubt about his capacity to mobilize the GOP base.

In Virginia the 2000 race began with an upbeat and confident Republican Party that believed it had an excellent shot of knocking off an incumbent and an uncertain Democratic Party that felt that it had a chance, but only a slight chance, of defeating George Allen. The GOP thought that the two primary dangers to the Allen campaign were (1) the possibility that overconfidence might breed complacency in the Republican base and (2) the potential threat that Robb's attacks on Allen would succeed in alienating a sufficient number of moderate, GOP-leaning voters, especially women. The Democrats believed that Allen's record on education, transportation, and the environment, as well as his excessively conservative positions on guns and abortion, provided an opening that an effective campaign could exploit.

From the campaign's outset, Robb did not have the fundraising advantage that incumbents often possess in terms of direct contributions to the campaign. The first financial report filed by the campaigns in April indicated that Allen had more than $3.75 million on hand, compared to Robb's $2.26 million.[2] To many observers of Virginia politics, these reports confirmed just how formidable a challenger Allen was. However, the Robb campaign noted that it had been in a similar position in 1994 when Ollie North had raised more than $20.6 million. But North was essentially a national candidate, whereas Allen's base was Virginia. Allen's capacity to raise so much money from individuals indicated both his popularity and the willingness of many Virginians to consider unseating Robb.

The initial fundraising advantage that Allen possessed remained intact for the remainder of the campaign. Robb's position on the Senate Finance Committee and his marital connections to former President Lyndon Johnson enabled him to generate $6.7 million, but Allen, without any of the advantages of incumbency, was able to maintain and extend his lead in the battle for candidate contributions. In the end, Allen's campaign was able to raise almost 50 percent more than Robb's. Allen's final total was $10,073,255 compared to Robb's $6,737,158.[3]

POLITICAL PARTY ACTIVITY

The dollars raised by the individual campaigns were only part of the money story in Virginia's 2000 Senate contest. It was clear from the outset that the race would garner the attention of the national parties because of its potential impact on the Senate's partisan composition. Republicans perceived Robb as the Democrats' most vulnerable incumbent in the Senate and probably the only Democratic incumbent who could be defeated. As Ed Matricardi, executive director of the Virginia Republican Party, put it, "Virginia was the only place where we had a chance to knock off a Democrat. We were the only game in town."[4] Democrats recognized that Robb was in trouble but felt that he might retain his seat by a razor-thin margin if the campaign broke just right. For this reason, there was always a sense that the candidates' fundraising would be generously supplemented by their parties.

Although the early financial reports indicated a blow-out for Allen, transfers from the Democratic Senatorial Campaign Committee (DSCC) to Virginia on Robb's behalf were essential to making the race financially competitive. These transfers totaled $9,101,287,[5] fully compensating for the fact that Robb's campaign fundraising ultimately ran slightly more than $3 million behind Allen's.

Total reported spending in the campaign, including candidate spending, national transfers, party-coordinated expenditures, and internal communication costs, was almost equal for both sides; spending for Allen totaled $17,634,618 and for Robb, $17,100,168.[6]

The National Republican Senatorial Committee (NRSC) transferred $5,355,900 to be used in the Virginia campaign,[7] and Virginia's Republican Party used the money to mount a full-service complement to the official campaign: It produced fourteen television ads, distributed dozens of mailings, placed more than 120,000 yard signs for Bush/Cheney and Allen across the state, and sent out more than 6 million mail pieces for federal candidates in Virginia, almost all of which prominently included George Allen; it bought significant radio time in the last weeks of the campaign; and it funded more than a million get-out-the-vote (GOTV) calls. Table 6.1 shows the money spent in the Virginia Senate race by the most active organizations for television and radio ad buys.

Table 6.1. The Air War: Most Active Organizations' Collected Ad Buy Data in the Virginia Senate Race

Type	*Organization*	*TV*	*Radio*	*Total Ad Buy $*	*CMAG TV*
Democratic Allies					
Candidates	Robb for the Senate	$2,396,497	$11,955	**$2,408,452**	$3,528,962
Political Parties	Democratic Party of Virginia	$ 428,809	$0	**$ 428,809**	$0
	Virginia Democratic Party	$ 343,287	$14,145	**$ 357,432**	$ 488,466
Interest Groups	League of Conservation Voters	$ 108,485	$0	**$ 108,485**	$ 263,595
	Sierra Club	$ 4,840	$ 9,155	**$ 13,995**	$0
	NAACP National Voter Fund	$0	$ 3,140	**$ 3,140**	$0
	Voters for Choice	N/A	$0	**$0**	$ 611,359
Republican Allies					
Candidates	Friends of George Allen	$2,418,504	$0	**$2,418,504**	$5,070,499
Political Parties	NRSC	$ 724,503	$0	**$ 724,503**	$0
	Virginia Republican Party	$ 572,156	$61,734	**$ 633,890**	$4,525,941
	Republican Party of Virginia/ Victory 2000	$ 56,457	$0	**$ 56,457**	$0
Interest Groups	U.S. Chamber of Commerce	$ 66,953	$ 5,675	**$ 72,628**	$ 130,389
	National Rifle Association	$ 34,880	$16,120	**$ 51,000**	$ 10,637

Source: Election Advocacy and *Campaign Media Analysis Group* databases.
Notes: See appendix B for a more detailed explanation of the data. This table is not intended to portray comprehensive organization spending in the VA Senate race. A more complete picture can be obtained by examining this table together with tables 6.2 and 6.3.

The party's campaign was closely coordinated with the Allen campaign, and it reinforced the basic themes that the campaign had developed. The issue ads contrasted George Allen's position with Chuck Robb's on issues such as taxes and drugs and also attempted to inoculate Allen from Democratic attacks on his education record. Republican statewide campaigns in Virginia were premised on the assumption that the GOP could not succeed if the public perceived it to be inadequate on education. Matricardi noted that if "we are seen as good on taxes, but poor on education, we lose. But if we're seen as good on taxes and sound on education, we win."[8] The issue ads produced for television distribution followed the legal guidelines and did not specifically endorse either of the candidates. But as Matricardi observed, "you would have to be an idiot, however, not to have understood who the ad implied was the preferred candidate."[9]

The Republican Party mailings and telephone calls were often more specifically targeted than the television ads. The Allen campaign believed that Robb could only win if he ran extraordinarily well among moderate, GOP-leaning voters in the suburban D.C., northern Virginia area. For this reason, much of the campaign's mail strategy, both the party's and the candidate's, was directed at maintaining the loyalty of GOP women in suburban northern Virginia. Initial mailings to acquaint voters with Allen and his family were disseminated in May and June to women who had voted in the GOP presidential primary. The ads also attempted to address Robb's expected attack on Allen's education record by noting that Allen's own children attended public schools and that he was committed to educational reform. Table 6.2 shows the number of unique ads that the most active organizations produced for Democratic and Republican allies in the Virginia Senate race.

The Robb campaign implicitly conceded from the outset that it would not be able to capitalize on many of the traditional incumbent advantages because all the early polls showed Robb trailing Allen, the popular former governor who was denied an opportunity to succeed himself by Virginia's one-term limit. Robb's problems were compounded by the Gore campaign's decision not to contest Virginia. For Robb to win, he needed a sizeable number of ticket splitters who would vote for Bush but not Allen. One estimate suggested that Robb would need 20,000 ticket splitters for every percentage point that Bush led over the combined Gore/Nader vote.[10]

For these reasons, Robb's campaign was framed more as an attack on Allen's record than as a defense of Robb's tenure in the Senate. Although the Robb campaign did spend some time speaking about Robb's biography, especially his service in Vietnam, the campaign never attempted to make the contest a referendum on his twelve-year Senate record. According to Craig Bieber, executive director of the Virginia Democratic Party, the Robb strategy was to convince Virginians that Allen was outside the mainstream on issues that mattered to them, especially on education, abortion, civil rights, and guns.[11] The Robb campaign and groups such

Table 6.2. The Ground War: Most Active Organizations' Observed Activity in the Virginia Senate Race

Type	*Organization*	*Mail*	*News*	*Person*	*Total Unique Ads*
Democratic Allies					
Candidates	Robb for the Senate	6	—	—	6
Political Parties	Democratic Party of Virginia	18	—	—	18
Interest Groups	Virginia Education Association	4	—	—	4
	Sierra Club	3	—	—	3
	League of Conservation Voters	2	—	—	2
	National Education Association	2	—	—	2
Republican Allies					
Candidates	Friends of George Allen	1	—	—	1
Political Parties	Republican Party of Virginia/Victory 2000	18	—	1	19
	Fairfax County Republican Committee	2	—	—	2
Interest Groups	National Federation of Independent Business	5	2	—	7
	National Rifle Association-Political Victory Fund	3	—	—	3

Source: Election Advocacy database.
Notes: See appendix B for a more detailed explanation of the data. Totals exclude all presidential data. Data include all ad campaigns that mentioned any VA Senate candidate, including those ads that simultaneously mentioned any presidential or VA House candidate. This table is not intended to represent comprehensive organization activity in the VA Senate race. A more complete picture can be obtained by examining this table and tables 6.1 and 6.3 together. Active organizations not listed above include (Democratic Parties) Arlington Democratic Joint Committee, DNC, Fairfax County Democratic Committee, Salem Democratic Party, VA Democratic Party; (Democratic Allies) ALF-CIO, Campaign for a Progressive Future, Coalition to Stop Gun Violence, Human Rights Campaign, Local 51 Painters Union No VA, People for the American Way, Planned Parenthood Blue Ridge Action Fund, Inc., VA Chapter of the Sierra Club, Virginia NOW; (Republican Parties) 11th Congressional District of VA Republican Committee, 6th District Republican Committee PAC, Virginia Republican Party; (Republican Allies) Christian Coalition, Commonwealth's Attorney for the City of Danville, NRA.

as the Sierra Club and the League of Conservation Voters (LCV) also made Allen's environmental record an issue.

The Robb campaign and the Democratic Party made targeted efforts to mobilize African Americans around civil rights issues. Significant radio buys on African American radio stations sent the message that Allen couldn't be depended on to protect the basic civil rights gains made in recent decades. A radio ad that ran on African American and "crossover" radio stations pointed out the differences between Robb and Allen on affirmative action, the Martin Luther King Jr. holiday, and the Confederate flag.[12]

THE PARTIES AND INTEREST GROUPS

Both the Democratic and Republican parties of Virginia have strong and important relationships with interest and activist groups. But the 2000 Senate campaign indicated that, at least at the present time, the nature of this relationship differs in at least one very important sense. The Republican Party of Virginia has had close ties with the National Rifle Association (NRA), the Christian Coalition, and the National Federation of Independent Business. Yet the GOP itself is also a strong grassroots organization. It turns out large numbers of volunteers, it organizes signage and bumper stickers effectively in large parts of the state, and it can serve as an effective mobilizing force for campaign events. By contrast, the grassroots capacity of the Virginia Democratic Party withered considerably during the 1990s. By the time the Senate campaign of 2000 began, the Virginia Democratic Party was dependent on its associated interest and activist groups for its grassroots mobilization. Labor, the teachers' association, environmental groups, African American ministers' organizations, and gay rights supporters are the grassroots of Virginia's Democratic Party. The Democrats did not possess the independent mobilizing power that the GOP had built up in the previous decade.

The importance of organized interest and activist groups to the Democratic campaign cannot be overstated. Indeed, some Republicans believed that the Democrats' reliance on groups was so extensive that when a group didn't exist to attack Allen, the Democrats attempted to create one. Ed Matricardi noted that he had never heard of "Voters for Choice," a group that sponsored pro-Robb and anti-Allen ads on the abortion issue. Matricardi felt that the group itself was largely a creation of the Democratic Party and pointed to the role that Senator Emily Couric, cochair of the state party, played in its commercials.[13]

In any case, the 2000 campaign indicated that both parties understood the importance of developing links that connected candidates, parties, and interest groups. For the Virginia Democratic Party, this link might have been even more important because the activist groups had essentially become the party grassroots.

INTEREST GROUP ACTIVITY

The level of interest group involvement in Virginia's Senate campaign may well have been unprecedented in terms of the number of groups involved, money spent, and resources utilized. Many of the hardest-hitting messages were delivered by interest groups. They covered a range of issues, from abortion to education and from gun control to taxes.

Almost all of the wide variety of interest groups active in the Virginia Senate race participated in the ground war; fewer participated in the air war. Most focused on motivating their members to vote, but others took a more proactive campaigning approach. Geographic targeting was a common strategy due to the different ideologies and issue salience of various regions within the state. Table 6.3 shows interest group advertising activities and the estimated spending involved.

Interest groups ran more than 2,315 television advertisements at a cost of over $2.5 million and nearly five hundred radio ads totaling more than $34,000.[14] The air war was led by the LCV, which aired 779 television spots; Voters for Choice (515 spots); the NRA with 378 spots; and the U.S. Chamber of Commerce (362 spots). Most of the groups focused their television efforts at the end of the campaign and purchased ads in the middle of October or later.

Radio ads began airing in early October, and the Sierra Club topped the list with 234 ads. The NRA was second at 155, and the NAACP National Voter Fund aired 62 spots. Although these numbers represent only a sampling of radio stations, our research shows that interest groups outspent the candidates on the radio by a three-to-one ratio, while the parties doubled the amount spent by the groups on the radio.

Pro-Allen Groups

One of the most active groups working for George Allen was the NRA. The NRA fought the battle in the air and on the ground, especially hitting the airwaves in the friendly territory of southwestern Virginia. They also spent significant resources targeting members throughout the state.

The NRA set up a volunteer network that worked with the leaders in northern Virginia as well as the Republican Victory 2000 campaign. Their volunteers manned phone banks, did literature drops, placed yard signs, and campaigned extensively by e-mail. Interviews with those involved in the campaign, including a volunteer coordinator, revealed that the organization does not fit the stereotype of the unsophisticated, gun-toting good-ol' boy.

In early October, the NRA placed billboards that simply read "Vote Freedom First." They added an Allen message to billboards closer to the election. The NRA also sent mailings to its members. In the end, the NRA reported over $606,407 to the Federal Election Commission (FEC) in independent expenditures supporting George Allen.[15]

National Right to Life (NRTL) mailed an oversized postcard with a picture of a baby urging the recipient to "[V]ote for George W. Bush and a Pro-Life Senator." The focus was on partial-birth abortions, but other policies were mentioned. The punch line of the mailing was "A vote for anyone else [other than Bush] is, in effect, a vote for Al Gore and a vote for abortion." The mailings also summarized

Table 6.3. **Organization Activity and Estimated Spending**

Group	*TV*	*Mail*	*Phone*	*Radio*	*News*	*GOTV*	*Money*
AFL-CIO		x	x			x	$227,000[1]
Campaign for a Progressive Future		x					?
Christian Coalition of America		x					?
Coalition to Stop Gun Violence		x					?
Handgun Control, Inc.	x	x	x			x	$165,000[2]
Human Rights Campaign		x				x	$100,000[3]
League of Conservation Voters	x	x				x	$543,279[4]
National Education Association		x				x	$ 27,500[5]
National Federation of Independent Businesses		x			x	x	$125,000[6]
National Rifle Association	x	x	x	x		x	$699,000[7]
National Right to Life PAC		x					$ 44,996[8]
People for the American Way		x					?
Sierra Club		x				x	$ 26,000[9]
U.S. Chamber of Commerce	x	x		x	x	x	$102,000[10]
Virginia Education Association		x				x	$ 57,500[11]
Virginia NOW		x					?
Virginia Partisans Gay/Lesbian Group		x					$ 50,000[12]
Voters for Choice	x						$600,000[13]

[1]Campaign Media Analysis Group (CMAG) reports.
[2]Greg Macias, telephone interview by Scott Keeter, 12 December 2000.
[3]Mark Perriello, telephone interview by Stephen Medvic, 28 November 2000. This figure is an estimate of funds raised for the Robb campaign, not of how much money the group spent.
[4]Glen Close, telephone interview by David B. Magleby, 13 November 2000.
[5]Rob Jones, e-mail interview by Scott Keeter, 2 November 2000.
[6]Matt Garth, telephone interview by Harry Wilson, 18 December 2000.
[7]CMAG reports (TV data), project database (radio data).
[8]FEC, "Disclosure Database," <ftp.fec.gov> [accessed 22 January 2001].
[9]Campaign Media Analysis Group (CMAG) reports.
[10]Ibid.
[11]Jones, interview by Keeter.
[12]"The Virginia Partisan," *Newsletter of the Virginia Partisans Gay and Lesbian Democratic Club* 9, no. 4 (August 2000).
[13]Maureen Berittel, telephone interview by Stephen Medvic, 21 November 2000.

candidate records. The NRTL also aired some television spots in the Roanoke (southwest Virginia) market only.

In support of Allen, the Christian Coalition of America distributed its renowned Voter Guide, offering choices between both presidential and senatorial candidates on a litany of issues. On the Sunday prior to Election Day, the guides were distributed in churches throughout Virginia. Our direct mail network received only one guide, so we are uncertain how many were actually distributed.

To tout the pro-Allen position of the business community, the National Federation of Independent Business (NFIB) stayed primarily on the ground, while the U.S. Chamber of Commerce took to the air as well as the ground. The NFIB spent about 90 percent of its efforts reaching its membership, primarily by mail and phone. The organization urged voters to support Allen and solicit volunteers. The NFIB also advertised in several newspapers in the commonwealth, attempting to reach beyond northern Virginia and Tidewater to the more rural areas.[16] The Chamber of Commerce focused on areas outside the northern Virginia corridor, using a range of direct mail pieces aimed at members and affiliates.

Pro-Robb Groups

The LCV and Voters for Choice actively campaigned on Chuck Robb's behalf. The LCV reported heavy early and late independent expenditures against George Allen ($224,000 on 20 September and $157,000 on 3 November).[17] It aired numerous television ads in northern Virginia and Norfolk, some in Richmond, and none in southwest Virginia. The LCV also sent mailings to its members, including both issue advocacy pieces and a GOTV postcard. It listed George Allen as one of its "Dirty Dozen" and emphasized independent expenditure campaigns over issue ads because regulations allow the former to be more direct, specific, and hard-hitting.

The LCV was aided in northern Virginia by the Sierra Club, which also fought the battle primarily in the air. The Sierra Club mailed targeted brochures to members in Tidewater and northern Virginia, asking, "It's Their [the children's] World. Who Will Keep It Clean?"

Voters for Choice, an abortion-rights political action group cofounded by Gloria Steinem, aired an ad in late October that featured state senator Emily Couric trying to convince the public that George Allen was in fact more extreme in his position on abortion than he had led voters to believe. The groups had planned to do GOTV rallies but canceled them in favor of the television ad campaign. There was no evidence of organized activity by NARAL or Planned Parenthood in the Virginia Senate race, although our network received one mailing from a local Planned Parenthood chapter.

Groups with the NRA in their sights included Handgun Control, Inc., Coalition to Stop Gun Violence, and Campaign for a Progressive Future. Campaign for a

Progressive Future mailed what may be the most creative literature in the campaign. The quad-fold brochure's cover was cut in the outline of a hammer-set revolver with children's faces superimposed on the weapon. Opening the fold revealed photos of U.S. currency and noted that the NRA has spent money to elect George Allen, who "support[ed] a law that increases gun violence in Virginia."

Handgun Control targeted moderate women, principally located in northern Virginia, who are concerned about handgun violence. The group ran ads in that area in early September and in early October sent about 25,000 mailings to members and others on lists believed to reflect potentially receptive voters, advocating a vote for Robb. Finally, the organization placed about 8,000 GOTV phone calls to members.

Both the National Education Association (NEA) and the Virginia Education Association (VEA) spent $72,921 mailing several pieces touting Robb's education record while assailing George Allen's.[18] One item was a report card on which Robb earned As while Allen had Cs, Ds and Fs on several education-specific issues. Another mailing urged support for the candidate "who supports children."

The VEA targeted its 57,000 members, while NEA provided $27,500 to the VEA for supporting Robb's candidacy, donated a full-time consultant for the race, and sent two direct mailings to VEA members. The NEA Fund for Children and Public Education endorsed Robb on the recommendation of the state affiliate (VEA), but the VEA itself did not endorse Robb. The VEA also staffed a statewide phone bank in addition to making direct contributions to the Robb campaign, the DSCC, and the Virginia Democratic Party.

People for the American Way suggested that "[Y]ou be the judge" on issues ranging from abortion and education to the environment, with the clear implication that the judgment would favor Robb.

The Human Rights Campaign focused on gay/lesbian, minority, and women's issues, using a GOTV phone bank, and targeted almost all its efforts at educating its members about candidate positions regarding issues of interest.

The AFL-CIO was active on labor issues at the grassroots level. It focused efforts on communication at the workplace, although it also did some door-to-door work, using both volunteers and paid staff toward the end of the campaign.

ASSESSMENT OF INTEREST GROUP IMPACT

Not surprisingly, most interest group representatives who were interviewed claimed that their strategies were successful and that they accomplished their goals. This is true both of groups who supported Allen and those who supported Robb. The ground war, which included both campaign mailers and GOTV efforts, such as phone banks and postcards, seems to have been the preferred method of campaigning, and this tactic was more widely used by the groups that supported Allen.

According to Bernadette Budde of BIPAC, interest groups are learning that some of their most effective communications are with their members, where the groups' credibility is greatest.[19] The ground war is the most cost-effective strategy for reaching members and producing votes.

We expected to see groups with fewer resources, like the Human Rights Campaign, concentrate more heavily on their target audience—usually members—and larger groups like the NRA, LCV, and Voters for Choice emphasize the air war because they can afford it. The latter did engage heavily in televised ads (Voters for Choice used television almost exclusively), but the NRA also organized a network of volunteers throughout the state and used them to personally contact likely Allen supporters. Add that to a large number of mailings to members and an election insert in *America's 1st Freedom* magazine, and one can begin to assess the level of effort expended by the NRA.

Probusiness groups, such as the NFIB and the Chamber of Commerce, also focused efforts on members and tried to reach their constituents in the areas beyond northern Virginia. As a point of comparison, neither Voters for Choice nor LCV aired any ads in the Roanoke market. Although southwest Virginia is more Republican and conservative, pockets of Democratic voters can be found in Roanoke and the southwestern coalfields.

To be sure, the groups that supported Robb were also active on the ground; the Human Rights Campaign was fairly typical in this regard. The HRC worked almost exclusively with members and others it was sure would support the cause. The group kept a low profile publicly because it believed that support of gay rights would be anathema to much of Virginia's relatively conservative electorate.

Membership size may also contribute to decisions to concentrate on internal communication and GOTV. Larger membership groups such as the AFL-CIO (approximately 200,000 in Virginia), NRA (about 100,000), and VEA (57,000) can potentially provide the winning margin in an election by turning out their members. Others like the Sierra Club (13,000), NFIB (10,000), and People for the American Way (1,400) will have a smaller but still important impact if they can persuade their members to vote.

CONCLUSION

Overall, the candidates, parties, and interest groups on each side all sang from the same page. This was particularly true of the Democratic side, where the Robb campaign, the Virginia Democratic Party, and the independent groups that expended money on Robb's behalf repeated the same mantra: George Allen could not be trusted to protect the basic rights and interests of a majority of Virginians. There was also considerable congruence between the issues that groups emphasized, such as abortion, the environment, and others highlighted by the party and the Robb campaign. This "team approach" suggests at least an implicit coordination among the three component parts. Indeed, Craig Bieber, executive director of the Democratic Party, noted that the Democrats felt they had a unified message and did not worry that the independent expenditures were in any way detracting from the themes that the Democrats and Robb's campaign were developing.[20] Any difference of opinion that arose among the campaign, parties, and groups had to do with tactics, not with the basic message. For example, Bieber felt that the LCV's early television buy was probably of little use because it was too small and too early in the campaign.[21]

On the Republican side, the messages of the Allen campaign and the Republican Party were coordinated and reinforcing. The Allen strategy rested on mobilizing Republicans with appeals based on his commitment to reducing taxes and on inoculating Allen from Robb's attempts to portray him as a conservative ideologue, out of touch with the public's real interests. The two-pronged strategy was evident in the themes contained in television and radio advertisements, in the direct mail sent to voters, and in the head-to-head debates between the candidates. The inoculation strategy was also evident in the manner in which both the campaign and the party targeted GOP-leaning women voters in northern Virginia. This effort was initiated in May and June and was never abandoned.

In one interesting way, however, the interest groups that worked on Allen's behalf articulated a message that differed considerably from the campaign's own pronouncements. Concerned that his position against various forms of gun control could undermine the inoculation strategy, Allen modified and moderated some of his previous public stances. Most important, he said that he would support the continuation of the assault weapons ban, legislation that he had publicly opposed when it was first introduced. In essence, the Allen campaign believed that he was better off defending a flip-flop than defending his opposition to the ban. At the same time, the NRA campaign's major effort on Allen's behalf across the state dovetailed with support for a ballot amendment that would offer constitutional protection for Virginians' right to hunt and fish. When the NRA and its high-profile supporters noted that Allen would be much more supportive of the right to bear arms than Robb, they worked strenuously to mobilize supporters. The NRA's message to supporters throughout Virginia was inconsistent with the theme the campaign was showcasing among moderate voters.

Nevertheless, the cooperation between the NRA and the Allen campaign with respect to tactics was, as NRA Election Volunteer Coordinator Dave Adams suggested, "the most coordinated effort I've seen."[22] Whether it was setting up booths at gun shows or organizing literature drops, "They [the Allen campaign] constantly stayed in contact with us [the NRA]."[23]

The efforts of interest groups and parties did differ from those of the candidates—both Allen and Robb—in one significant way. Parties and interest groups were more willing to "go negative" than were the candidates. The political parties were more likely to attack the opponent than were the candidates or interest groups (Democrats, 40 percent; Republicans, 26 percent); the candidates themselves primarily praised themselves (Robb, 45 percent; Allen, 56 percent), while the interest groups provided messages that compared the candidates (groups supporting Robb, 56 percent; groups supporting Allen, 67 percent). This finding—that candidates can now stay positive while parties and groups do their "dirty work"—comports with recognized trends nationally.[24]

With respect to the tone of the entire campaign, including all types of communication from the candidates, the parties, and interest groups, we found that communications on Robb's behalf could be categorized as follows: 23 percent were strictly positive, 51 percent compared Robb's positions with those of Allen, and 26 percent only attacked Allen (N = 47). Allen's communications were 16 percent positive, 60 percent contrast, and 19 percent attack (N = 43).

When only ads (television, radio, and newspaper) were analyzed, we found that those for Robb (N = 14) were more likely to be only attacks (43 percent) than either comparative (36 percent) or positive toward Robb (21 percent). Allen's (N = 24) were more likely to feature comparisons with Robb (71 percent) than to attack Robb (17 percent) or praise Allen (13 percent). Interestingly, however, one study of the Virginia Senate race found that voters perceived no difference in negativity between Robb and Allen ads.[25]

In the end, we might ask, what impact did these efforts have on the outcome of the election? Answering that question is complicated because it requires comparisons both over time and against expectations. Any evaluation of a campaign must, for instance, take into account the partisan environment of the state. Although Virginia has become strongly Republican throughout the 1990s, the Democratic Party has been reasonably competitive in presidential years.[26]

In one sense, Chuck Robb's 48 percent of the vote represents a continuation of the pattern of Republican wins in close races during presidential years.[27] Alternatively, the results suggest that Allen's campaign successfully minimized the substantial incumbency advantages that Robb should have enjoyed. Allen's social conservatism and controversial record on education and the environment could have given Robb an opening; instead, the Allen campaign managed to turn the election into a referendum on Robb.

Nevertheless, the trend in public opinion polls throughout the race demonstrates that Robb cut deeply into an early Allen advantage. The race began with Allen leading by double digits. Election Day polls by Voter News Service showed that Robb received the same percentage of the vote among Democrats (91 percent) as Allen did among Republicans. Democrats also represented the same percentage of the Virginia electorate in 2000 (35 percent) as they did in 1996 and 1994. Allen added to his natural base by securing a solid majority among Virginia's Independents, who tend to be slightly more conservative than Independents nationally. On the other hand, Robb had a slight majority among self-described moderates, but this was not enough to overcome the fact that conservatives outnumbered liberals.

These considerations allow us to draw several conclusions about the impact of the campaign and the relationship among the candidates, parties, and interest groups that participated. First, the Robb campaign, along with the effort of the Democratic Party and allied interest groups, succeeded in mobilizing the Democratic base to competitive levels. Exit polls also indicated that the electorate was more moderate and less conservative than the pre-election polls suggested. The one disappointing feature to Democrats was that exit polls indicated that Robb obtained 83 percent of the African American vote, a percentage considerably below the 92 percent that Al Gore received nationally.

Second, the "team approach" employed by the pro-Robb forces extended beyond mobilization to message congruence. Robb relied heavily on numerous interest groups, as well as the Democratic Party, to take his basic message to their various audiences. Rather than create conflicting messages, these groups reinforced Robb's campaign theme and helped emphasize the issues he was addressing. Although voters may have had a difficult time identifying the sponsor of the message, Robb undoubtedly benefited from this consistent drumbeat heard throughout the state.

Third, late spending on Robb's behalf seemed to reduce the size of Allen's margin. Reports on the total number of television ads run in the last week of the campaign indicate that Robb had a considerable advantage. The Robb campaign and the Virginia Democratic Party purchased 1,432 television ads at an estimated cost of $1,214,590. The Allen campaign and the Republican Party of Virginia purchased 1,034 ads at an estimated cost of $903,847.[28] Both Republicans and Democrats believe that, contrary to conventional wisdom, many of the late deciders in the campaign broke for Senator Robb, the incumbent, not former Governor Allen, the challenger. Although late spending subsidized by the DSCC was not enough to propel Robb to victory, it did help reduce Allen's winning margin.

Fourth, Allen's strategy of inoculation was sufficiently successful in the urban-suburban areas of the state, especially in vote-rich northern Virginia. Allen's decision to target northern Virginia women early in the campaign successfully reduced the slippage experienced when the Robb campaign and Democratic interest groups launched their full-scale assault on his record. This also demonstrates the critical importance of examining the ground war, even in races with statewide constituencies. The mail battle over the support of northern Virginia women was critical to the race's outcome.

Finally, Allen was not damaged by the inconsistencies between the message his campaign directed toward the suburbs and the message the NRA delivered in rural Virginia. Indeed, the NRA's communication and mobilization efforts in the less-populated areas of the state helped Allen significantly. The Robb campaign had difficulty articulating a response to the inconsistencies since the group message was carried out on the ground and, therefore, "under the radar."

On November 8, Virginia Republicans congratulated themselves for knocking off the only Senate Democrat defeated in 2000 and defeating the last Democrat in Virginia who held a statewide office. It was the culmination of an extraordinary decade of GOP success in the Old Dominion. Virginia Democrats were understandably disappointed, but they were not entirely displeased with Robb's showing, one that convinced them that they had an excellent chance of regaining the governorship in 2001. They were able to accomplish this task in another $30 million election in which a centralist candidate and millionaire businessman, Mark Warner, outpolled Republican Mark Earley in a race in which he outspent Earley by almost 2 to 1.

NOTES

1. Roll Call, "Interactive Election 2000 Map," <election.capwiz.com/rollcall/emap/search/?outlook=4&chamber=S>.
2. Federal Election Commission (FEC), "Quarterly Report of Receipts and Disbursements," *Robb for Senate and Friends of George Allen*, press release, 15 April 2000.
3. Federal Election Commission (FEC), "Candidate Summary Reports," <herndon1.sdrdc.com/cgi-bin/cancomsrs/>, 2001 [accessed 13 August 2001].
4. Ed Matricardi, telephone interview by Robert Holsworth, 2 January 2001.
5. Federal Election Commission (FEC), "FEC Reports Increase in Party Fundraising for 2000," press release, <www.fec.gov/press/051501partyfund/tables/cong2state2000.html>, 15 May 2001 [accessed 27 August 2001].
6. Data for independent expenditures, internal communication, and party coordinated expenditures were obtained from the FEC, "Disclosure Database," <ftp.fec.gov> [accessed 22 January 2001].
7. Federal Election Commission (FEC), "Party Fundraising Escalates," press release, 12 January 2001.
8. Matricardi, interview by Holsworth.
9. Ibid.
10. Estimate by Robert D. Holsworth. The estimate was premised on the assumption that a small proportion of Gore voters (5 percent) would split their tickets and vote for Allen.
11. Craig Bieber, telephone interview by Robert D. Holsworth, 5 December 2000.
12. Radio ad, paid for by the Democratic Party of Virginia, narrated by Delegate Dwight Jones.
13. Matricardi, interview by Holsworth. In fact, Gloria Steinem created Voters For Choice over twenty years ago, and the organization backs pro-choice candidates of any party.
14. Television data are taken from Campaign Media Analysis Group (CMAG) reports. Radio ads include only those stations that are part of the project database. The latter do not include all broadcast media in Virginia; they should therefore be interpreted as low estimates.
15. FEC, "Disclosure Database."
16. The NFIB also sponsored a PAC meet-and-greet that was attended by several candidates, including Allen, and a "couple hundred" PACs.
17. Federal Election Commission (FEC), "Independent expenditures reported after 20 days before the election," press release, 8 November 2000.
18. Ibid.

19. Bernadette Budde, Expert Panel on "Election Advocacy: Soft Money and Issue Advocacy in the 2000 Congressional Elections," The National Press Club, 5 February 2001.

20. Bieber, interview by Holsworth.

21. Ibid.

22. Dave Adams, telephone interview by Harry Wilson, 13 December 2000.

23. Ibid.

24. See Brennan Center for Justice, press release, <www.brennancenter.org/presscenter/pressrelease_2001_0313cmag.html>, 13 March 2001 [accessed 15 March 2001].

25. L. Dale Lawton and Paul Freedman, "Beyond Negativity: Advertising Effects in the 2000 Virginia Senate Race," paper presented at the 2001 Annual Meeting of the Midwest Political Science Association, Chicago, 19–22 April 2001.

26. Bill Clinton, for example, ran much stronger in both 1992 and 1996 than Democratic gubernatorial candidates did in 1996.

27. Interestingly, Robb's showing was also the best by a Democrat since Don Beyer received 54 percent in his 1993 race for reelection as lieutenant governor.

28. CMAG, "Candidate Television Spending," report, 2–8 November 2000.

7

The Montana 2000 Senate and House Races

Craig Wilson

Political party soft money and issue advocacy group activity were integral factors in shaping Montana's 2000 competitive U. S. Senate and House races.

In the Senate contest Republican incumbent Conrad Burns defeated Democratic challenger Brian Schweitzer by a margin of 51 to 47 percent, and Reform Party candidate Gary Lee received 2 percent of the vote. The Senate race was significant for a number of reasons: Burns became the state's first popularly elected Republican senator to win election to a third term, more Montanans voted in the U.S. Senate race than in the presidential contest, the $10.1 million spent by the major party candidates and their allied parties made the Senate contest the most expensive political race in state history, and Burns's two-to-one advantage over Schweitzer in official campaign spending shrunk to a 14 percent difference when political party spending was factored in. In fact, for every vote cast, the parties and candidates spent the equivalent of $24.74.

The 2000 contest for Montana's sole U.S. House seat, the second largest district in geographic area and the most populous district in the country, was both close and contentious. Republican Dennis Rehberg (51 percent) won the open-seat race, defeating Democrat Nancy Keenan (47 percent) and Libertarian James Tikalsky (2 percent), who was not a real factor in the race. The $5.6 million spent by major party candidates and by political parties made the U.S. House race the most expensive in state history. The equivalent of $13.56 was spent for every vote cast in the contest.

Brian Schweitzer, Nancy Keenan, and the Democratic gubernatorial candidate were all subsumed by the Republican electoral tide that swept Montana. Keenan carried only twelve, and Schweitzer eleven, of the state's fifty-six counties. The day following the election some Democratic Party operatives claimed their candidates had been "Bushed."[1] In reality, the losing Democrats appeared to have been

"Gored"; one Montana reporter concluded that Gore was "as popular in Montana as a game warden at a hunting camp."[2] The vice president ran like a strong third-party candidate, winning only 33 percent of the state's popular vote. In comparison, in 1992, third-party candidate Ross Perot attracted 26 percent of the vote, and Bill Clinton won Montana with 38 percent of the vote, while in 1996 he lost the state to Bob Dole, who garnered 44 percent of the popular vote. In 2000 Gore's negative coattails in Montana were too closely related to his ties to President Clinton. The nationally directed Election Day exit poll found that in Montana, 54 percent of the voters interviewed disapproved of President Clinton's job performance and 73 percent held an "unfavorable" personal opinion of him.[3]

MONTANA'S POLITICAL BACKGROUND

The results of the last general election of the twentieth century demonstrated that many of Montana's historic political tendencies were no longer applicable as the state had begun to mirror the Republican dominance found in Wyoming and Idaho.

In supporting George W. Bush, Montana continued its tradition of being a presidential weather vane; in only four instances in the twentieth century has the state not supported the winning presidential candidate. Montana has also often been cited as an example of a two-party competitive state, characterized by ticket-splitting voters. But the post-World War II tendency of divided party control of the state house and at least one legislative chamber appears to no longer be valid.

In 2000, Republicans won the gubernatorial race for the fourth time in a row, and the 2001 legislature marked the fourth consecutive biennial session with GOP majorities in both houses. Beginning with the 1996 primary election, more Republicans than Democrats started casting votes in major office races. And a variety of objective polls consistently find more Republican than Democratic voters in Montana.

Although Montana may have become more Republican because of changes in its political culture, the transformation also appears related to population change and growth. Several of the fastest-growing counties in the central and western parts of the state are heavily Republican, while three of the four Democratic-leaning urban counties have had stagnant or moderate population growth.

THE SENATE CANDIDATES AND THEIR CAMPAIGNS

Most political observers felt that two-term Republican Senator Conrad Burns would be difficult to defeat in 2000. In 1988, Burns, sixty-five, a native of Missouri, became only the second popularly elected Republican senator from Montana, and he easily won reelection in 1994. Burns's principal opponent, Democrat

Brian Schweitzer, forty-five, a Montana native and farmer/rancher, was an unknown political neophyte when he announced his candidacy in March 1999. As a party outsider, he continued to maintain his distance from Democratic presidential candidate Al Gore and state party leaders. Schweitzer's campaign theme was "Plain talk, Good ideas," and he easily defeated a primary opponent who did little campaigning.

Early in the primary, the Trial Lawyers Association attracted significant publicity when Senator Burns was slow to react to the issue of industry-caused asbestos pollution. In 1999, Burns cosponsored legislation, supported by various business groups, which limited corporate liability for asbestos-caused illness. But in mid-November 1999, the *Seattle Post-Intelligence* ran an investigative report revealing that 192 individuals had died as the result of asbestos contained in vermiculite mined at Libby, Montana.[4] Despite this revelation, Burns continued to support the controversial legislation, arguing that it would improve the litigation process.

Schweitzer was quick to pick up on the Trial Lawyers' agenda and used the allegation in his Senate campaign. The issue attracted state and national media coverage and focused attention on Schweitzer, who charged that the legislation was favorable to corporations and noted that asbestos companies had contributed $29,000 to Burns's campaign. In the end, Senator Burns withdrew his sponsorship of the legislation, which died in April.

Early in 2000, Schweitzer also received state and national media attention as well as attacks from issue advocacy groups for organizing senior citizen bus trips to Canada to purchase prescription drugs that are significantly cheaper there than in the United States. Schweitzer's goal was to embarrass Congress into allowing less-expensive prescription drugs to be re-imported into the United States.

For several months following the primary, prescription drug and medical issues continued to be major campaign issues. Although some criticized Schweitzer for being a one-issue candidate, the Burns campaign largely let him set the agenda by mimicking his focus on prescription drug and medical issues. In late September and early October, this preoccupation with health issues was supplemented by debates about economic development and about Montana's place in a high-tech world and agricultural policy.

The 2000 Montana Senate contest was the most expensive in state history. Conrad Burns raised $3.9 million and spent $4.3 million, and Brian Schweitzer raised $2.1 million and spent over $2 million. About 43 percent of Burns's and almost 17 percent of Schweitzer's funds came from political action committees (PACs).[5] Political parties and issue advocacy groups spent millions of additional dollars on the race.

The outside campaign money appeared to help Schweitzer the most. First, the issue advocacy expenditures for and against his positions on asbestos pollution and the price of pharmaceutical drugs during the primary solidified his legitimacy as a candidate. Second, during the general election, Democratic Party spending on Schweitzer's behalf represented a greater percentage of his campaign funds than Republican Party spending on Burns's campaign.

The parties were also incredibly active when it came to advertising. The number of mass mailings identified as coming from both campaigns was fewer than those financed for the candidates by party soft money. And while television advertising was costly for both campaigns, the Democratic Party sponsored more ads for Schweitzer than Schweitzer's campaign produced. This did not appear to hold true for Burns.

The Schweitzer campaign began running a significant number of television ads in August, prior to Burns, and during a period when political "noise" from other campaigns was at a minimum. At the time Schweitzer said that he would be able to maintain this level of advertising until the election, but later admitted that he took "a risk" because he only had $320,000 in campaign money.[6] In contrast, by mid-summer, Burns's campaign had raised millions of dollars, but decided to postpone early television commercials in favor of a later blitz. Although Burns delayed his television ad campaign, by early September he had spent $500,000 on radio advertising, purchased $200,000 of cable television time (a large purchase in Montana), and bought a large block of expensive nonpreemptible television advertising for the final weeks of the campaign.

Many of the campaign television commercials led to charges and countercharges, but the greatest controversies arose over ads about prescription drugs, the single most important campaign issue. In August, Schweitzer ran an ad featuring him discussing the cost of the breast cancer drug Tamoxifen and saying, "Veterinarians prescribe the exact same medicine for dogs and charge half as much." Burns's campaign responded with an ad featuring breast cancer survivors, one of whom said, "Brian Schweitzer misleads women into believing they can get Tamoxifen and other life-saving drugs from their veterinarians at half-price." After the election, Schweitzer concluded that Burns made a decision to focus on the Tamoxifen issue and spent several hundred thousand dollars attempting, with some success, to confuse voters about Schweitzer's position on reducing pharmaceutical drug costs.[7] The Democratic challenger felt the issue also placed him on the defensive and delayed his ability to address new issues.[8]

By the end of the campaign, Burns had spent several million dollars on television ads and $600,000 on radio ads, whereas Schweitzer spent about $800,000 on television commercials and considerably less on radio advertising.

In his victory speech Burns attributed his reelection to face-to-face campaigning, while Schweitzer entertained the possibility of running for office again.

THE HOUSE CANDIDATES AND THEIR CAMPAIGNS

In August 1999, Montanans were surprised when two-term Republican congressman Rick Hill announced in August 1999 that he would not seek reelection. This left Democrat Nancy Keenan, who had announced her candidacy in May, running unopposed in an open-seat contest.

The Democrats' satisfaction with having a well-known candidate in an open-seat race was short-lived; Dennis Rehberg, a Republican with political credentials, soon announced his candidacy for Hill's seat.

Nancy Keenan, forty-eight, known as a relatively liberal politician, was a native Montanan, raised in the heavily unionized town of Anaconda, where her father was a blue-collar worker for the company of the same name. She was elected to the state house in 1982, and in 1988 was elected to serve the first of three terms as superintendent of public instruction.

Republican Dennis Rehberg, forty-four, was also a native Montanan with family ties to the state's agricultural and business communities. Rehberg established his conservative credentials after being elected to the Montana house in 1984. He was appointed lieutenant governor in 1991 and served in that position until 1996, when he undertook a bitter and unsuccessful effort to unseat Democratic U.S. Senator Max Baucus.

Early in the 2000 campaign, it appeared that Keenan and Rehberg were consciously working to tone down their prior reputations as feisty politicians. They also appeared to have purposely moderated their past conservative and liberal personas and made ideological U-turns, permitting them to run to the political center.

In terms of issues, both Keenan and Rehberg agreed that improving Montana's economy and creating jobs was a top priority. Both also assumed the safe position for Montana politicians by strongly opposing gun control. On some issues, however, they held polar opposite positions: Rehberg was pro-life, Keenan pro-choice; she opposed establishing permanent normal trade relations with the People's Republic of China, while he supported the policy; he backed privatizing part of Social Security, and she spoke against this plan.

Because of the narrow Republican U.S. House majority, the relatively low cost of Montana campaigns, the open seat, and the perception of a close race, the Montana House race attracted national attention. Democratic U.S. House Minority Leader Dick Gephardt visited the Great Falls to stump for Keenan, as did former Texas Governor Ann Richards. Republican U.S. House Speaker Dennis Hastert appeared twice for Rehberg, and National Republican Campaign Committee chairman Representative Tom Davis (R-Va.) went to Missoula on Rehberg's behalf.

Nancy Keenan and Dennis Rehberg raised and spent similar amounts of money, \$1.9 million for Keenan and \$2.1 million for Rehberg. Whereas 35 percent of Rehberg's support came from PACs, 29 percent of Keenan's funding came from these groups.[9]

Both candidates began and ended their campaigns with softer television commercials talking about their Montana roots and their families. Rehberg's first ad, and many of his later ads, featured his two-year-old daughter, Elsie. Rehberg said he purposely showed his daughter to stress the importance he placed on the family issue.[10] Left unsaid was that as a single woman, Keenan found it difficult to counter the family image projected by Rehberg.

Having been state superintendent of public instruction for almost twelve years meant that education was Keenan's strongest issue. A great deal of her advertising showed her with children, featured her discussing schools, or focused on teachers trumpeting her commitment to quality education. Rehberg felt that he had to counteract the numerous ads of Keenan positively interacting with children. He said he began employing negative advertising later in the campaign because "it works" and because Keenan gave him the opportunity to do so by violating her own clean campaign pledge when she falsely accused him of supporting school vouchers.[11]

The campaign became contentious at about the same time the television advertising blitz began in late September and early October. Many of Rehberg's ads attempted to merge Keenan and Al Gore into a single polyglot liberal candidate. Rehberg explained his strategy as follows: "It's a conscious effort because I believe that the Bush-Cheney team better reflects . . . the values, principles, and philosophies of Montanans. . . . For the very reasons that Al Gore isn't popular, Nancy Keenan espouses the same philosophies."[12]

Initially, Keenan responded to her opponent's attacks by showing television ads featuring award-winning teachers shaming Rehberg for his attack ads. Her campaign manager said: "It's very ugly. . . . This is Dennis Rehberg. It's the kind of campaign he runs. He'll say or do anything to win."[13]

By the end of the campaign, ads were running claiming that Keenan was "desperate in attacking" Rehberg and not being "honest" about her position on taxes, while others claimed Rehberg was willing "to say anything to get elected" and had moved "beyond shame" in his campaign tactics.

On election night the Keenan campaign concluded that they were undermined by Al Gore's abysmal showing in the state, while Dennis Rehberg felt his strong campaign organization was responsible for his victory.

POLITICAL PARTY ACTIVITY

The national parties transferred a record amount of hard and soft money, $6.9 million, to their Montana affiliates for the Senate and House races. These transfers represent 50 percent of the total campaign funds raised by the four major party candidates. All four campaigns got more "bang for the buck" from their campaigns, due to this political party spending on their behalf.

The Democratic Senatorial Campaign Committee (DSCC) sent $2.7 million in hard and soft money to the state party to assist Schweitzer. The National Republican Senatorial Committee (NRSC) transferred $1.3 million in hard and soft money assistance for Burns.[14] The Republican transfer amounted to 32 percent of the money raised by the Burns campaign, while the Democratic national party monetary assistance amounted to 129 percent of what the Schweitzer campaign raised.

In the House contest, the Republicans spent about $725,000 (34 percent of the amount Rehberg's campaign raised) and the Democrats about $878,000 (equivalent to 46 percent of Keenan's campaign funds) on behalf of their candidates.[15]

Party money paid for a majority of the mass mailings and a significant percentage of the television advertising for both candidates.

The Senate Race

During the general election period, the parties often sponsored more ads for their candidates than the candidates sponsored themselves. Schweitzer's campaign ran at least ten different official campaign television ads, compared to sixteen party-sponsored television ads. The comparable figures for Burns were ten official and nine soft money advertisements. Table 7.1 shows the money spent on television and radio ads by both sides in the Senate race.

In the ground war, both parties ran phone banks for voter identification and get-out-the-vote (GOTV) efforts, and the number of party-sponsored, soft money mass mailings exceeded those sent by the campaign organizations: nine Republican party mass mailings sent for Burns were identified, and the Democrats mailed at least thirteen on behalf of Schweitzer. Most Republican mailings

Table 7.1. The Air War: Most Active Organizations' Collected Ad Buy Data in the Montana Senate Race

Type	*Organization*	*TV*	*Radio*	*Total Ad Buy $*	*CMAG TV*
Democratic Allies					
Candidates	Schweitzer for US Senate	$252,794	$ 1,344	**$254,138**	N/A
Political Parties	Montana Democratic Party	$109,485	$ 8,283	**$117,768**	N/A
Republican Allies					
Candidates	Friends of Conrad Burns 2000	$266,425	$10,968	**$277,393**	N/A
Political Parties	Montana Republican Party	$ 59,528	$0	**$ 59,528**	N/A
	Montana Republican State Central Committee	$ 26,850	$25,718	**$ 52,568**	N/A

Source: Election Advocacy database.

Notes: See appendix B for a more detailed explanation of the data. This table is not intended to portray comprehensive organization spending in the MT-AL race. A more complete picture can be obtained by examining this table together with table 7.2. Because ad buy content was often nondescriptive, a portion of these data was possibly bought for the MT At-Large race. Unfortunately, it was not possible to parse the MT AL data from the MT Senate data. CMAG did not cover a market in Montana.

were standard fare, such as endorsements by Governor Racicot and George W. Bush and comparisons of the candidates' positions on multiple issues. The Democratic Party mailings for Schweitzer usually addressed single issues and had bullet statements on the outside. Table 7.2 shows the money spent on the ground war by both sides in the Senate race.

Table 7.2. The Ground War: Most Active Organizations' Observed Activity in the Montana Senate Race

Type	*Organization*	*Mail*	*News*	*Person*	*Phone*	*Total Unique Ads*
Democratic Allies						
Candidates	Schweitzer for US Senate	5	—	—	—	5
Political Parties	Montana Democratic Party	17	—	—	—	17
Interest Groups	Montana AFL-CIO	7	1	—	—	8
	Montana NARAL	5	—	—	—	5
	MT Conservation Voters	4	—	—	—	4
	MT Education Association	3	—	—	—	3
	MT St Bldg & Construction Trades Council	3	—	—	—	3
	NARAL	1	—	—	2	3
	Public Citizen, Inc.	2	—	1	—	3
	NEA	2	—	—	—	2
	Planned Parenthood Action Fund	2	—	—	—	2
	Sierra Club	1	1	—	—	2
Republican Allies						
Candidates	Friends of Conrad Burns 2000	1	1	—	—	2
Political Parties	MT Republican Party	7	—	—	—	7
	RNC	6	—	—	—	6
Interest Groups	NFIB	2	1	—	—	3
	NRA -Political Victory Fund	3	—	—	—	3
	NRA	2	—	—	—	2

Source: Election Advocacy database.

Notes: See appendix B for a more detailed explanation of the data. Totals exclude all presidential data, and include all e-mail observations. Data include all ad campaigns that mentioned any MT Senate candidate, including those ads that simultaneously mentioned any presidential or MT-AL candidate. Therefore, this table and the table for MT-AL are not mutually exclusive. This table is not intended to represent comprehensive organization activity in the MT Senate race. A more complete picture can be obtained by examining this table and table 7.1 together. Active organizations not listed above include (Democratic Allies) AFL-CIO, Council for a Livable World, MT Federation of Teachers, Youth Vote 2000; (Republican Parties) NRSC, Voter Consumer Research; (Republican Allies) AMA, Americans for Job Security, Business Roundtable, Cellular Telecommunications Industry Association, Christian Coalition, COMPAC, Free IM, Gray PAC, League of Rural Voters Action Fund, MT Citizens for Better Medicare, MT Right to Life PAC, MT Shooting Sports Association, National Association of Health Underwriters, NRSC, National Right to Life PAC, National Right to Work Committee, National Taxpayers Union, Rocky Mountain Research, U.S. Chamber of Commerce; (Nonpartisan) MT Hunters and Anglers Political Action Committee, Interfaith Alliance of Billings, WC Research.

Many of the controversies over party soft money television ads again dealt with medical/prescription drug issues. For example, in September, a Montana Democratic Party ad claimed, "The big insurance companies are getting access to your medical records and selling them to the highest bidder and Conrad Burns is helping them."[16] When Burns said the ad unfairly presented his position on privacy, the executive director of the Montana Democratic Party labeled the allegation "a crock" and said the senator's campaign had attempted to "confuse the issues, hide the votes, and bury the record."[17] Also in September, the Montana Republican Party sponsored a television advertisement linking Gore and Schweitzer in support of what was called an excessively expensive prescription drug plan. Schweitzer labeled the ad "fake and misleading," but a Burns spokesman said the campaign had no influence over third-party ads and accused Schweitzer of being "a guy who loves to dish it out, but who cannot take it."[18] These and other brouhahas over outside money ads led the *Helena Independent Record* to editorialize: "What is getting most boring is the practice of candidates, when asked about negative [third-party] ads, to shrug their shoulders and explain that their campaign had no control over those ads."[19]

In early October, a spokesman for the Montana Democratic Party said his organization had spent $980,000 on television ads for Schweitzer, which at the time was almost twice as much as the official campaign; he also added that they were prepared to spend $400,000 more. The Montana Republican Party estimated its soft money television ad spending for Burns at $400,000. Burns justified the soft money party ads in terms of attacks against him by issue advocacy groups: "The Republican party doesn't have those little groups around. They get the idea that Montanans think this seat is for sale by outside interests."[20]

In late October, a *Missoulian* editorial explained the external money race in the Burns-Schweitzer contest in the following terms: "For better or worse, Montana has become a national political battleground and always will be. The reason is simple. A Senate seat can be purchased cheap in Montana."[21]

The House Race

As was the case in Montana's U.S. Senate contest, outside groups spent more on behalf of House candidates than the candidates spent themselves. In terms of the air war, during the general election period, there were more Republican Party-sponsored television commercials for Rehberg than the number funded by his campaign. Table 7.3 shows the money spent on the air war in the congressional district race by both sides.

However, the Keenan campaign appeared to have sponsored a few more distinct ads than the Democratic Party did on Keenan's behalf. The number of political party-sponsored mass mailings exceeded the number sponsored by the official campaigns. Table 7.4 shows the money spent by both sides on the ground war in the congressional district race.

Table 7.3. The Air War: Most Active Organizations' Collected Ad-Buy Data in the Montana At-Large Congressional District Race

Type	*Organization*	*TV*	*Radio*	*Total Ad Buy $*	*CMAG TV*
Democratic Allies					
Candidates	Nancy Keenan for Montana	$152,565	$ 3,136	**$155,701**	N/A
Political Parties	Montana Democratic Party	$109,485	$ 8,283	**$117,768**	N/A
Republican Allies					
Candidates	Rehberg for Congress	$ 66,775	$10,044	**$ 76,819**	N/A
Political Parties	Montana Republican Party	$ 59,528	$0	**$ 59,528**	N/A
	Montana Republican State Central Committee	$ 26,850	$25,718	**$ 52,568**	N/A

Source: Election Advocacy database.

Notes: See appendix B for a more detailed explanation of the data. This table is not intended to portray comprehensive organization spending in the Montana AL race. A more complete picture can be obtained by examining this table together with table 7.2. Because ad buy content was often nondescriptive, a portion of these data was possibly bought for the MT Senate race. Unfortunately, it was not possible to parse the MT Senate data from the MT AL data. CMAG did not cover a market in Montana.

Ads and mailings sponsored by the various parties and outside groups were often indistinguishable from those sponsored by the candidates. These soft money mailings and television advertisements led to multiple disputes. For example, during the general election period, the Republican Party sponsored a mailing and television commercial stating that while superintendent of schools, Keenan had once said she had not opposed placing *Playboy* magazines in school libraries. Keenan responded that as school superintendent, she lacked the authority to remove materials from school libraries and asked Rehberg to end his negative campaigning on this issue: "The people of Montana expect more from this campaign than the typical political mudslinging that dominated your '96 Senate campaign."[22] Keenan also responded by portraying Rehberg as a conservative who would not fight for average Montanans or work to protect vital federal programs.

Likewise, when the Rehberg campaign ran a television ad accusing Keenan of supporting a state sales tax on home sales while she was a state legislator, she denied it, and the Democratic Party replied with an ad attacking Rehberg for once having backed a general state sales tax. Viewing back-to-back television commercials accusing each candidate of having supported this controversial tax was not unusual. Both political parties also sponsored mailings addressing this issue.

In a state where few voters identify themselves as liberals, the Rehberg campaign and Republican Party cross-supported each other in mailings and television commercials linking Keenan to "liberal" organizations like NARAL and People for the American Way. For their part, the Keenan campaign and the Democratic Party portrayed Rehberg as an uncaring conservative who favored the rich and would not work to protect Social Security or Medicare or to improve education.

Table 7.4. **The Ground War: Most Active Organizations' Observed Activity in the Montana At-Large Congressional District Race**

Type	*Organization*	*Mail*	*News*	*Phone*	*Total Unique Ads*
Democratic Allies					
Candidates	Nancy Keenan for Montana	7	—	—	7
Political Parties	Montana Democratic Party	20	—	1	21
Interest Groups	National Education Association	8	—	1	9
	Montana AFL-CIO	7	1	—	8
	Montana NARAL	5	—	—	5
	United Brotherhood of Carpenters and Joiners of America	5	—	—	5
	AFL-CIO	3	—	—	3
	Montana Conservation Voters	3	—	—	3
	Montana Education Association	3	—	—	3
	Montana State Building and Construction Trades Council	3	—	—	3
	Planned Parenthood Action Fund	2	—	—	2
Republican Allies					
Candidates	Rehberg for Congress	6	1	—	7
Political Parties	Montana Republican Party	16	—	—	16
	NRCC	2	—	—	2
Interest Groups	National Federation of Independent Business	4	—	—	4
	Christian Coalition	1	—	—	1
	National Rifle Association	1	—	—	1

Source: Election Advocacy database.

Notes: See appendix B for a more detailed explanation of the data. Totals exclude all presidential data. Data include all ad campaigns that mentioned any MT-AL candidate, including those ads that simultaneously mentioned any presidential or MT Senate candidate. Therefore, this table and the table for MT Senate are not mutually exclusive. This table is not intended to represent comprehensive organization activity in the MT-AL race. A more complete picture can be obtained by examining this table and table 7.1 together. Active organizations not listed above include (Democratic Parties) Missoula New Party; (Democratic Allies) Emily's List, Montana Federation of Teachers, Montana Sierra Club, NARAL, PRIDE!, Sierra Club, Youth Vote 2000; (Republican Parties) MT Republican State Central Committee; (Republican Allies) Gray PAC, League of Rural Voters Action Fund, MT Citizens for Better Medicare, MT Right to Life PAC, MT Shooting Sports Association, National Right to Life PAC, National Right to Work Committee, National Taxpayers Union, SBA List Candidate Fund; (Nonpartisan) MT Hunters and Anglers PAC, Interfaith Alliance of Billings.

Toward the end of the campaign, the shortage of television commercial time had an impact on both campaigns but probably affected the Democrats somewhat more than the Republicans. The manager of the largest group of television stations in Montana said that in "most cases" they had been able to honor candidate requests for air time, but this occurred "at the expense of outside soft money groups that have tried to pour in money this year. We haven't been able to handle their advertising."[23] The executive director of the Montana Republican Party said his party had to deal with some sold-out markets, even though they had bought as much time as possible in advance. The executive director of the Montana Democratic Party said he had been unable to buy all the time he wanted for Nancy Keenan and that this forced the party to do more direct mail and door-to-door campaigning.

The campaign ended with tired candidates, many frustrated voters, and some complaining newspapers. A *Missoulian* editorial noted that many ads had been "wrong or so manipulative that they insult. . . . Take TV advertisements with slow-motion video of the demonized politician. These clips make the opposition look stupid and slow, and the image is usually fuzzy and of poor quality, suggesting someone who is not quite all together . . . Enough!"[24]

INTEREST GROUP ACTIVITY

A national article on Montana's Senate race, entitled "Montana an Unlikely Target for Out-of-State Campaign Cash," failed to recognize that with every state having two senators, Montana represents a good value for interest groups because it has the fifth cheapest television advertising rates in the country.[25] In fact, thirty-four interest groups were identified as independent participants in the Senate campaign. Although a majority of groups active in the ground war favored Schweitzer, or issues he supported, a slight majority of the groups participating in the air contest and/or running newspaper advertisements directly or indirectly backed Burns. No group participated in all aspects of the campaign. Unions and abortion rights groups exhibited a penchant for the ground game, while business groups leaned toward the air war. It is difficult to estimate the total spending of issue advocacy groups. Some are reluctant to make estimates, and others exaggerate when estimating expenses. Objective estimates gathered from multiple sources place issue group spending on the race at $2 to $4 million.

On Election Day, a national article about Montana's House race stated, "Seldom before have so many outside interests devoted so much time and money to so few voters."[26] At least twenty-six interest groups were active in the House contest. In many instances these groups engaged in "shotgun" advertising that covered other races, and in multiple instances both national organizations and their state affiliates participated in the campaign. A majority of the groups were active for Keenan. Almost all of the issue groups favored ground war activities over television, radio, or newspaper advertising. Dennis Rehberg commented about the external interest in the race, saying, "I'm in the eye of the storm . . . [outsiders] have a lot of influence. What influence, I can't tell. You won't know until you look back."[27]

Nancy Keenan received significant support from pro-choice groups, blue-collar and education unions, and environmental interests. Dennis Rehberg was backed by pro-life, business, resource development, and hunter/sportsmen groups. Based on news articles and interviews, interest groups appear to have spent about $1 million in indirect support of Keenan and Rehberg.

Interest group activity in both the Senate and House contests undoubtedly helped shape many voters' opinions about the candidates on the issues but did not appear to be a determining factor in the outcome of either race. Collectively, group activity was less significant than the actions supported by soft money party and official campaign spending undertaken on behalf of the four candidates. And in both the Senate and House elections the Republican landslide was too overwhelming to be slowed by group activity.

SENATE RACE GROUP ACTIVITY

Environmental Groups

As mentioned previously, during the Senate Democratic primary, Brian Schweitzer attracted attention for criticizing Conrad Burns's support of legislation dealing with corporate responsibility for asbestos pollution after the situation in Libby became public. In mid-January, Montanans for Common Sense Mining Laws, an environmental group supported by more than $200,000 in Trial Lawyer money, began airing three emotional television advertisements, set in a cemetery, which called on Burns to drop his support for the bill. One ad featured the wife and mother of a family of Libby victims stating: "It took the life of my husband. And, four of my children have it [Asbestosis]." In return, several industry groups, including the Coalition for Asbestos Resolution, bankrolled by asbestos and roofing companies, sponsored counter television ads also set in a cemetery, which attacked Trial Lawyers for their greed and litigiousness. The U.S. Chamber of Commerce also paid for newspaper ads supporting the bill.

In September, the League of Conservation Voters (LCV) received significant publicity when it named Senator Burns one of its "dirty dozen" members of Congress and pledged $250,000 to help defeat him. The president of the LCV accused Burns of "protecting polluters rather than families, for voting against the interests of Montanans. . . . His record is consistently terrible."[28] But the LCV had a difficult time spending the amount of money it had pledged in the way that it planned. Although a League spokesperson said that increasing ad rates made it difficult to buy the television ad time the LCV wanted, the ad manager at one television station reported that the organization bought a block of time and ran some ads, but then cancelled the remainder of its buy.

Health Care

Brian Schweitzer received additional media attention when he began taking Montana senior citizens to Canada to purchase cheaper prescription drugs. In

March, Citizens for Better Medicare, a 527 group supported by pharmaceutical companies, began running generic television ads opposing politicians taking seniors to Canada to purchase prescription drugs. The group next sponsored its first television ad naming an individual, Schweitzer, for wanting "Canadian-style government controls on prescription medications here in America." Schweitzer said that Citizens for Better Medicare forced him to commit $65,000 of his campaign funds to run his first television ads when he only had "$100,000 in the bank," but he felt he had to "take a risk."[29]

The Citizens for Better Medicare advertisements led to increased media attention for Schweitzer and additional scrutiny of the organization. A *Missoulian* editorial concluded that Schweitzer had been "zinged . . . by cleverly worded, but inaccurate, messages financed by a national group with a name that doesn't represent the forces behind it."[30] The *Billings Gazette* labeled one ad "a total misrepresentation of Schweitzer's position. It had the credibility of a cockroach."[31]

Conrad Burns's campaign also opposed Citizens for Better Medicare's ads, feeling that they focused too much attention on Schweitzer's prescription drug issue. The Burns campaign tried unsuccessfully to get the group to suspend its Montana advertising.[32]

Gun Control

In September, Charlton Heston, president of the NRA, traveled to Montana to campaign for Conrad Burns. Although Brian Schweitzer also opposed gun control and submitted the organization's survey, the NRA said it had no record of receiving it. The organization sponsored billboards, radio and television ads, and an active campaign of mass and targeted mailings and e-mails.

HOUSE RACE GROUP ACTIVITY

Women's Groups

Even prior to the primary, controversy arose over interest group tactics when an Emily's List fundraising mailing made on behalf of Keenan called Rehberg a "Knee-jerk Conservative" because in 1994 he had commented about AIDS: "You get it, you die, why are we spending any money on people who get AIDS?" Rehberg pointed out that he had apologized for the remark and accused Keenan of having violated her clean campaign pledge. Keenan then asked the group to quit using the statement.[33] Emily's List raised about $50,000 on this mailing.

During the general election, there were multiple examples of dueling groups. Seven groups, four pro-life and three pro-choice, endorsed one or the other of the candidates. While a mailing from the Susan B. Anthony List Candidate fund (SBA) backed the pro-life Rehberg because a "[c]hild's dreams will never come true . . . if the child is never born," the National Abortion Rights Action League (NARAL) spent $82,528 on independent expenditures supporting Keenan, and the Montana chapter of the organization said it supported the pro-choice Keenan because since "1995, Congress has voted over 130 times to restrict a woman's right to choose."[34] And while the Montana Christian Coalition Voter Guide accused Keenan of supporting "Special Civil Rights Protection Based on Sexual Preference," the PRIDE Voter Guide backed her based on her positive responses to two questions regarding gay rights.

Unions and Business Groups

Almost all of the unions working to elect Keenan employed multiple mailings, some targeted and some not, and many also ran phone banks. The Montana State Building Trades Council sent three mailings from Washington, D.C., and the United Brotherhood of Carpenters and Joiners of America sent five mailings, similar in design, solely on behalf of Keenan. But when a Montana member of this union attended a local meeting to inquire why his union had chosen the House race to participate in, no one knew why. This seems to indicate that the rank-and-file members of this union had little or no input into the political decisions made by their leadership. Education groups active for Keenan buttressed the emphasis on quality schools, initiated by her campaign and Democratic Party soft money advertising. The NEA conducted a direct mail, radio, and limited television campaign, spending a total of $165,482 for Keenan, and sent a field organizer to work with all three major statewide races in Montana.[35]

Similarly, the National Federation of Independent Business (NFIB) sent a field organizer to Montana to support Rehberg and to work on developing a personal contact political pyramid of probusiness voters that actively supported Rehberg.[36] An NFIB mailing supported Rehberg because he "understands the challenges of Montana's small business owners," but noted that Nancy Keenan "is heavily supported by labor unions and trial lawyers." And the National Association of Home Builders sponsored a television ad in which they charged that Keenan "supports higher taxes."

Gun Control

In late September, the NRA formally endorsed Rehberg for his "unwavering and unquestioned support of law abiding citizens' Right to Keep and Bear Arms."[37] In accepting this endorsement Rehberg said: "I will not waver, I will not flip flop, I will not change by mind with the changing times. I will never vote for any encroachment on our Second Amendment rights." But in October, NRA-ally Michigan Democratic Representative John Dingell convinced the NRA not to activate pro-gun voters for Rehberg because Keenan had also received an "A" rating from the organization.[38] The Republican Party then stepped in and sponsored several mailings for Rehberg touting his support of gun rights and his "A" rating from the NRA. In the end, given the way the gun question played out, Rehberg probably did not gain as much political mileage from the issue as he had hoped.

CONCLUSION

The Montana Senate and House races took place in the context of the presidential contest, a contentious gubernatorial race, and other statewide and local elections. Prior to Election Day many households were receiving up to twelve daily mass mailings, watching television programs that often featured back-to-back commercials for opposing candidates, and being interrupted every several days by a phone bank call. One television station reported that in an eighteen-hour period it ran 163 political commercials. By the first week in October, many Montana television stations reported having no additional political advertising to sell. Even though Pat Buchanan was the only presidential candidate buying television ads, the scale of purchases by the official campaigns began to lock out interest group and party soft money advertising, unless they had purchased time in advance. One station manager reported that he could easily have sold another $100,000 (a significant amount in Montana) if he had had the inventory.[39] Between August and late October, several stations doubled the price of ads run on their early evening news program and added additional spots to some news shows. Late in the campaign, some issue groups were forced to find alternative ways to deliver their messages. This contributed to an unprecedented level of mass political mailings. In Billings, the largest city in the state, the volume of pre-election mail was compared to the Christmas rush period, and people complained about late mail deliveries.[40] On Election Day, political mail continued to arrive, phone banks were active, and the evening news featured political commercials.

Public irritability with the cacophony of the campaigns was mirrored on the editorial pages of the state's newspapers. The *Bozeman Daily Chronicle* noted: "This may well be the most gladly departed campaign season in U.S. history. . . . Even the most casual observer can see our state has been overrun with money from outside special interests who clearly perceive that Montana's elected offices are for sale to the highest bidder."[41] The *Billings Gazette* wrote: "Voters had their space invaded on the streets, on television, in newspapers and at home with calls from out-of-staters spewing garbage that most of us wouldn't dare dump in our own trash cans."[42]

Despite the irritability surrounding the record number of campaign ads, the late October "MSU-Billings Poll" found that, to some extent, 79 percent of Montana's likely voters interviewed were interested in the "upcoming election." And 78 percent of the survey respondents reported that it was "very" or "somewhat important" for them to know who "pays for or sponsors a political ad," while a majority (51.9 percent) agreed with the statement that "elections in the

U.S. are usually for sale to the candidate who raises and spends the most money."[43]

The negativity of the Senate race assumed comic overtones at the end of the campaign when Burns and Schweitzer could not agree if they had ever met briefly at Schweitzer's home to have a beer. Burns denied the meeting and when Schweitzer produced pictures of it, he said, "I have never been to his house in my life. . . . (Schweitzer) makes up everything."[44]

Brian Schweitzer's crusade for cheaper prescription drugs was the single most important issue debated during the Senate campaign, but proved not to be a seminal issue with voters. The national exit poll found that in Montana, almost 60 percent of voters over age sixty-five supported Burns, and only 6 percent of the electorate in the presidential race identified Medicare and prescription drugs as the most important campaign issue.[45]

In the final period of the House campaign, objective polls reported the race "too close to call." For example, the "MSU-Billings Poll" found that among likely voters, Rehberg held a statistically insignificant 2 percent lead over Keenan. And even though a plurality (35.7 percent) of those interviewed were "undecided" about which candidate had "run the most negative campaign," more respondents felt that Rehberg (25 percent), rather than Keenan (15 percent), had been the most negative. And although quality schools was a linchpin issue for Keenan and a plurality (49 percent) of the poll respondents identified her as being the candidate most likely to improve education, the electoral results suggest that it was not a decisive factor with the voters.[46]

On election night Keenan's campaign manager blamed her defeat on George W. Bush's political coattails in Montana, while Rehberg attributed his victory to his successful work in building strong volunteer organizations in all of the state's counties. But in the end, the only definite thing is that Rehberg's two-year-old daughter, Elsie, who had been featured in many of his advertisements, spoke for a majority of Montanans voting in the House race when she said, "I vote for Papa."[47]

The more than $6.9 million in national party money transferred to Montana's Republican and Democratic parties was employed to finance a majority of the four major party House and Senate candidates' campaign mass mailings and a significant percentage of the television advertising run on their behalf. In both absolute, as well as percentage, terms, political party hard and soft money spending helped Brian Schweitzer more than Conrad Burns or other major candidates. In the House race, the money the national Democratic Party committed to help Nancy Keenan was somewhat more in real and percentage terms than the financial aid the national Republican Party sent to assist Dennis Rehberg's campaign. In the interest group ground war, more entities assisted Democrats Schweitzer and Keenan than their Republican opponents, Burns and Rehberg. Air war group activity divided fairly equally for and against both Senate candidates but was a much less significant factor in the House race. In the end, however, both Conrad Burns's reelection to the Senate and Dennis Rehberg's victory in the House contest probably had less to do with outside money and more to do with the reality that the Montana electorate has become more Republican.

NOTES

1. A term used by the executive director of the Montana Democratic Party. See Charles S. Johnson, "Democrats: We Were Bushed," *Missoulian*, <www.missoulian.com/display/inn_news/news02.txt>, 9 November 2000, [accessed 9 November 2000].

2. Carol Bradley, "Candidate's Efforts Creating Tight Senate Race," *Great Falls Tribune*, <www.greatfallstribune.com/news/stories/20001031/topstories/36440.html>, 31 October 2000 [accessed 31 October 2000].

3. Voter News Service, "Exit Polls for Montana," <www.cnn.com/ ELECTION/2000/epolls/MT/P000.html>, 8 November 2000 [accessed 5 December 2000].

4. Andrew Schneider, "A Town Left to Die," *Seattle Post-Intelligencer*, <www.seattlep-i.com/uncivilaction/lib18.shtml>, 18 November 1999 [accessed 1 May 2000].

5. "Total Raised and Spent: 2000 Race: Montana Senate," *Center for Responsive Politics*, <www.opensecrets.org/2000elect/dist_total/MTS1.htm>, 10 January 2001 [accessed 10 January 2001].

6. Brian Schweitzer, discussion with author, Billings, Montana, 23 August 2000; and Brian Schweitzer, telephone interview by author, 16 November 2000.

7. Schweitzer, interview by author, 16 November 2000.

8. Brian Schweitzer, telephone interview by author, 10 January 2001.

9. "1999–2000 U.S. House and U.S. Senate Candidate Info for State of Montana, *FEC Infor*, <www.fecinto.com/cgi-win/graphpg.exe?MT012000H>, 9 January 2000 [accessed 9 January 2001].

10. Dennis Rehberg, discussion with author, Montana State University, Billings, 6 November 2000.

11. Ibid.

12. Erin P. Billings, "Republicans Trying to Use Coattails to Their Advantage," *Billings Gazette*, <www.billingsgazette.com/content/local/1tails.php>, 16 October 2000 [accessed 16 October 2000].

13. Emily Pierce, "Attack Ads Turn Montana House Race 'Ugly'," *Congressional Quarterly*, <www.washingtonpost.com/ac2/wo-dyn/A52481-2000Oct31?language=printer>, 31 October 2000 [accessed 31 October 2000].

14. Federal Election Commission (FEC), "Party Fundraising Escalates," press release, <fecweb1.fec.gov/press/011201partyfunds.htm> [accessed 15 January 2001].

15. This was both hard and soft money. And a National Democratic Party official placed expenditures for Keenan at $905,000. See Brad Martin, Executive Director, Montana Democratic Party, estimated party spending for Rehberg at about $900,000, telephone interviews by author, 9 January 2001.

16. Kathleen McLaughlin, "Burns Says Demo Ads Distort Record, Blames Schweitzer," *Lee State Bureau*, <www.mt.thepulse2000.com/top_stories/burnsbrian.shtml> [accessed 29 September 2000].

17. Ibid.

18. Kathleen McLaughlin, "Schweitzer Charges Republican TV Ads Inaccurate," *Lee State Bureau*, <www.mt.thepulse2000com/topstories/schweit.shtml>, 18 September 2000 [accessed 18 September 2000].

19. "Opinion: Negative Ads Already Are Old," *Helena Independent Record*, 28 September 2000.

20. Kathleen McLaughlin, "Sea of Money," *Missoulian*, 17 October 2000.

21. "Burns Is a Proven Voice in D.C. for Montanans," *Missoulian*, 2 November 2000.

22. Erin P. Billings, "Keenan Asks Rehberg to Pull 'Negative' Flier," *Billings Gazette*, 28 September 2000.

23. This and the following quotations in this paragraph may be found in Erin P. Billings, "No More TV Ad Time Left for Pols," *Lee State Bureau*, <www.mt.thepulse2000.com/topstories/tvads/shtml>, 29 October 2000 [accessed 29 October 2000].

24. "Campaigns Degrade and Got On Our Nerves," *Missoulian*, <www.mt.theulse2000.com/rednews/2000/11/05/buildtopstories/opedbadads.shtml>, 5 November 2000 [accessed 5 November 2000].

25. Kathyrn Wallace, "Montana an Unlikely Target for Out-of-State Campaign Cash," *The Public I*, <www.public-i.org/adwatch_01_102500.htm>, 25 October 2000 [accessed 25 October 2000].

26. Greg Hitt, "For Sale House Seat, Montana Is Swamped with Special Interest," *Wall Street Journal*, 7 November 2000.

27. Ibid.

28. League of Conservation Voters, "Deb Callahan's Statement Announcing Senator Conrad Burns to the LCV Dirty Dozen List," <www.lcv.org/news/091200-statement.htm>, 13 September 2000 [accessed 14 September 2000].

29. Schweitzer, interview by author, 16 November 2000.

30. "Finding Your Way Through the Ad Maze," *Missoulian*, 19 April 2000.

31. "Ads Dump Political Garbage in Montana," *Billings Gazette*, 21 April 2000.

32. Burns for Senate, staff employee, background discussion with author, 6 December 2000.

33. Erin P. Billings, "Rehberg Accuses Keenan of Misusing Old Quotation," *Billings Gazette*, 25 May 2000.

34. Data for independent expenditures, internal communication, and party coordinated expenditures were obtained from FEC, "Disclosure Database," <ftp.fec.gov> [accessed 26 January 2001]. Information is current through 22 January 2001.

35. See Jack Polidori and Jack Pacheco, interviews by David B. Magleby, Washington, D.C., 7 December 2000; and FEC, "Disclosure Database."

36. Hitt, "For Sale House Seat."

37. This and the following quotation in this paragraph may be found at "NRA Weighs in for Rehberg," *Rehberg 2000*, <www.rehberg2000.com/>, 5 October 2000 [accessed 23 October 2000].

38. "The Gun Lobby Muzzles Its Firepower in Two Key House Races," *Wall Street Journal*, 20 October 2000.

39. Television station advertising manager, background interview with author, Great Falls, Montana, 31 November 2000.

40. Pat Bellinghausen, "Politicians' Junk Mail Causes Gridlock," *Billings Gazette*, 8 November 2000.

41. "Now That It's Over, Let's Try to Fix It," *Bozeman Daily Chronicle*, 7 November 2000.

42. "Election Process Needs Cleansing," *Billings Gazette*, 6 November 2000.

43. Craig Wilson and Joe Floyd, co-directors, "The MSU-Billings Poll," October 2000 (Montana State University-Billings, Montana), 4–8.

44. Kathy McLaughlin, "Burns-Schweitzer Race Gets Ugly," *Billings Gazette*, 5 November 2000

45. Voter News Service, "Exit Polls for Montana."

46. Wilson and Floyd, "The MSU-Billings Poll," 10–12.

47. Daryl Gabdow, "Rehberg Wins State's Lone House Seat," *Missoulian*, <www.missoulian.com/display/innnews/news03txt>, 8 November 2000 [accessed 8 November 2000].

8

Opening the Floodgates: Campaigning without Scarcity in the 2000 California Twenty-Seventh Congressional District Race

Drew A. Linzer and David Menefee-Libey

The 2000 election contest in California's Twenty-seventh Congressional District between Democratic state Senator Adam Schiff and incumbent Republican Jim Rogan was the most expensive U.S. House race ever. The case illustrates many of the trends Magleby explores in chapter 1. The candidates were able to raise and spend nearly unlimited amounts of money from a variety of sources. State and national party organizations and outside interest groups allocated millions of dollars to the race and spent their money on state-of-the-art strategies and tactics. The various participants waged ground wars, air wars, even star wars in this show business district, opening the floodgates to inundate voters with campaign contacts and materials. All this may have been a wash, however, as the changing political and demographic fundamentals of the district outweighed the money.

Rogan had been one of the most visible and outspoken members of the House Judiciary Committee and a House manager during President Bill Clinton's 1999 impeachment trial in the Senate, and the Democratic Party wanted to defeat him for reasons that were as much symbolic as strategic. The Republican Party refused to cede Rogan's seat to the Democrats and rallied to his defense. Meanwhile, Rogan's district was undergoing profound demographic changes: Young Democrats were moving in, and the district's traditional Republican base was either moving out or dying. As a result, the race was one of few in the country in which two candidates as different as Rogan and Schiff each had a legitimate chance of victory—if they had the resources to stay competitive.[1]

In the end, the candidates raised and spent $11.5 million; political parties spent approximately $5.5 million; and outside organizations spent over $2 million, bringing the total price tag to over $19 million.[2] Both campaigns hired a full staff of professional consultants and operatives and generated voter persuasion material at a staggering rate. In addition to the political parties, outside groups saw a unique opportunity in the Twenty-seventh District to affect the outcome of a close race between two sharply contrasting candidates, so a large number of independent advocacy organizations entered the fray with television ads, mailers, and phone calls.

On Election Day, both candidates and outside groups mounted large-scale efforts to ensure that their identified voters went to the polls. Amid all this activity—and with nearly complete information about the electoral choice at hand—voters chose Schiff over Rogan, 53 to 44 percent.

INSIDE THE TWENTY-SEVENTH DISTRICT

The Twenty-seventh District, which extends along the northeastern borders of Los Angeles, through Burbank, Glendale, and Pasadena, had indeed changed substantially even since Rogan was first elected in 1996. By 2000, registered Democrats outnumbered Republicans 139,905 to 117,945. Increasing numbers of voters from the traditional white conservative base in the district had died or moved. In their place, black communities in Pasadena and Altadena had expanded; young couples had moved into South Pasadena; Iranian, Korean, and Filipino immigrants had settled throughout the district; and Glendale had become home to the largest Armenian community in the nation.[3] The district is also a base for the entertainment industry—including NBC Studios and Disney headquarters—which had grown increasingly close to the Democratic Party under Clinton's presidency.

THE CANDIDATES AND THEIR CAMPAIGNS

Newly elected in 1996, Jim Rogan spent much of his first term in Congress researching legal precedent for congressional inquiries into the executive branch, and from his seat on the House Judiciary Committee he aggressively pursued impeachment charges against President Clinton. After being reelected to a second term, Rogan became an even more visible spokesman for the efforts of the House Republicans, appearing frequently on cable television news channels and weekly network news programs. Attention on Rogan intensified when he became a House manager during the Senate's trial of the president.[4] As reported in one local television news report, Rogan had earned "a degree of fame and notoriety unusual for a second-term Congressman."[5]

State and national Democrats, outraged at the impeachment proceedings, placed Rogan at the top of their targeted, vulnerable incumbents list for 2000.[6] Many Democrats believed that Rogan's impeachment zealousness would be, if not a dominant campaign theme, then at least a cue to district voters that Rogan did not represent their increasingly moderate Democratic district. As early as February 1999, California Democratic party chair Art Torres declared: "Jim Rogan is done. . . . People didn't really know him until this impeachment issue. He had painted himself as a moderate. Now he has been exposed as the far-right zealot he is."[7]

Democratic state Senator Adam Schiff wasted little time announcing that he would challenge Rogan in 2000. As in other races explored in this volume, national party organizations also got involved at a very early stage. The Democratic Congressional Campaign Committee (DCCC) started looking for a winning candidate early, hoping to preempt alternative challengers and settle the Democratic nomination quickly in order to focus on the two-party contest. After meeting with leaders of the DCCC in March 1999, Schiff declared himself a candidate for Congress in early April and began fundraising immediately. In a trend that continued throughout his campaign, Schiff's announcement made no mention of Rogan's role in the impeachment proceedings, focusing instead on Schiff's desire to pay closer attention to local interests.[8]

Many considered Adam Schiff a major recruiting success for the Democrats.[9] A popular state senator first elected in 1996, Schiff represented a district of 800,000 people that completely encompassed the Twenty-seventh Congressional District. Thus, Schiff began the race with exactly the same base as Rogan; any deficit in name recognition he may have suffered at the outset was quickly remedied as both candidates began raising funds at a record-setting pace and earning a great deal of media attention.

Neither Rogan nor Schiff was a novice when it came to running professional, competitive, and expensive campaigns. Rogan had already won two hard-fought congressional races—with 51 percent of the vote in 1996 and 50 percent in 1998—and had raised and spent over $1.2 million in his 1998 reelection campaign. Likewise, in Schiff's first state senate race for in 1996, he raised and spent about $1.7 million, winning his race with just under 52 percent of the vote.[10]

Schiff's campaign strategy was to show that Rogan had abandoned the interests of the district. In an early interview with the *Los Angeles Times*, Schiff emphasized this theme, saying: "I think our district has really been ill-served; a lot of local needs have gone unmet. Our constituents are unrepresented in Congress, and I'd like to change that."[11] This strategy was likely a calculated decision to woo Democrats as well as crossover Republicans.[12]

In contrast, Rogan's campaign never settled on a single message to voters about why he was the better candidate. Attempting to make the case that Schiff was too liberal for the district, Rogan's campaign presented a series of attacks, first on Schiff's stances on issues such as HMO reform, immigration, and education; then on his record in the state senate; then for bills that he had authored or supported but which had been vetoed by California Governor Gray Davis, a staunch Schiff ally in the campaign.

As the campaign progressed, Rogan also shifted the way he presented himself to the district. For much of the campaign, he campaigned as a moderate on issues such as education and gun control, prompting DCCC spokesperson, John Del

Cecato, to comment: "I haven't seen anyone attempt to reinvent themselves to this extent, ever."[13] However, with two months left in the campaign, Rogan behind in the polls, and neither candidate having mentioned impeachment as a campaign issue, Rogan unveiled a new television ad that addressed his role in impeachment head-on. Impeachment soon became a recurring theme for Rogan.[14]

Voter Contact

There was little about either candidate that was not communicated through the campaigns' direct mail programs. Schiff and Rogan each mailed at least forty-five different mail pieces, the majority of which were glossy, full-color, and multiple-fold. Rogan's mail began hitting around ten weeks before the election, while Schiff's started six weeks before.

Issues emphasized by Schiff included education, HMO reform, drug coverage for seniors, gun control, abortion rights, and Schiff's personal commitment to the district's Armenian American community. Rogan's ads emphasized his differences from Schiff over issues of gun violence, taxes, patients' rights, education reform, veterans' issues, and seniors' issues.

The mail programs were so immense that both candidates could regularly attack each other as well as respond to each other's attacks. In Schiff's rebuttals of Rogan's charges, Schiff pulled no punches, calling Rogan a liar, a hypocrite, and an embarrassment to the community. Rogan fought back aggressively; one particularly venomous mailer sent to local Armenian Americans accused Schiff of being complicit with the "Turkish Lobby."

Schiff and Rogan were also extremely visible on television. Schiff purchased a total of 21,072 units from Charter Communications, the Twenty-seventh District's cable television company, for nearly $600,000. Rogan's cable buy went even further: 54,080 units from Charter Communications at a cost of over $1 million. These purchases included seventeen different ads from Rogan and six from Schiff. An anonymous Charter Communications employee remarked that the two campaigns were "buying all available airtime."[15] Shattering precedent for the district, in the last week of the campaign, both candidates' advertisements appeared on the usually prohibitively expensive Los Angeles broadcast television stations to reach the broadest possible television audience. Schiff spent $400,000 to Rogan's $150,000 on broadcast ads throughout the entire Los Angeles basin. Parke Skelton, Schiff's lead campaign consultant, said, "I had more money than I knew what to do with,"[16] while Jim Nygren, Rogan's chief strategist, explained that they began running television advertisements so early in the campaign because "Fundamentally . . . we had the budget to do it."[17]

The campaigns also waged large-scale field operations that were partially coordinated with the local party organizations. Rogan operated phone banks out of his two campaign offices, the local Republican office, and some realty offices. "We [made] about 1,000 calls a night," said Rogan field representative Moyra Wright.[18] Skelton indicated that Schiff had "approximately 2,000 volunteers" working on his campaign, resulting in "between 80,000 and 100,000 phone contacts and approximately 50,000 contacts canvassing."[19] Leading up to Election Day, supporters previously identified by the campaigns received upwards of four phone calls or personal visits to remind them to vote.

Fundraising

Both candidates could mount such comprehensive and responsive campaigns because they had practically unlimited financial resources at their disposal—a record total of over $11 million (see table 8.1).

Total contributions from political action committees (PACs), although large compared to most congressional races, represented only a small proportion of the candidates' total receipts. The number of contributing PACs and the amount of money they had available to contribute simply could not keep pace with the candidates' ever-expanding circle of individual donors, whose contributions made up the vast majority of both candidates' fundraising. Each candidate received approximately $240,000 from "single-issue" PACs; Schiff took in $316,334 from organized labor, and Rogan netted over $600,000 from business PACs representing finance, technology, retail, health care, energy, and real estate interests.[20]

Because Rogan decided to strategically invest large amounts of campaign funds into national direct mail prospecting to expand his donor base,[21] 35 percent of his itemized contributions from individuals came from outside California, compared to only 14 percent for Schiff. But this immense expenditure also meant that while Rogan consistently outraised Schiff, the two almost always had similar amounts of cash-on-hand.

POLITICAL PARTY ACTIVITY

Due to the demographic changes in the Twenty-seventh District as well as the symbolic value of defeating or reelecting an impeachment "celebrity" like Jim Rogan, national and state Democrats and Republicans pledged complete support to their candidates. The DCCC chair Patrick Kennedy placed Rogan at the top of his targeted incumbents list: "House GOP: Faces of Failure."[22] His counterpart, NRCC chair Tom Davis, called the Rogan-Schiff contest "probably the premier

Table 8.1. Rogan and Schiff Fundraising and Total Disbursements through 27 November 2000

Name	*Receipts*	*Disbursements*	*From PACs*	*From Individuals*
Jim Rogan	$ 6,871,077	$ 6,889,947	$ 1,046,695	$5,640,866
Adam Schiff	$ 4,352,754	$ 4,351,025	$ 722,324	$3,563,953
Totals	**$11,223,831**	**$11,240,972**	**$1,769,019**	**$9,204,819**

Source: FEC, "Disclosure Database," <ftp.fec.gov> [accessed 22 January 2001].

House race in the country."[23] Consequently, both national Democrats and Republicans transferred large amounts of cash to the California party organizations: The DNC, DCCC, and DSCC contributed a combined total of $14.3 million, and the RNC, NRCC, and NRSC transferred a combined total of $13.2 million.[24] Total spending by the parties in the Twenty-seventh District race totaled approximately $4.9 million on television advertising and $500,000 on direct mail.[25] Local Democrats funded an additional four mail pieces of their own.

Because both campaigns were professionally staffed and raised millions of dollars on their own, national party activity was limited to collaborating with the campaign, sharing research, assisting with fundraising, and financing their own television ads and direct mail.[26]

Political party efforts also targeted specific demographic groups. State and national Democrats, working in concert, spent $1.6 million on television ads and sent five direct mail pieces in English and Spanish just to Latino households. These mailers complemented Schiff's mail program, which, despite its size and sophistication, contained no ads targeted at Latino issues. Both Danny Medress of the California Democratic Party and Karin Johanson of the DCCC said that they believe Latinos were the Democrats' base in the Twenty-seventh District.[27]

Johanson also noted that they had wanted to avoid going on television but felt that they needed to respond to the substantial levels of pro-Rogan spending in the district. Democratic Party ads first appeared on cable television in July, eighteen weeks from Election Day; in fact, the DCCC launched its national television ad campaign with an ad in the Twenty-seventh District attacking Rogan for voting against funding to reduce classroom size. In total, the Democratic Party aired six different ads from July through November on five network television stations and local cable.

The Republican Party outspent the Democratic Party in the Twenty-seventh District, both on television ads and direct mail. Republicans aired five different ads on six network television stations and local cable at a cost of $3.3 million. The NRCC was also the race's single leading producer of outside direct mail, sending nine pieces that attacked Schiff over the course of the campaign. These mailers alternately linked Schiff to drug companies, picked apart Schiff's record in the state senate, and accused Schiff four times of lying about Rogan's record. Some of the NRCC pieces that referred to a *Glendale News-Press* editorial were so contrived that Rogan filed a complaint with the NRCC, saying, "We've got so much stuff on Schiff that we don't have to have people send things out that are sort of twisting the truth any way or just not presenting it in a fair light."[28] The California Republican Party and local Republicans sent out an additional seven mailers that either contained traditional anti-Schiff negative messages or compared Schiff and Rogan on a wide array of issues.

ROLE OF INDEPENDENT GROUPS

Independent advocacy organizations got involved in the Twenty-seventh District congressional race for much the same reason that PACs, individual donors, and the political parties did; they saw it as one of the few competitive congressional races in which the two candidates differed significantly on issues that concerned their groups. Nonparty-affiliated outside groups spent an additional $2.1 to $2.3 million in the race.

Excluding commercial voter guides that were subsidized by the candidates,[29] twenty-nine different nonparty-affiliated outside groups either sent campaign mail—fifty-seven pieces in all (see table 8.2)—or aired ads on local television or radio (see table 8.3). Most outside groups, including those whose issue advocacy ads could not explicitly advocate the election or defeat of any particular candidate, clearly preferred Schiff to Rogan. Of the twenty-nine nonparty affiliated outside groups, twenty-one favored Schiff (representing forty-two mailers) and seven preferred Rogan (thirteen mailers). Table 8.4 aggregates all mail communications for the opposing sides in this campaign tallying the number of unique candidates, party committee, and interest groups mail observed in the campaign. The proportion of negative or positive mail was consistent between the two sides. Like the mailers from candidates and parties, mail from outside groups was professionally

Table 8.2. Mail from Outside Groups and Party Organizations

Organization Name	*Number of Pieces Sent*	*Preferred Candidate*
National Republican Congressional Committee	9	Rogan
League of Conservation Voters	8	Schiff
California Republican Party	6	Rogan
California Democratic Party	5	Schiff
National Education Association	4	Schiff
Planned Parenthood	4	Schiff
California Labor Federation AFL/CIO	3	Schiff
Citizens for Better Medicare	3	Rogan
Los Angeles County Federation of Labor	3	Schiff
Neighbor to Neighbor PAC	3	Schiff
27th Congressional District Democratic Club	2	Schiff
Amer. Assoc. of Retired Persons (AARP)	2	None
Congress of California Seniors	2	Schiff
NARAL	2	Schiff
National Federation of Independent Business	2	Rogan
National Taxpayers Union	2	Rogan
Seniors Coalition	2	Rogan
Traditional Values Coalition	2	Rogan
Armenian National Committee	1	Schiff
California Federation of Teachers	1	Schiff
California League of Conservation Voters	1	Schiff
California Nurses Association	1	Schiff
California Peace Action	1	Schiff
Campaign for a Progressive Future	1	Schiff
Coalition to Stop Gun Violence	1	Schiff
Hispanic Business Roundtable	1	Rogan
Human Rights Campaign	1	Schiff

Table 8.2. (*Continued*)

Organization Name	*Number of Pieces Sent*	*Preferred Candidate*
Independent Voters League	1	Schiff
Los Angeles County Democratic Party	1	Schiff
National Jewish Democratic Council	1	Schiff
National Right to Life PAC	1	Rogan
Sierra Club	1	Schiff
Pasadena Republican Club	1	Rogan
Pasadena United Democratic Headquarters	1	Schiff
United Farm Workers of America	1	Schiff
Voter Information Guide	1	Schiff
36 Total Outside Groups	**82**	
29 Total Nonparty-Affiliated Groups	**57**	

Source: Election Advocacy database.
Note: See appendix B for a more detailed explanation of the data. Party organizations in italics.

Table 8.3. The Air War: Most Active Organizations' Collected Ad Buy Data in the California Twenty-seventh Congressional District Race

Type	*Organization*	*TV*	*Radio*	*Total Ad Buy $*	*CMAG TV*
Democratic Allies					
Candidates	Schiff for Congress	$1,745,035	$0	**$1,745,035**	$625,720
Political Parties	California Democratic Party	$1,184,186	$0	**$1,184,186**	$962,181
	DCCC	$ 239,931	$0	**$ 239,931**	$0
Interest Groups	AFL-CIO	$ 64,845	$0	**$ 64,845**	$0
	California Peace Action	$ 2,563	$0	**$ 2,563**	$0
Republican Allies					
Candidates	Rogan Campaign Committee	$1,181,237	$0	**$1,181,237**	$224,912
Political Parties	California Republican Party	$3,295,001	$0	**$3,295,001**	$0
	NRCC	$ 43,650	$0	**$ 43,650**	$546,691
Interest Groups	U.S. Chamber of Commerce	$0	$518,425	**$ 518,425**	$0
	Citizens for Better Medicare	$ 159,901	$0	**$ 159,901**	$0

Source: Election Advocacy and *Campaign Media Analysis Group* databases.
Notes: See appendix B for a more detailed explanation of the data. This table is not intended to portray comprehensive organization spending in the CA 27 race. A more complete picture can be obtained by examining this table together with table 8.4.

Table 8.4. The Ground War: Most Active Organizations' Observed Mail Activity in the California Twenty-Seventh Congressional District Race

Type	*Organization*	*Total Unique Mail Pieces*
Democratic Allies		
Candidates	Schiff for Congress	53
Political Parties	California Democratic Party	5
	27th Congressional District Democratic Club	2
Interest Groups	League of Conservation Voters	8
	National Education Association	4
	Planned Parenthood	4
	California Labor Federation AFL/CIO	3
	Los Angeles County Federation of Labor	3
	Neighbor to Neighbor PAC	3
	Congress of California Seniors	2
	NARAL	2
Republican Allies		
Candidates	Rogan Campaign Committee	46
Political Parties	National Republican Congressional Committee	9
	California Republican Party	6
Interest Groups	Citizens for Better Medicare	3
	National Federation of Independent Business	2
	National Taxpayers Union	2
	Seniors Coalition	2
	Traditional Values Coalition	2
Nonpartisan		
Interest Groups	AARP	2

Source: Election Advocacy database.

Notes: See appendix B for a more detailed explanation of the data. Totals exclude all presidential data; totals include all newspaper ads observed. Data include all mail pieces that mentioned any CA 27 candidate, including those pieces that simultaneously mentioned any presidential candidate. This table is not intended to represent comprehensive organization activity in the CA 27. A more complete picture can be obtained by examining this table and table 8.3 together. Active organizations not listed above include (Democratic Parties) LA County Dem Party, Pasadena United Democratic Headquarters; (Democratic Allies) American National Committee, CA Federation of Teachers, CA LCV, CA Nurse Association, CA Peace Action, Campaign for a Progressive Future, Coalition to Stop Gun Violence, Human Rights Campaign, Independent Voters League, National Jewish Democratic Council, Sierra Club, United Farm Workers of America, and Voter Information Guide; (Republican Parties) Pasadena Republican Club; (Republican Allies) Hispanic Business Roundtable, National Right to Life PAC.

produced—multicolored with multiple-folds. The estimated median cost of $20,000 for producing and mailing one piece of mail[30] suggests that outside groups spent well over $1.1 million on direct mail.

The flood of mail from the candidates and these outside groups was literally staggering. A *Los Angeles Times* reporter found that the U.S. Postal Service's north Glendale station saw a 42 percent increase in mail volume in the final weeks of the campaign. On a daily basis, mail carriers in the district filled their bags to the

Postal Service limit of thirty-five pounds and had to come back for more to cover their routes. Between hand-sorting the nonstandard sized mailings and doing multiple runs, they worked an average of two hours overtime every day. "I can't wait until November 8," the postal station manager told the reporter, echoing the sentiments of many inundated voters.[31]

Furthermore, three of the groups that sent mail—Citizens for Better Medicare, AFL-CIO, and California Peace Action—also aired ads on local cable television at an aggregate cost of $232,576, not including production or buyers' fees. Radio advertising was largely avoided, although the U.S. Chamber of Commerce spent $518,425 to air a radio spot for five weeks that attacked Schiff's position on providing prescription drug coverage under Medicare.[32] Finally, outside groups spent an estimated $50,000 on field organizing, including telephone persuasion, voter identification calls, and Election Day get-out-the-vote (GOTV) reminders.

All outside groups faced the difficulty of influencing a race dominated by large-budget candidate and party messages. Successful outside groups followed one of two strategies: either they planted their message so firmly in the minds of voters that the candidates were forced to respond, or they targeted a specific subgroup of voters with a message and a voter identification program tailored to the unique characteristics of that subgroup. Outside groups whose campaign presence was either broad in scope or limited in reach had little incremental effect on voters, who were already completely overwhelmed with campaign messages. As one voter commented on Election Day regarding the seemingly endless stream of ads, "I've taken to just shutting them out—they are more confusing than useful."[33]

Citizens for Better Medicare/U.S. Chamber of Commerce

Only Citizens for Better Medicare's efforts through television and direct mail, combined with the U.S. Chamber of Commerce's radio ads, made Schiff spend more time on Medicare prescription drug coverage than he had planned.[34] In one of his mailers, Schiff confronted these attacks, identifying Citizens for Better Medicare as "the pharmaceutical industry's misnamed front group." Getting Schiff's campaign to respond cost the two groups approximately $750,000 and had questionable effects. On the one hand, both Rogan and Schiff were already addressing the issue in their own campaign ads, so voters who truly intended to base their vote on the candidates' positions on this issue did not need any outside groups to introduce the issue into the campaign dialogue or reveal the candidates' positions. On the other hand, if the media campaign by Citizens for Better Medicare and the U.S. Chamber of Commerce was intended to cast doubt on Schiff's integrity and force Schiff to adjust his campaign strategy, it accomplished that goal.

NARAL/Planned Parenthood

Pursuing an alternate and successful strategy, pro-choice groups focused their efforts on discrete voter groups within the district whom they believed would trust and be affected by their message.[35] National Abortion Rights Action League (NARAL) political director Gloria Totten commented, "We consider it our role to go to people who might be predisposed to Jim Rogan . . . and take them away from him and give them to Adam Schiff."[36] NARAL used paid phone banks to identify Schiff supporters from a file of 10,000 pro-choice voters it had accumulated over years of telephone identifications. After three or four rounds of persuasive calls, NARAL identified "close to the national average, 86 percent to 88 percent" of the file as Schiff supporters. These voters then received GOTV calls on Election Day, reminding them to vote.[37]

Planned Parenthood had a similar plan for its campaign because the organization felt that abortion rights were a key issue. Martha Swiller, executive director of the Planned Parenthood Advocacy project in Los Angeles, said she thought voters would vote for Schiff "if they considered [the issue of] choice."[38] Planned Parenthood's calling strategy did not include voter identifications, but the local chapter did pay for approximately 15,000 GOTV calls to voters in its pro-choice voter file, using a taped message from Barbara Streisand. Planned Parenthood also recruited celebrities Sarah Jessica Parker and Whoopi Goldberg to send e-mails about Rogan and Schiff to voters on Planned Parenthood's distribution list.[39]

Both groups supplemented their telephone activity with direct mail; NARAL sent two express advocacy pieces, and Planned Parenthood of California sent 32,000 of each of three mailers to Independent and Republican women, a group they considered persuadable on choice, although they conducted no polling.[40] Planned Parenthood of Los Angeles mailed a fourth piece, a slate card including Schiff and other pro-choice candidates endorsed by the organization. Based on interviews with representatives of both groups, we estimate that NARAL and Planned Parenthood together spent approximately $100,000 on direct mail and $20,000 on telephone identifications and GOTV calls. Martha Swiller added that Planned Parenthood would have spent more, but polls made public by the Schiff campaign showed him comfortably ahead with a month remaining in the campaign.[41]

Organized Labor

Organized labor in the Twenty-seventh Congressional District was highly successful in mobilizing union members for Schiff through a methodical program of telephone identifications and precinct-level canvassing. Dave Sickler, lead organizer with the Los Angeles County Federation of Labor for the Twenty-seventh District, explained that it was "easier to sell the issue than the candidate," so local unions organized a member-to-member voter persuasion campaign that would get union voters to "think about things where you know they care."[42]

Each week, on average, one hundred union volunteers placed nightly telephone calls to fellow union members. Volunteers recorded members' voting preferences and uploaded them to a central labor database in Sacramento every Tuesday night. A list of undecided voters was returned to the district office every Thursday. An additional one hundred to two hundred union volunteers canvassed these undecided voters door-to-door with a persuasive message and a packet of literature every Saturday and Sunday. Undecideds were then called back to see if they had settled on a candidate.

Sickler estimates that approximately 130 members per precinct were being canvassed in the first week; by late October, this number had fallen to around 50.[43] Of the roughly 32,000 union members living in the Twenty-seventh District, 75 percent ultimately committed to voting for Schiff. Organized labor's program also included GOTV calls to committed Schiff voters on Election Day.

The national AFL-CIO supplemented the local groundwork with an early $64,845 cable television buy, running four different ads attacking Rogan. In addition, the California Labor Federation and Los Angeles County Federation of Labor each paid for three mail pieces, sent to a targeted subgroup of district households. Attaching a dollar figure to the massive field campaign mounted by the Los Angeles County Federation of Labor is difficult, especially considering that it was conducted on a completely volunteer, strictly member-to-member basis. In cash terms, including mail, television, campaign literature, and telephone costs, organized labor spent an estimated $150,000 to $200,000, plus $285,650 in itemized PAC contributions to help Schiff win the election.

Other Groups

Plenty of other groups were also active in the campaign; although they may not have enjoyed such high degrees of relevance, some attracted attention for other reasons. For example, the League of Conservation Voters (LCV) named Jim Rogan to their "Dirty Dozen" list of incumbents targeted for defeat and followed through, spending $297,698 on a comprehensive program of eight full-color mailings supporting Schiff.[44] "Congressman Rogan is vulnerable," said LCV political director Betsy Loyless. "We're real pragmatic about the political races we'll go into."[45]

In Rogan's support, the Traditional Values Coalition (TVC), a conservative Christian group, sent 15,000 to 20,000 of each of two mail pieces to the district's Armenian community, which is almost monolithically Christian. One warned that "State Senator Adam Schiff supports gay marriages," and another questioned whether Schiff, who is Jewish, represents "our Christian family values." Schiff criticized the mailers for being "divisive, bigoted, and destructive," but Rogan refused to denounce the two pieces that had been sent out on his behalf.[46] The TVC also conducted a phone bank in the district.

Many groups that conducted their own voter persuasion campaigns appeared prominently in the candidates' campaign literature. Most of the candidates' positive pieces—and many of their negative pieces—contained endorsements from prominent outside groups. For example, Schiff publicized his backing from "local classroom teachers," Planned Parenthood, the California Police Chiefs Association, the Armenian National Committee, the California Nurses Association, Sierra Club, and the National Council for Senior Citizens. Rogan, a former prosecutor and judge, seemed most proud of his support from law enforcement and crime victim organizations. Female voters received a copy of a letter from Handgun Control, Inc., thanking Rogan for his work on gun control legislation. In a piece devoted to seniors' issues, Rogan mentioned support from the Seniors Coalition, the 60 Plus Coalition, and the United Seniors Association.

Ironically, the massive involvement of outside groups aided both Rogan's and Schiff's fundraising and likely drove the cost of the campaign higher than it would have been otherwise. In their fundraising pleas, both candidates referred to the activity of outside groups as a major reason why they needed more money to "stay competitive." For example, in one fundraising mailer, Rogan pointed to $54,460 spent by the DCCC on television commercials, as well as ads aired by the AFL-CIO and the "leftist Washington group" Human Rights Campaign. Meanwhile, Schiff's material mentioned the price and scale of the California Republican Party's negative campaign, saying, "The California Republican Party has filled the mailboxes of district residents with distorted and untruthful allegations about Adam Schiff's record. Landing once a day, the attack mail has exceeded a quarter of a million dollars already—and it keeps on coming." Schiff also linked attack mailers from the NRCC to "soft money contributions from HMO's, the NRA, big tobacco, and corporate polluters [who] just wired $1.4 million dollars for a network-TV ad buy to prop-up Rogan for the final two weeks of the campaign." With such high stakes in this race and the already elevated spending, contributions kept pouring into the two campaigns.

CONCLUSION

The 2000 congressional race in California's Twenty-seventh District provided unique insight into what can happen when candidates are not limited by practical monetary considerations. Because the campaigns can wage a complete and professional program of voter persuasion, identification, and GOTV operation without any outside help, outside groups can choose to contribute little directly to the candidates. However, at great expense in this particular race, some outside groups altered the issue dialog of the campaign; other groups mobilized targeted subgroups of voters; but for the most part, to mix metaphors, outside group activity reverted to an arms race, in which groups spent increasing amounts of money simply to avoid being outspent and overwhelmed by their opponents' campaign material. The campaigns themselves became caught in the trap. If they unilaterally gave up outside group assistance, the sheer volume of opposing messages would drown out their own campaign message. Alternatively, if outside spending continued to escalate, the campaigns would increasingly lose control of their message to the clutter and confusion that naturally arises from the nearly constant—and frequently contradictory and misleading—bombardment of campaign material. In this race, allied groups sometimes even pushed their own candidates off message, as the NRCC did to Rogan. Schiff field director Julie Nielson said that their campaign found outside groups' ads in support of Schiff "annoying," as they did not conform to the campaign's message and would sometimes use words that the campaign would not have chosen.[47]

Nevertheless, one of the most striking aspects of the contest was the two campaigns' overwhelming skepticism about whether all the spending by the campaigns and outside groups actually changed the outcome of the race. Ultimately, given the rough parity of the two sides, the underlying political and demographic dynamics of the district probably had a greater impact on the outcome than the campaigns did. No matter how much was spent, "It probably wouldn't be much different," said Rogan fundraiser Matt Keelen a few weeks before Election Day.[48] Schiff consultant Parke Skelton later agreed: "I don't believe that the large amounts of money going to the race affected the outcome. . . . I really don't think all of the money did anything but upset a lot of voters."[49] Jeff Solsby, Rogan's press secretary, explained that the unusually large amounts of money put into the campaigns did not substantially change their strategies or tactics: "It just allows us to do more of what works. . . . Communicating with voters is still the key to winning an election."[50] Past some threshold income level, both candidates' extra fundraising accomplished marginal or zero electoral gain.

Assuming that two competing candidates remain evenly financed, evidence from this race suggests that optimal campaigns should not invest further resources in fundraising past the threshold. The evidence also suggests that outside groups without either the substantial resources necessary to alter the candidates' dialogue over the issues or the ability to target and identify supporters among select subgroups of voters are likely wasting their money.

NOTES

With the invaluable research assistance of M. Kirby Borthwick, Andrew Flores, Eric Freborg, Adam Rick, David Rion, and particularly Matthew Muller. We also thank residents of the district who generously collected and sent us information about the campaign.

1. Political journalist Charles E. Cook Jr. predicted in 1999 that "this is likely to be the most competitive and closely watched race for 2000." See Michael Barone et al., *The Almanac of American Politics 2000* (Washington, D.C.: National Journal Group, 1999), 248.
2. The spending by political parties and outside groups was estimated from the authors' research. For spending by candidates, see FEC data at <herndon1.sdrdc.com/cgi-bin/canccomsrs/?_00+CAN+CA> [accessed 13 August 2001].
3. Barone, *Almanac of American Politics 2000.*
4. Among the memorable comments Rogan made at the time was his reply to a White House attorney during the Senate trial: "I believe the appropriate legal response to your

request is that it is none of your damn business what the other side is going to put on." This Rogan comment has been quoted extensively; see Steven Mikulan, "Impeachment Loser: Rogan Desperately Seeks the Center," *LA Weekly*, 13–19 October 2000.

5. News report on KCRA-TV, Sacramento, California, 22 February 1999.

6. The president himself was reported to have been "so furious at House Republicans over his impeachment . . . that he . . . vowed to mount an all-out offensive to knock out many of his foes and win back the House for Democrats in 2000." See Richard L. Berke and James Bennet, "The President's Trial: The House Race; Clinton Vows Strong Drive to Win a House Majority," *New York Times*, 11 February 1999.

7. Quoted in Lee Condon, "Prosecutor Rogan May Be Facing Trouble at Home," *Los Angeles Daily News*, 7 February 1999.

8. Schiff for Congress, campaign release, 9 April 1999.

9. The Schiff recruitment is deemed a "success" in *Cook Political Report*, 25 September 1999. Schiff is called "first tier" in Barone, *Almanac of American Politics 2000*, 248.

10. *Cook Political Report*, 12 November 1999.

11. Bob Rector, "Adam Schiff," *Los Angeles Times*, 10 October 1999.

12. "A little-known fact about the 27th is that Rogan does not even enjoy the monolithic support of district Republicans. . . . And many in the local GOP . . . discovered Rogan to be balky when it has come to taking the initiative on local interests." See Mikulan, "Impeachment Loser."

13. Quoted in Jean Merl, "Rogan Cites Role in Impeachment in Ad," *Los Angeles Times*, 14 September 2000.

14. Rogan explained, "My campaign folks tried for months to get me never to talk about the 'I-word.' I systematically refused. . . . Being silent might somehow communicate that I am sorry. . . . If I lose, I won't enjoy having to pack up and move out of my office, but I will move out with my head held high." Patrick McGreevy and Jean Merl, "3 Debates Underscore Sharp Differences," *Los Angeles Times*, 11 October 2000.

15. Anonymous employee of Charter Communications, interview by author, Los Angeles, California, 5 October 2000.

16. Parke Skelton, interview by author, Pasadena, California, 12 November 2000.

17. Jim Nygren, quoted in James Bennet, "Is the Choice Between These Two Guys Worth $10 Million?" *New York Times Magazine*, 22 October, 2000, 66.

18. Moyra Wright, interview by author, Glendale, California, 14 October 2000.

19. Skelton, interview by author.

20. Federal Election Commission (FEC), "Disclosure Database,"<ftp.fec.gov> [accessed 22 January 2001].

21. Rogan campaign manager Jason Roe acknowledged that their high spending "is related to Rogan's effort to raise funds" from national Republicans; quoted in Lee Condon, "Rogan's Primary Spending Soars Beyond $2.5 Million," *Los Angeles Daily News*, 25 February 2000. Rogan's donor list ultimately grew to include 50,000 people from forty-six states.

22. Patrick Kennedy, e-mail to author, 9 September 2000.

23. Tom Davis, quoted on *Inside Politics*, CNN, 31 August 1999.

24. Federal Election Commission Reports, <ftp.fec.gov>, 31 December 2000 [accessed 20 August 2001].

25. Party spending and television advertising spending estimated from authors' research.

26. This collaboration is consistent with current patterns of national party involvement in congressional campaigns. In the absence of such skilled, experienced campaigners, the

national party organizations often offer substantial guidance. See David Menefee-Libey, *The Triumph of Campaign-Centered Politics* (New York: Chatham House Publishers, 2000), chapter 9.

27. Karin Johanson, interview by David B. Magleby, Washington, D.C., 20 November 2007. See also Danny Medress, telephone interview by author, 1 November 2000.

28. Jim Rogan, quoted in Claudia Peschiutta, "Rogan Camp Says GOP Ad 'Misleading,'" *Glendale News-Press*, 30 October 2000.

29. At least eleven different voter guides were sent that urged support for Adam Schiff or Jim Rogan. The candidates subsidized all but two. Voter guides are commercial ventures, targeted to various segments of the electorate, and candidates pay to appear as though they have been "endorsed" by the group producing the guide. These groups are not political organizations. Compared to most congressional races, eleven is an unusually large number of voter guides.

30. Estimate based on interviews by author with representatives from groups sending literature.

31. Quoted in Sue Fox, "Political Combat Fatigue Engulfs Voters in Hotly Contested District," *Los Angeles Times*, 3 November 2000.

32. These ads were broadcast on KRTH-FM 101.1 and KNX-AM 1070, Los Angeles, California. KRTH-FM has an "oldies" music format and a target demographic of adults aged thirty-five and older; KNX-AM has a news format. The ads also attacked neighboring Democratic congressional candidate Jane Harman.

33. Anonymous voter, interview by author, Pasadena, California, 4 November 2000.

34. Skelton commented, "The prescription drug issue became much larger in this race than it would have without these expenditures. . . . We couldn't compete with the money that was being spent on Rogan's behalf and much of our natural advantage was eroded. The expenditures turned it from an issue that we could go on the offensive with to one that we had to defend against." Skelton, interview by author.

35. For example, DCCC official Karin Johanson, who commented "every group" was involved in the Twenty-seventh District, added that NARAL and Planned Parenthood were "particularly effective." See Karin Johanson, Democratic Congressional Campaign Committee (DCCC), interview by David B. Magleby, Washington, D.C., 20 November 2000; Rogan Press Secretary Jeff Solsby also noticed that "Planned Parenthood and labor unions are doing a huge amount of mailing," interview by author, Glendale, California, 14 October 2000.

36. Gloria Totten, telephone interview by author, 17 November 2000.

37. Ibid.

38. Martha Swiller, telephone interview by author, 14 December 2000.

39. Ibid.

40. David Alois, Director of Electoral and Legal Affairs for Planned Parenthood affiliate of California, telephone interview by author, 14 December 2000.

41. Schiff defeated Rogan in the March 7, 2000, open primary election 49 to 47 percent. Schiff's polling firm, The Feldman Group, made public three polls conducted between August and October that each showed Schiff ahead by 5 to 6 percent. However, with a week remaining in the campaign, Rogan pollster Dresner, Wickers and Associates released a contradictory (and ultimately incorrect) poll that showed Rogan *leading* by 5 percent. Swiller, interview by author.

42. Dave Sickler, interview by author, Burbank, California, 28 October 2000.

43. Ibid.

44. Data for independent expenditures, internal communication, and party coordinated expenditures were obtained from the FEC, "Disclosure Database," <ftp.fec.gov> [accessed 22 January 2001].

45. Quoted in Gina Keating, "Rogan Named to Environment Group's 'Dirty Dozen,'" *Pasadena Star-News*, 22 June 2000.

46. Gina Keating, "Election 2000: Rogan Slams Christian Group, but Not Anti-Schiff Mailer," *Pasadena Star-News*, 24 October 2000.

47. Julie Nielson, interview by author, Pasadena, California, 2 October 2000.

48. Quoted in Bennet, "Is the Choice Between These Two Guys Worth $10 Million?," 67.

49. Skelton, interview by author.

50. Solsby, interview by author.

9

The 2000 Michigan Eighth Congressional District Race

Eric Freedman and Sue Carter

The November 1994 election brought two ambitious politicians from adjacent districts, Mike Rogers and Dianne Byrum, to the Michigan state senate together. Their careers tracked in another way: Both small-town natives are part-owners of small family businesses, but before the 1994 election, Republican Rogers had never held elective office, while Democrat Byrum had been a county commissioner and state representative.

The November 2000 election drove Rogers, thirty-seven, and Byrum, forty-seven, apart as adversaries in one of the year's most expensive House battles. A few hours after polls closed, Byrum prematurely claimed victory in the Eighth District. But not many hours later, when a fuller tally was available, it looked like Rogers would head to Washington as representative-elect and Byrum would stay in Lansing, at least for the next two years.

When the state Board of Canvassers certified the results, Rogers held a 160-vote edge. After a recount, the margin was 111—the closest House margin in the nation.

THE GREEN FACTOR

One explanation for the extremely close race is Green candidate Bonnie Bucqueroux, who ran a Web-based campaign with a ground operation in about a dozen precincts. "Part of what I was looking for is whether it's possible for a third-party candidate to substitute a cybercampaign for a traditional ground campaign," she said. She reported receipts of $2,060 from her Web-based campaign. Early in her campaign, she e-mailed environmental groups about potential support but stopped when their national groups endorsed the Democratic ticket.[1] Although she got some press and appeared with Ralph Nader, her opponents, the parties, and independent groups largely ignored her.

However, she drew almost 3,500 votes—far above the Rogers-Byrum margin. But she strongly disputes angry Democrats' assertion that she's responsible for Byrum's defeat and argues that most Green-oriented voters wouldn't have voted because they were "disaffected" or would have voted Republican if she and Nader weren't on the ballot.[2]

Bucqueroux's 1.1 percent vote share was lower than that of Green nominees in three other Michigan congressional districts, and the Libertarian drew more than 2,400 votes in the Eighth, the Natural Law nominee more than 700, and the U.S. Taxpayers candidate almost 700—all well over the Byrum-Rogers margin.

Moreover, the Sierra Club's national executive director and president appeared in the Eighth for Byrum. Dan Farough, the Sierra Club's environmental voter education campaign coordinator in the race, said bluntly, "The Green Party candidate did not figure prominently in the conversation."[3]

To Bucqueroux, the real impact of soft money came with efforts "to demonize the Greens." She cited ads with Gloria Steinem and the Sierra Club executive director's trip to Michigan to push Gore. "It's unfortunate because it showed up some of the nonprofit groups as not being as ideologically driven as they said they were. They were basically soft money extensions of the Democratic campaign, masquerading as independent."[4]

Although most officials affirm that Bucqueroux had little effect on the race, Mark Brewer, the state Democratic chair, insists that most Bucqueroux votes would have gone to Byrum but denies that Democrats were behind attacks on the Greens: "Our attitude has been that any party can get on the ballot and we didn't see it would promote us to attack the Greens."[5]

THE CANDIDATES AND THEIR CAMPAIGNS

Although GOP-oriented in its general voting pattern, the Eighth District is a ping-pong district, held more often by Democrats than by Republicans. Democrat Bob Carr won it in 1974 but lost it in the 1980 Reagan landslide. Two years later, he ousted GOP incumbent Jim Dunn. In 1992, Carr defeated GOP challenger Dick Chrysler, but gave it up in 1994 to make a failed U.S. Senate bid. Chrysler grabbed it in 1994, but lasted only one term before Democrat Debbie Stabenow—Byrum's predecessor in the state senate—defeated him. Stabenow then left it to challenge Republican U.S. Senator Spencer Abraham—a contest Byrum had explored earlier while Stabenow equivocated.

The Eighth District is important because it covers all of Livingston County, the state's fastest growing county and Rogers's stronghold; Ingham County, headquarters of state government in Lansing and the home of General Motors Corporation plants; Michigan State University, which Byrum represents in the senate, parts of Oakland, Washtenaw (some of suburban Ann Arbor), Genesee (some of suburban Flint), and largely rural Shiawassee counties make up the rest. Located in mid-Michigan between Detroit and Grand Rapids, much of the district falls within the Detroit broadcast market.

Although both candidates portrayed themselves as moderates, and despite similarities in personal backgrounds and constituencies, not surprisingly, their legislative report cards from unions and business groups differ dramatically. For example, Byrum voted right in the eyes of the Michigan Chamber of Commerce 40 percent of the time while Rogers pulled an 85 percent approval rating.[6]

Yet they were closer from some perspectives; the Michigan Farm Bureau, which endorsed Rogers for Congress, gave Byrum an 80 percent score and Rogers a 100 percent score, perhaps reflecting large rural constituencies in both U.S. Senate districts.[7] These scores represent how well the candidate's beliefs agree with the group's beliefs.

Big Spending

The race proved one of the most expensive in the nation. According to a Federal Election Commission (FEC) report, Rogers for Congress raised $2,224,233, with $937,385 from nonparty committees and political action committees (PACs) and $44,033 from party committees. The FEC also reported that Byrum for Congress received $2,392,324 in receipts, with $714,518 from nonparty committees and PACs and $18,782 from party committees.[8] Another way to look at this race is that neither side had a marked partisan advantage in available resources, and that the margin in spending—directly by the candidate committees and through soft money—was almost as narrow as the margin of votes.

More than a half-dozen industry PACs buttered both sides of the toast by donating to both committees. These PACs include those associated with the American Dental Association, American Health Care Association, American Podiatric Medical Association, General Motors, Conagra, and Jackson National Life Insurance.

Issues

Despite the axiom that all politics is local, the Eighth District rivals mirrored their presidential and U.S. Senate candidates on the principal national issues of the year—almost exclusively dominated in the Eighth by such domestic policy concerns as prescription drugs, Social Security, taxes, Medicare, health coverage, and education. The two opponents disagreed dramatically on gun control, affirmative action, worker rights, and abortion, which was reflected in heavy independent expenditures and issue advocacy from pro-life and pro-choice groups.

In debate, the tone was generally amicable. Yet Byrum campaign manager Tom Russell observed that while the candidates stayed mostly civil, "this race got pretty negative" near the end, primarily due to the independent organizations and party committees.[9]

The Governor at Bat

Third-term GOP Governor John Engler played a significant role, helping Rogers secure funding and endorsements in a year when there were huge demands on traditional pro-Republican PAC and individual donors. In addition, he gave longtime speechwriter John Nevin a leave of absence to manage Rogers's campaign. Engler's press secretary, John Truscott, said that when the governor visited Washington, "he talked Mike up to some of the groups there."[10] Engler also was the chief draw at some of Rogers's fundraisers.

Byrum's campaign was also well aware of the governor's campaigning efforts on Rogers's behalf. Russell, Byrum's campaign manager, said, "The governor made personal calls on behalf of Mike back when some of those organizations were making decisions on endorsements." As a result, "we hit a lot of walls. We had a real fight over the Realtors' endorsement [that Rogers won] and over a lot of law enforcement endorsements" that the candidates split. Russell also attributes "the governor's weight" for Rogers' securing the Michigan Chamber of Commerce endorsement, although Byrum was endorsed by its biggest affiliate in the district.[11]

THE POLITICAL PARTY BATTLE

Some of the harshest negative ads—and the biggest spending—came from state and national party committees, and both sides used and abused the opponents' legislative records to fuel those fires. Both state parties released a barrage of slick materials, much of it funded with pass-through money. There were multimillion-dollar transfers from national party organs to the Michigan parties; FEC records show the following: $789,819 in hard money and $1,673,634 in soft money from the Democratic Congressional Campaign Committee (DCCC)[12] and $941,543 in hard money and $1,209,888 in soft money from the National Republican Congressional Committee (NRCC). The Rogers committee reported $66,500 in party-coordinated expenditures by the NRCC, while Byrum's committee logged $65,871 in party-coordinated expenditures and $45,983 in independent expenditures by the DCCC.[13]

Tables 9.1 and 9.2 list the most active organizations in the Michigan Eighth Congressional District race. Table 9.1 tallies the amount of money spent on television and radio ad buys. Table 9.2 tallies the number of unique mail and phone ads.

Democratic Barrages

Byrum's campaign chair, Mark Brewer, said the state Democratic Party didn't coordinate activities with pro-Byrum groups because that would be illegal. But obvious questions arise concerning the close convergence of messages in education, environment, and health shared by candidate committees, party organs, and

Table 9.1. The Air War: Most Active Organizations' Collected Ad Buy Data in the Michigan Eighth Congressional District Race

Type	*Organization*	*TV*	*Radio*	*Total Ad Buy $*	*CMAG TV*
Democratic Allies					
Candidates	Byrum for Congress	$ 561,555	$0	**$ 561,555**	$681,190
Political Parties	Michigan Democratic Party	$1,196,730	$0	**$1,196,730**	$ 42,568
	Michigan Democratic State Committee	$ 277,490	$0	**$ 277,490**	$0
	Democratic Victory 2000	$ 24,500	$0	**$ 24,500**	$0
Interest Groups	AFL-CIO	$ 769,240	$0	**$ 769,240**	$567,959
	Michigan Democrats	$ 533,200	$0	**$ 533,200**	$0
	Emily's List	$ 526,220	$0	**$ 526,220**	$0
	Planned Parenthood	$ 461,245	$0	**$ 461,245**	$0
	Coalition for the Future Am Worker	$ 259,500	$0	**$ 259,500**	$122,785
	Sierra Club	$ 119,675	$0	**$ 119,675**	$0
	League of Conservation Voters	$ 104,250	$0	**$ 104,250**	$0
	Handgun Control	$ 68,525	$0	**$ 68,525**	$0
	NAACP National Voter Fund	$ 57,300	$0	**$ 57,300**	$0

Table 9.1. *(Continued)*

Type	*Organization*	*TV*	*Radio*	*Total Ad Buy $*	*CMAG TV*
Republican Allies					
Candidates	Rogers for Congress	$ 294,400	$0	**$ 294,400**	$785,962
Political Parties	Michigan Republican State Committee	$1,682,425	$0	**$1,682,425**	$0
	Republican Party of Michigan	$ 185,800	$0	**$ 185,800**	$0
	National Rep State Central Comm	$ 70,485	$0	**$ 70,485**	$0
	2000 GOP	$ 51,725	$0	**$ 51,725**	$0
	NRCC	$ 11,300	$0	**$ 11,300**	$114,349
Interest Groups	U.S. Chamber of Commerce	$ 921,335	$0	**$ 921,335**	$709,820
	Business Roundtable	$ 415,680	$0	**$ 415,680**	$171,250
	Michigan Chamber of Commerce	$ 323,175	$0	**$ 323,175**	$0
	Citizens for Better Medicare	$ 302,325	$0	**$ 302,325**	$452,205
	Alliance for Quality Nursing Home Care	$ 88,850	$0	**$ 88,850**	$0
	Americans for Job Security	$ 67,900	$0	**$ 67,900**	$0
	Committee for Good Common Sense	$ 27,850	$0	**$ 27,850**	$0

Source: Election Advocacy and *Campaign Media Analysis Group* databases.

Notes: See appendix B for a more detailed explanation of the data. This table is not intended to portray comprehensive organization spending in the MI 8 race. A more complete picture can be obtained by examining this table together with table 9. 2. Because ad buy content was often nondescriptive, a portion of these data was possibly bought for the MI Senate race. Unfortunately, it was not possible to parse the MI Senate data from the MI 8 data; the addition of the CMAG data helps allay this problem. Active organizations not listed include (Democratic Parties) DNC; (Democratic Allies) NARAL; (Republican Parties) NRSC, RNC; (Nonpartisan) American Society of Anesthesiologists, Michigan Information.

Table 9.2. The Ground War: Most Active Organizations' Observed Activity in the Michigan Eighth Congressional District Race

Type	*Organization*	*Mail*	*Phone*	*Total Unique Ads*
Democratic Allies				
Candidates	Byrum for Congress	9	1	10
Political Parties	Michigan Democratic State Committee	8	—	8
	DCCC	2	—	2
Interest Groups	League of Conservation Voters	4	—	4
	AFL-CIO	2	1	3
	American Federation of State, County, and Municipal Employees (AFSCME)	2	—	2
	Emily's List	2	—	2
	NARAL	1	—	1
	Public Citizen, Inc.	1	—	1
Republican Allies				
Candidates	Rogers for Congress	2	—	2
Political Parties	Michigan Republican State Committee	3	—	3
Interest Groups	National Federation of Independent Business	3	1	4

Source: Election Advocacy database.
Notes: See appendix B for a more detailed explanation of the data. Totals exclude all presidential data. Data include all ad campaigns that mentioned any MI 8 candidate, including those ads that simultaneously mentioned any presidential or MI Senate candidate. Therefore, this table and the table for MI Senate are not mutually exclusive. This table is not intended to represent comprehensive organization activity in the MI 8 race. A more complete picture can be obtained by examining this table and table 9.1 together.

independent groups. According to Brewer, "Those issues resonated in the research" on both sides. Brewer described his responsibility as keeping in touch with the campaign. He said, "I view my role as keeping tabs on things, not to micromanage, and to pass on what I see on the road."[14]

This close convergence of campaigns included a number of negative ads. The Michigan Democratic State Central Committee played rough. For example, the committee sent out one direct mail ad titled, "A Safe Place," which features a large gun, a church, and children playing. Then it criticized Rogers for an anti-gun control vote "against zero tolerance for guns in churches, schools and day care centers." A "Bad Medicine" mail piece also hit Rogers for "voting against allowing patients the right to sue their HMOs" while "That's Garbage," another mailer, slammed a Rogers vote to allow out-of-state trash to be land-filled in Michigan.

In addition, a television commercial claiming that Rogers "would raid Social Security" drew fire from the American Association of Retired People (AARP), which asked the state party to withdraw it. The commercial cited AARP's voting guide as its source, but the association told Brewer that "The ad falsely implies that AARP takes partisan positions." In fact, the guide laid out AARP's position on Social Security, Medicare, managed care, and long-term care and gave both major candidates equal space to explain their own positions in their own words.

Another commercial supporting Byrum, paid for by the Michigan Democratic State Central Committee, stressed her support for early childhood education while attacking Rogers's position. The ad opened with happy children bouncing off a school bus, and then a voice-over began: "Investing in them means investing in our future." Suddenly, the screen was transformed into a background of ripped black-and-white horizontal sections overlaid with a picture of Rogers. The voice-over continued: "Someone should tell Mike Rogers because Mike Rogers voted against early childhood education." By now, the announcer's words were synoptically displayed next to his picture. "Mike Rogers voted twice against reducing class size. He even voted against ensuring our children have the best possible teachers." The scene then shifted again to the image of a vigorous young white male teacher in a classroom, with the voice-over reporting, "But Diane Byrum supports early childhood education and Byrum's fighting to put more quality teachers in Michigan classrooms. The commercial concludes that Byrum "knows better education means better opportunities."

Because of President Clinton's continued popularity in Michigan, the state party used a letter from him, much of it boasting of Clinton administration accomplishments in health, minimum wage, Head Start funding, and appointments of African Americans. To aid Byrum's campaign the letter called Byrum a "strong supporter" on education and prescription drugs and urged recipients to write to her at the campaign committee Web site.

The campaign was skillfully run. In fact, Karin Johanson of the DCCC observed that it was, "The best-run campaign that we lost."[15] Rogers provided the only party turnover in Michigan and the only new face in Michigan's House delegation.

Republican Assaults

The Michigan GOP put resources into only two Michigan House districts, the Eighth where Rogers was running, and the First, where Democratic incumbent Bart Stupak defeated his challenger. In the Eighth, the party budgeted more than $300,000 for broadcast aids, direct mail, phone banks, and yard signs. State Chair Rusty Hills said much of the direct mail carried the state party's name but was actually financed with pass-through money. The state party also put considerable effort into identifying Republican voters; Hills said, "We did a lot more canvassing than before to find people, whether they were Republicans or identified with us on certain issues."[16]

Hills and state GOP executive director, Mark Hoffman, said the state party didn't coordinate efforts with Rogers or outside groups and didn't share mailing lists. "The FEC says you can't coordinate" with candidate committees, Hills said, and Hoffman said groups such as Right to Life, the National Rifle Association (NRA), and business organizations "may talk with us [but] you don't talk too much because you've got your own game."[17] But, perhaps confusingly for voters, the Republican state committee's mailings used the Rogers candidate committee campaign logo next to the return address.

The state committee pursued a pro-Rogers rather than anti-Byrum theme, covering Rogers's position on consumer protection, tax, and Internet pornography issues. A "Dear Friend" letter from Roger's wife lauded her husband as a hard-working leader and legislator. The mailer "Common Sense Health Care Agenda" called for protecting Social Security and promised more money for "classroom instruction" and less for "wasteful Washington bureaucracy." One of the few campaign pieces on foreign policy came from the state GOP: The mailer "The World Is a Dangerous Place" talked about members of the U.S. military who were killed on duty and summarized Rogers's proposal to strengthen the military.

Meanwhile, the NRCC took an alternative route and issued a heavy anti-Byrum attack with about a half-dozen direct mail ads, about the same number as the state party's pro-Rogers mailings. The NRCC issue advocacy ads attacked Byrum's vote against the state's $37.5 million Elder Prescription Insurance Coverage Program, "which will provide affordable drug coverage for Michigan seniors." It urged: "Call and tell [Byrum] to stop voting against Michigan seniors and their health care needs." The NRCC's "Failed for Lack of Attendance" piece slammed Byrum for missing a key vote when attending a fundraiser "held at a casino." It urged, "Call and ask her why she turned her back on Michigan schools to go to a casino." In "Better Teachers or Bigger Bureaucracy," a glaring stogie-smoking man denounced her votes against a ban on teacher strikes and a state takeover of the Detroit public schools.

The GOP party funding for commercials came from two sources: the Michigan Republican State Committee and the NRCC. For its ads, the state committee went into attack mode. One ad made no reference to Rogers but sharply criticized Byrum's vote to borrow money from the state Veterans' Trust Fund, extrapolating that she'd join other Democrats in Washington in staging a similar raid on Social Security. It opened with stirring military music, split-screen images of World War II, and profiles of helmeted soldiers. A sonorous male intoned: "We have always been there for our veterans." The voice-over script then appeared on the screen. "So how can Byrum tell us she'll protect Social Security if she won't even repay the Veterans' Fund?" Now the call to action: "Tell Diane Byrum to repay the Veterans' Trust Fund," with her state senate office number on the screen.

In a much softer pitch, paid for by the NRCC and authorized by Rogers for Congress, Rogers sat before a fireplace, a fire dancing lightly in the background. New Age piano music underlined an on-camera message that sought to boost him while claiming not to attack Byrum. The candidate began: "I believe in bringing people together, not tearing down others." The implication is clear. Rogers, still on-camera as the shot tightened to a medium close-up, recited programs he would vote for, and concluded, "I'm Mike Rogers [lean slightly into camera]. I'm not asking you to vote against my opponent. I'm asking you to vote for me. Give me two years, and we can make a difference." The appeal for two years is noteworthy, given the ping-pong nature of the Eighth.

BEYOND THE CANDIDATES: THE ROLE OF INTEREST GROUPS

Money flowed from abortion, anti-abortion, labor, environment, and women's groups. When it came to independent expenditures and issue advocacy, Lansing pollster Ed Sarpolus observed, "There was equality in soft money. Neither one had the edge."[18]

Abortion Interest Groups

The abortion issue was one magnet for such spending; the Eighth was a prime district because abortion rights advocates wanted to protect the seat held by pro-choice Stabenow. The state affiliate of National Abortion Rights Action League (NARAL) endorsed Byrum, but "the money that was spent was all national money," said Rebekkah Warren, executive director of the Michigan Abortion and Reproductive Rights Action League.[19] NARAL reported $72,907 in independent expenditures on Byrum's behalf.[20] It ran phone banks and sent several mail pieces, including one comparing Byrum and Rogers and one linking Byrum with Stabenow. One piece read, "Since 1995, Congress has voted over 130 times to restrict a woman's right to choose" and promised that Byrum "will protect a woman's right to choose."

"We have a lot of pro-choice voters and believe the district has a majority of pro-choice voters," said Chris Mather, NARAL's deputy political director. "NARAL's niche in the pro-choice movement is we do the best targeted voter contract work. We don't open a phone book." In the Eighth, there are "close to 25,000 pro-choice identified voters," and "we worked 10 percent of the voters needed to win the election."[21]

On the opposite side, the National Right to Life PAC reported $3,819 in independent expenditures on Rogers's behalf. The Right to Life of Michigan PAC reported $8,611 in independent expenditures on his behalf.[22] It sent two 35,000-piece mailings to its own list of pro-life households. The first focused on Rogers's record and the need to reclaim a pro-life seat, referring to ex-Representative Chrysler. The second contrasted the candidates' positions on partial-birth abortions, parental consent, assisted suicide, and fetal tissue research, citing Byrum's endorsement by "the extreme pro-abortion group Emily's List" and her acceptance of "more than $100,000 from Emily's List members." Right to Life of Michigan PAC director Larry Galmish said, "It's a swing district. We try to get the pro-life candidate identified and get our people motivated to vote." The state Right to Life did get-out-the-vote (GOTV) calls on behalf of all endorsed candidates, including Rogers.[23]

Right to Life wasn't the only pro-life player. Support came from Susan B. Anthony List, which is "committed to increasing the percentage of pro-life women in Congress through our Candidate Fund." United States Senator Spencer Abraham's wife is president. Its PAC spent $38,218 in the district for direct mail and radio spots, and executive director Jennifer Bingham said it distributed 50,000–60,000 copies of a mailer that said, "Liberal Dianne Byrum supports Partial Birth Abortions," and "Senator Mike Rogers would ban partial birth abortions."[24]

Labor and Business Interest Groups

Unions representing teachers and autoworkers were strong Byrum supporters, with much of their activity—mailings and phone calls—directed at union households.

The National Education Association's Fund for Children and Public Education reported $183,117 in expenditures backing Byrum, in addition to $10,000 in PAC contributions to her committee.[25]

Rogers made an unusual bid for the endorsement of the Michigan Education Association (MEA), which has 14,000 members in the Eighth. Rogers had a "great interview," union government affairs director Al Short said: "Afterwards, he thanked the committee for interviewing him and said that if he won, he'd like to work with us. In the past, the Republican [nominees, such as Chrysler] wouldn't show up." Short commented that one result was that "We didn't run any negatives against him." Despite Rogers's efforts, the MEA promoted Byrum in its magazine, sent direct mail pieces, and called every member at least once—and some as many as two or three times. Short said the state senate GOP leadership helped set Rogers up as pro-public education by letting him sponsor relevant legislation once he decided to run.[26]

As a major form of internal communication, some union pieces sounded a class theme. For example, a United Auto Workers Region 1C Community Action Program (CAP) mailing morphed a smiling mug shot of Rogers onto a cartoon-like drawing of formal wear and a top hat; Rogers was holding a money bag and the ad read, "It's about time Michigan's working families got a break." It added, "If you really don't think you'll need your Social Security checks when the time comes, then Mike Rogers is your man" and labeled him a "Big Insurance supporter" who backs privatization.

Meanwhile, the National Federation of Independent Business (NFIB) ran a half-page newspaper ad citing Rogers for his "NFIB Certified pro small-business voting record." That record, which included votes to repeal Michigan's estate and intangibles tax, reform workers' compensation, and provide business tax credits, earned him an "A" on his report card.

The state Chamber of Commerce proved a comparatively small player and wasn't as active in its Rogers endorsement as some had expected. For one thing, as a small business owner, Byrum had chamber backing in her first state Senate race and secured the backing of the Greater Lansing Chamber in the House race. The state Chamber's endorsement of Rogers in 2000 meant direct mail to members and favorable mentions in internal publications but no independent expenditures or issue advocacy for Rogers. Robert LaBrant, the executive vice president for political affairs, attributed the lack of expenditures to the Chamber pouring its money into Abraham's unsuccessful reelection bid and into reelecting three GOP conservatives to the state supreme court. According to LaBrant, "We did an awful lot more in the Senate race" than in the Eighth.[27]

Environmental Issue Groups

The League of Conservation Voters (LCV) Action Fund provided a deep pocket, reporting $74,095 in independent expenditures against Rogers.[28] The LCV "A Cool Drink Shouldn't Worry You" mail piece was based on five Senate votes by Rogers and its "Dirty Dozen" flyer tarred him as one of the nation's "twelve worst legislators." Details of Rogers's record appeared on the LCV's Web site. Nationally, LCV spent $3.5 million in independent expenditures in Dirty Dozen Senate and House races and another $1 million in six "Environmental Champion" races. Entities related to the LCV also spent money on soliciting absentee ballots, polling, GOTV drives, and noncandidate television ads.[29]

The Sierra Club's newsletter, an internal communication for 17,000 to 18,000 members, highlighted endorsed candidates, such as Byrum, and its local chapter mailings went to members.[30] The Sierra Club also donated Dan Farough, a staff member, to Byrum for several weeks. Farough came from the Sierra Club's environmental voter education campaign and "worked a lot with Byrum's field staff, helping coordinate bird-dogging efforts to turn out our supporters to Rogers events to make sure the Byrum presence was felt." He organized college students and linked Byrum to a land preservation bond issue on the ballot in Washtenaw County.

Other Players

Emily's List put the Eighth District high on its priority list and operated as Michigan WOMENVOTE. It ran a Web site and mailed "Call Mike Rogers Today" attack pieces; one read, for example, to tell Mike Rogers "that medical decisions should be made by patients and doctors—not HMO bureaucrats," and pointed to $43,000 in contributions to Rogers from the Health Benefits Coalition.

When it came to independent spending, the NRA was absent in the Eighth.[31] In an attempt to placate Representative John Dingel, the NRA endorsed Rogers but also gave Byrum an "A" rating and sat out the race.[32] However, the NRA's district coordinator worked with about two hundred volunteers using e-mail and phone calls to advise members about campaign events, such as appearances by NRA-backed Rogers, and to discuss the candidates' positions on gun issues.[33]

CONCLUSION

In this big-money contest with its resulting flood of television and radio commercials, direct mail pieces, and incessant phone calls; the boundaries between direct expenditures, volunteer efforts, soft money, and independent expenditures blurred and dissolved. Without the fine print, it would be impossible for voters to distinguish the nominal source—let alone the funding—for much of the material and many of the calls. At the same time, national attention, coupled with the 2000 election environment in Michigan, made it imperative to raise and spend on a record level, whether in the name of the candidate committees, party entities, or independent organizations.

There are multiple theories—beyond the presence of the Green candidate—about why Byrum lost. One is the Democrats' failure to properly predict turnout in the Rogers stronghold. Mark Brewer acknowledged, "We may have underestimated the turnout in Livingston County by a fraction of a percent, but that may be enough in a close race. We needed higher vote goals in Lansing to balance that out."[34] Byrum campaign manager Russell agreed, saying, "We had the percentage we needed in Livingston County but Livingston turned out 12,000 more voters than in 1996. Otherwise, we would have won by a point and a half."[35] Pollster Sarpolus said Byrum also lost on personality, not issues: "Rogers won more Democratic male votes than Byrum won Republican female votes. Rogers came across as much more congenial and personable."[36]

As always in a nearly balanced district where the major candidates have access to roughly equal financial support, it's impossible to measure the role any one component in the mix plays. Asked about the impact of soft money and issue advocacy in the race, Russell observed that "most of our tracking polls were basically simple horse race polls," so it's difficult to judge the effectiveness of independent issue-related expenditures.[37] The obvious questions arise: Would more money have changed the results, and if so, how much more would it have taken? And how would it have been spent? According to Russell, "You couldn't rule out" that a little more for commercials would have enabled Byrum to "sway" enough votes.[38]

Media consultants who prepared the television commercials were reluctant to talk about the messages they molded. Those at firms serving both candidates either declined comment or didn't return phone calls. One firm, National Media in Alexandria, Virginia, referred an inquiry to an advocacy group it had worked for, Citizens for Better Medicare (CBM). Dan Solinski of the CBM sounded surprised that his group had run commercials in the Eighth, saying the twenty-six districts it focused on all had incumbents. Solinski did acknowledge that the mid-Michigan media buy was most likely to shore up support for the pharmaceutical industry's view of Medicare and prescription drugs. He said, "We believe the debate over prescription drugs has been presented as a one-sided issue, framed as either supporting the government program or being against seniors. We absolutely disagree with that statement." Overall, CBM wanted to help construct the national debate and to neutralize what looms for the industry as a negative issue.[39]

In reality, though, these are unanswerable questions in a contest where both sides raised and spent ample resources to get their messages out over and over through a variety of media. In fact, the environment raises questions about how more money could have been spent beyond simply throwing $10 bills into the air and letting voters catch them as they drifted in the wind. It would have been difficult to use more money for television ads. The presidential, U.S. Senate, state house, and state supreme court races and two expensive ballot issues made it tough near the end to even buy television time.

At the same time, independent expenditures made it possible for partisans to use scorched-earth advertising in a way that purportedly insulates the candidates and their official committees from allegations of dirty politics. But on another level, it's unclear whether those distinctions are too nuanced for most voters.

Johnston Mitchell, director of the nonpartisan Michigan Campaign Finance Network, pointed to the "deluge of junk mail" with similar design and tone. "You look at it and you're befuddled." One consequence is that "Prospective voters have to spend too much time to sort through a new yellow journalism. It's sensationalism. They always criticize the press so much when the independent expenditures by these groups are no better."[40]

As for the impact of direct mail, Engler aide Truscott observed, "I don't think most people read them when you're getting five or six of these a day in the different elections. If *I'm* looking at it and pitching it, I can't imagine ordinary voters reading them."[41]

Were a lot of those millions of dollars in essence flushed down the toilet? Perhaps. Discussing NRA efforts, district coordinator Dieball said, "We found out the grassroots efforts were far more valuable than any money spent on ads and campaigns."[42]

NOTES

1. Bonnie Bucqueroux, telephone interview by Eric Freedman, 13 November 2000.
2. Ibid.
3. Dan Farough, telephone interview by Eric Freedman, November 2000.
4. Bucqueroux, interview by Freedman.
5. Mark Brewer, telephone interview by Eric Freedman, 13 November 2000.
6. Michigan Chamber of Commerce, "1999–2000 Job Providers Index."
7. Michigan Farm Bureau, "1995–1998 Voting Record."

8. FEC data through 31 December 2000 obtained from "Candidate Summary Reoprts," <herndon1.sdrdc.com/cgi-bin/cancomsrs/?_00+CAN+MI>, 2001 [accessed 13 August 2001].

9. Tom Russell, telephone interview by Eric Freedman, 20 November 2000.

10. John Truscott, telephone interview by Eric Freedman, 4 December 2000.

11. Ibid.

12. The DCCC spent over $2.1 million on the Eighth according to Karin Johanson, political director, DCCC, telephone interview by Jason Beal, 10 January 2001.

13. Party transfers were obtained from "FEC Reports Increase in Party Fundraising for 2000," FEC press release, <www.fec.gov/press/051501partyfund/tables/cong2state2000.html> [accessed 13 August 2001]. Coordinated expenditures were obtained from "1999–2000 U.S. House and U.S. Senate Candidate Information," <www.fecinfo.com/cgi-win/x_candpg.exe?DoFn=HOMI08042*2000> [accessed 20 August 2001].

14. Brewer, interview by Freedman.

15. Karin Johanson, interview by David B. Magleby, Washington, D.C., 20 November 2000.

16. Rusty Hills and Mark Hoffman, telephone interview by Eric Freedman, 13 November 2000.

17. Ibid.

18. Ed Sarpolus, telephone interview by Eric Freedman, 10 November 2000.

19. Rebekkah Warren, telephone interview by Eric Freedman, 29 November 2000.

20. Data for independent expenditures, internal communication, and party coordinated expenditures were obtained from FEC, "Disclosure Database," at <ftp.fec.gov> [accessed 22 January 2001].

21. Chris Mather, telephone interview by Eric Freedman, 30 November 2000.

22. PAC independent expenditures are from "PAC Summary Reports," <herndon1.sdrdc.com/cgi-bin/can_give/1999_H0MI08042> [accessed 13 August 2001].

23. Larry Galmish, telephone interview by Eric Freedman, 13 November 2000.

24. Jennifer Bingham, telephone interview by Eric Freedman, 4 December 2000.

25. The NEA spent $137,174 on independent expenditures and $45,943 on internal communication. FEC, "Disclosure Database."

26. Al Short, telephone interview by Eric Freedman, 6 December 2000.

27. Robert LaBrant, telephone interview by Eric Freedman, 29 November 2000.

28. FEC, "Disclosure Database."

29. Lisa Wade, communications director, interview by David B. Magleby, Washington, D.C., 13 November 2000.

30. Farough, interview by Freedman.

31. Johanson, interview by Magleby.

32. "The Gun Lobby Muzzles Its Firepower in Two Key House Races," *Wall Street Journal*, 20 October 2000.

33. Dave Dieball, telephone interview by Eric Freedman, 7 December 2000.

34. Brewer, interview by Freedman.

35. Russell, interview by Freedman.

36. Sarpolus, interview by Freedman.

37. Russell, interview by Freedman.

38. Ibid.
39. Dan Solinski, telephone interview by Sue Carter, 7 December 2000.
40. Johnston Mitchell, telephone interview by Eric Freedman, 21 November 2000.
41. Truscott, interview by Freedman.
42. Dieball, interview by Freedman.

10

The 2000 New Jersey Twelfth Congressional District Race

Adam J. Berinsky with Susan S. Lederman

The race in New Jersey's Twelfth District was one of the hardest fought congressional elections in 2000. On election night, the Republican candidate, former Congressman Dick Zimmer, was declared the winner over Democratic incumbent Rush Holt. But a recount in the weeks following the election overturned this result, and on November 29, Zimmer conceded the race. By a margin of 672 votes, Rush Holt retained his seat for another two-year term.

INSIDE THE TWELFTH CONGRESSIONAL DISTRICT

New Jersey's Twelfth Congressional District stretches from the Delaware River almost to the Jersey Shore and straddles U.S. 1, the highway that connects the communities surrounding Rutgers and Princeton as well as many of New Jersey's pharmaceutical and telecommunications companies. The Twelfth District is now a largely suburban district, running from Hunterdon and Somerset counties, where once-bucolic farms are giving way to corporate headquarters and three-garage McMansions, through parts of Mercer, Middlesex, and Monmouth counties.

The district was redrawn in 1991 by the Republican state legislature to ensure that it would provide safe Republican majorities for the then-incumbent Congressman Richard Zimmer.[1] Although there are some Democratic-leaning communities, notably liberal Princeton and some of the working class suburbs of Middlesex County, the Twelfth District has the lowest percentage of registered Democrats of any New Jersey congressional district. Even though President Clinton carried the district in 1996 and Democrat Rush Holt eked out a narrow win in 1998, national observers still label the district "Republican-leaning."[2]

The district's voters are concerned with suburban sprawl and the resultant daily traffic jams. Education is also of prime importance; the district has the largest percentage of college graduates of any in the state and boasts some of the state's best public schools. In addition to Rutgers University in New Brunswick, the flagship campus of New Jersey's largest public university, the district is also home to Princeton University, Rider University, Monmouth University, the College of New Jersey, and three community colleges. The incumbent candidate, Rush Holt, a Princeton University physicist, may typify the high-tech, high-education image of the district. Yet the vestiges of "working" farms and "horse country" persist; it is, after all, the home district of Governor Christie Whitman and her family farm, Pontefract; and its former congressman, Dick Zimmer, lives in the western part of the district on a working farm.

THE CANDIDATES AND THEIR CAMPAIGNS

Republican candidate Dick Zimmer's political career began in the 1970s when he was head of New Jersey Common Cause and continued in 1981 with his election to the state legislature, where he acquired a reputation for being a fiscal conservative and an open-space preservationist. In 1990, he won the Twelfth District in the most expensive House race in the nation, defeating Marguerite Chandler, his Democratic opponent, who freely spent her own money.[3] Zimmer's moderate views on cultural and foreign policy issues (he supported abortion rights, for example), his fiscal austerity, and his good government voting record were mixed with his support for conservative causes. For example, he supported Newt Gingrich's crime bill and, as a member of the Ways and Means Committee, was a Republican loyalist on major issues.[4] He was reelected to the House in 1992 and 1994, with over 60 percent of the vote both times. In 1996, Zimmer ran for the U.S. Senate seat vacated by Bill Bradley. He lost an expensive and acrimonious race to Congressman Robert Toricelli.

Rush Holt, the Democratic candidate, narrowly won the district in 1998. Holt's emphasis on gun control, abortion rights, Social Security preservation, and environmental protection attracted sufficient voter interest to secure 50 percent of the votes, a 3 percent victory over Republican Congressman Mike Pappas.[5] Holt was also "careful to stress his independence and emphasize his Princeton University physicist credentials in that first campaign."[6]

Holt's political lineage is colorful. His father, Rush D. Holt, was elected to the Senate in West Virginia at age twenty-nine and had to wait six months to turn thirty before he could take his seat. Holt's mother served as a top official in the Federal Housing Agency. Holt, as a first-term representative, championed education issues, serving on the Education and Workforce Committee and on the Budget Committee. Yet he exercised some independence, bucking the Democrats' party-line vote to oppose the federal estate tax repeal.[7] He also continued to stress environmental issues, particularly issues related to urban sprawl.

Republicans considered Holt to be a "one-term accident"[8]and saw Zimmer as the most likely candidate to win back the district. Rush Holt, however, had different plans. Both parties considered the Holt-Zimmer contest for the Twelfth District crucial. The Green Party, represented by wealthy Princeton resident Carl Mayer (who unsuccessfully ran in several prior Democratic congressional primaries), ratcheted up the competition.

The Zimmer-Holt contest was one of the most expensive races in 2000. The Holt campaign raised $2,659,446 and spent $2,595,080, while the Zimmer campaign raised $2,223,722 for the primary battle with Pappas and the general election but only spent $2,196,588. Green Party candidate Carl Meyer raised $259,257 and spent $259,519.[9]

In the general election, Holt had more money than Zimmer, so he was able to spend more hard money on his campaign. Holt's campaign bought a good deal of time on the New York television stations, in particular WABC (see tables 10.1 and 10.2). We estimate that Holt ran about 325 ads at a cost of just over $1 million. Most of the ads ran during the week preceding the election. The ads included a spot in which Bill Bradley announced his support of Holt. The Holt campaign believes this Bradley ad was particularly effective in generating public support for Holt.[10]

Outside groups also participated in the race. The consulting firm Message and Media took the lead on campaign mailings and radio advertisements for Holt. The

Table 10.1. The Air War: Most Active Organizations' Collected Ad Buy Data in the New Jersey Twelfth Congressional District Race

Type	*Organization*	*TV*	*Radio*	*Total Ad Buy $*	*CMAG TV*
Democratic Allies					
Candidates	Rush Holt for Congress, Inc.	$1,077,975	$24,706	**$1,102,681**	$ 252,675
Political Parties	DCCC	$ 977,400	$ 5,700	**$ 983,100**	$2,560,448
Interest Groups	Sierra Club	$0	$35,380	**$ 35,380**	$0
Republican Allies					
Candidates	Zimmer 2000	$ 380,946	$31,437	**$ 412,383**	$ 564,623
Political Parties	Victory2000	$0	$ 3,500	**$ 3,500**	$0
	NRCC	$0	$0	**$0**	$1,136,426
	NRSC	$0	$0	**$0**	$ 27,360
Interest Groups	Republicans for Clean Air	$ 26,300	$0	**$ 26,300**	$0

Source: Election Advocacy and *Campaign Media Analysis Group* databases.

Notes: See appendix B for a more detailed explanation of the data. This table is not intended to portray comprehensive organization spending in the NJ 12 race. A more complete picture can be obtained by examining this table together with table 10.2.

Table 10.2. The Ground War: Most Active Organizations' Observed Mail Activity in the New Jersey Twelfth Congressional District Race

Type	*Organization*	*Total Unique Mail Pieces*
Democratic Allies		
Candidates	Rush Holt for Congress, Inc.	23
Political Parties	Democratic Congressional Campaign Committee	5
	Eatontown Democratic Club	1
	Shrewsbury Borough Democrats	1
Interest Groups	National Education Association	4
	League of Conservation Voters	2
	NARAL	2
Republican Allies		
Candidates	Zimmer 2000	2
Political Parties	New Jersey Republican State Committee	10
	National Republican Congressional Committee	4
	NJGOP/Victory 2000	3
Interest Groups	National Federation of Independent Business	4
Nonpartisan		
Interest Groups	AARP	1

Source: Election Advocacy database.

Notes: See appendix B for a more detailed explanation of the data. Totals exclude all presidential data. Data include all ad campaigns that mentioned any NJ 12 candidate, including those ads that simultaneously mentioned any presidential candidate. This table is not intended to represent comprehensive organization activity in the NJ 12 race. A more complete picture can be obtained by examining this table and table 10.1 together. Active organizations not listed above include (Democratic Allies) American Federation of Teachers, Handgun Control, NEA Fund for Children and Public Education, NJ Education Association, NJ Environmental Federation, NJ State AFL-CIO, Planned Parenthood Action Fund; (Republican Parties) College Republican National Committee, Hunterdon County Republican Committee, Monmouth Republican Committee, RNC, Republican Pro-choice Coalition PAC.

mailings were targeted at four specific groups: independents, independent seniors, Republican women, and Democrats. Because the Republican primary was contested, the mail campaign did not begin in earnest until Labor Day but increased in intensity as the election drew nearer. Addresses for the mailings were generated by combining labels and lists from the list broker and records from the National Committee for an Effective Congress, a private firm that works for the Democratic House Caucus.[11]

Zimmer's campaign sought a broad appeal in the district, largely because Zimmer had a strong record and high name recognition from his time as a representative. The television ads, therefore, used the theme "Dick Zimmer, a respected congressman." Although Zimmer's campaign had much less money available for advertising than Holt's campaign did, Zimmer's advertising was heavily augmented by commercials paid for directly by the National Republican Congressional Committee (NRCC). The Zimmer campaign itself ran almost three hundred ads in the New York media market at a cost of over $350,000. In addition, the Campaign Media Analysis Group reports that the NRCC spent more than $1.1 million on television and radio advertising focused on the Twelfth District.[12]

The New Jersey Republican State Committee, in coordination with the Zimmer campaign, sponsored mailings.[13]The state committee worked directly with Zimmer's Princeton-based, Republican consulting firm, Jamestown Associates. To comply with federal election law, volunteers recruited by the Zimmer campaign handled every piece of mail sent by the state Republican Party.[14] The New Jersey Republican State Committee, a nonprofit organization, financed the mailings, allowing them to be sent with the relatively inexpensive bulk rate postage. The funding for the mailings came from the state party's federal fund.[15] The mailings cost from $20,000 to $30,000 to send.[16]

Jamestown Associates, which produced the campaign mailings and television ads, believed that the mailings were the most effective means of reaching voters.[17] Many of the mailings attempted to appeal to a wide spectrum of voters, emphasizing Zimmer's role in writing the federal Meagan's Law and his opposition to raising taxes. The campaign, however, also targeted specific constituencies with mailings. For example, one mailing sent by the New Jersey State Republican Committee to senior citizens stated that Zimmer "has been a consistent champion for New Jersey Seniors" concerning drug issues. Other mailings, emphasizing Zimmer's record on support for education, were targeted to women.[18] The campaign also coordinated a get-out-the-vote (GOTV) effort with the Republican State Committee; this effort was paid for by the state party's federal fund.[19]

POLITICAL PARTY ACTIVITY

The national parties played large roles in both candidates' campaigns. The Campaign Media Analysis Group reports that the NRCC financed a large portion of the media advertising supporting Zimmer.[20] In addition, Zimmer's campaign manager, John Holub, said that the NRCC sent a number of mailings to residents of the Twelfth District. Holub said these mailings emphasized Zimmer's accomplishments in Congress and attacked Holt's record.[21] The NRCC also transferred $328,000 to the New Jersey Republican State Committee, almost certainly to finance the mailings and the GOTV effort described previously.[22]

The Democratic Congressional Campaign Committee (DCCC) was a major player in the New Jersey Twelfth District contest as well. The DCCC spent aggressively in the New York City media market, with large ad buys in September.[23] In that month, we estimate that the DCCC ran over four hundred commercials in the New York area at a cost of almost $1 million. Many of the ads supported Holt. All told, the DCCC spent $2.6 million on advertising buys, and beginning in

September the DCCC spent $200,000 sending out glossy fliers[24] praising Holt "as an advocate of HMO reform and a defender of personal privacy."[25]

However, the DCCC involvement did not always benefit Holt. In August, the DCCC ran a television advertisement on Comcast Cable, which characterized GOP candidate Dick Zimmer as an enemy of education. In particular, the ad asserted that when Zimmer was a representative, he "never voted for a single education funding bill. Not one." Zimmer quickly fought back, calling the ad a "flat-out lie." After Comcast researched Zimmer's claim, the cable provider concluded that the ad was inaccurate and pulled it (the DCCC later modified the ad and reran it). The advertisement, however, created quite a stir in the media. The *Trentonian* criticized both Holt and the DCCC with an editorial accusing the DCCC of "playing the role of 'Liars for Holt.'" Holt's campaign believes they made a tactical error in not immediately recognizing that the DCCC ad contained some technical errors. However, they believe that the ad was thematically correct even before the DCCC reworked it.[26]

Even more controversial was a DCCC campaign brochure that accused Zimmer of voting to deny expanded mammogram coverage to older women. Specifically, the mailer claimed that "Dick Zimmer voted against funding the Office on Women's Health again and again" and concluded with a plea to "Tell Dick Zimmer to quit voting against women's health." This mailer became a media target when it was revealed that Zimmer's mother died of lymphoma when he was in high school and that all three of his sisters are breast-cancer survivors. The *Currior News* decried the mailing as "in very bad taste,"[27] and Hunterdon Regional Breast Care Center director Ruth Feldman said Holt's mailers "attacking Zimmer's record are 'blatant lies.'" Zimmer swiftly called on Holt to denounce the spots, saying that the three votes Holt used to attack his record "were based on fiscal, not health considerations."[28] Holt instead defended the ad, disclosing that his mother also had breast cancer. The ad against Zimmer was, Holt argued, based purely on the votes that Zimmer cast.

The DCCC campaign's effect on the race is unclear. As in Kentucky's Sixth District race, inaccurate ads by the DCCC put the Democratic candidate on the defensive and made him vulnerable to media attacks. The DCCC ads also gave the Zimmer campaign a great deal of ammunition to use in its own ads. Despite these problems, the Holt campaign believed that the ads had the intended effect of "softening up" Zimmer; internal polling data showed that Zimmer's negatives went up after the education and cancer ads.[29]

Overall, party activity played a very large role in both candidates' campaigns. A great number of the mailings supporting Zimmer's efforts were sent out by state or national party organizations. A significant portion of Holt's mailings also came from party organizations. Regarding television and radio advertising, it is difficult to make precise conclusions about what proportion was paid for by party organizations because our research team's data are often in conflict with the data from the Campaign Media Analysis Group. But one conclusion seems clear: Party organizations financed a significant portion of the advertising for both candidates.

INTEREST GROUP ACTIVITY

The battle for the Twelfth District attracted a variety of interest groups, including the National Federation of Independent Business (NFIB), the Sierra Club, the AFL-CIO, the U.S. Chamber of Commerce, the National Education Association (NEA), and the National Abortion and Reproduction Rights Action League (NARAL). Some groups, such as the AFL-CIO and the Chamber of Congress, were involved because they strongly supported their candidates. But other groups apparently had their eye on a higher prize—a majority in Congress. Groups like NARAL and the Sierra Club may have supported Holt, even though he differed little from Zimmer on key issues, because they desired a Democratic majority. All told, the interest group presence in the race was substantial.

National Federation of Independent Businesses

The NFIB decided early to support Zimmer in the Twelfth District. It spent $75,000 on Zimmer's behalf in addition to raising a $5,000 direct PAC campaign contribution for the Republican candidate.[30] The NFIB sent out an endorsement letter in September to its members in the district. Most of its campaign activity, however, was concentrated in the last thirty days.[31] The NFIB targeted two particular business communities: member businesses and small nonmember businesses.

First, the NFIB asked member businesses to help stimulate voter turnout and sent mailings and absentee ballot request forms to those businesses. It encouraged member businesses to put Zimmer literature and signs in their stores and ran what it called the "Value Added Voter Program," sending packets to member business owners and asking them to recruit nine other people to vote for Zimmer.[32] The NFIB also sent members a joint Zimmer/Franks mailing termed a "foldout." The foldout unfolded into a poster, but the mailing was not called a poster because it was sent as an internal communication using hard dollars and was not explicitly meant to be seen by the general public.[33] Between the turnout effort and the "Value Added Voter Program," the NFIB sent out ten different mailings as well as making phone calls and sending faxes to members during the campaign. The NFIB also organized a "walk around," where Zimmer personally walked around to meet local member businesses.[34]

Second, the NFIB targeted small nonmember businesses in the district, using "small business lists" purchased from a list broker. Nonmember businesses were sent mail to encourage them to support and vote for Zimmer. In its literature, the NFIB emphasized that Dick Zimmer was a former NFIB member and was therefore a particular friend of small business. In addition to these mailings, in late October the NFIB published a half-page advertisement in the *Trenton Times* costing $3,500.[35] In the advertisement, the NFIB claimed that Holt was "against repeal of the death tax" and "against expanding deductibility of small business owners' health insurance." The NFIB ad prompted a strong and quick response from the Democrats: "The Liars for Zimmer propaganda machine has struck again," said DCCC spokesman John Del Cecato.[36] The NFIB also made periodic press releases during the campaign supporting Zimmer.

The U.S. Chamber of Commerce

The U.S. Chamber of Commerce produced three mailings on Dick Zimmer's behalf, totaling an estimated 5,000 pieces of mail. It also sponsored two fundraisers and conducted an e-mail GOTV campaign from its Washington office. Even though the national, state, and local chambers of commerce are separate organizations with different mailing lists, if local chapters agreed, the U.S. Chamber used the local mailing lists to send material supporting Zimmer.[37]

National Abortion and Reproduction Rights Action League (NARAL)

The NARAL took an active role in the Twelfth District race. It considered Holt one of its "friends" in Congress and supported the incumbent candidate. The League's research indicated that Holt was a vulnerable incumbent, and the organization knew that the Republican Party was going to put a great deal of money into the race. NARAL's involvement was therefore designed to protect a friendly candidate (Holt) rather than attack an abortion opponent (because Zimmer was not opposed to abortion).

The NARAL spent about $22,000 in independent expenditures on mailings and phone calls supporting Holt.[38] In addition, it donated $7,500 directly to the Holt campaign.[39] NARAL targeted 8,300 voters who were mostly pro-choice, independent, or undecided Republican women, or voters who were, in NARALs estimation, likely to support Holt. The League used some phone banking firms to develop these lists. In early September, NARAL began to directly contact potential supporters by phone. Most of the phoning was focused on persuading Independent and Republican undecided voters rather than mobilizing strong supporters. NARAL thought these people could be persuaded to support Holt because of his strong stance on the abortion issue. Some of the phone calling was done in-house, but NARAL also paid Winning Connections, a Washington, D.C., political firm, about $1,700 to do some of the calls.[40]

NARAL decided to wait until the end of the campaign to release its mailings, sending three mailings in the last two weeks of the campaign. The League put together the content of the mailings in-house, but the flyers were produced by Strategy Source, a Washington, D.C.-based graphics design firm. The tone of these mailings reflected the lack of meaningful differences between the candidates on the abortion question. One mailing labeled Holt "pro-choice" in comparison to Zimmer. This strategy directly contrasts with that used in a similar mailing in the New Jersey Thirteenth District, where the Democratic candidate, Maryanne Connelly, was labeled "pro-choice" and her opponent Mike Ferguson was labeled "anti-choice." A second mailing combined pro-choice endorsements for Holt with an identical endorsement for the Senate Candidate Jon Corzine. NARAL also used e-mail in attempting to mobilize its supporters.[41]

The Sierra Club

There was not much difference between the two candidates on environmental issues. When Zimmer ran for reelection in 1994 and 1996, the League of Conservation Voters (LCV) and the New Jersey chapter of the Sierra Club both endorsed him over his Democratic opponent.[42] This time, however, the Sierra Club actively supported Holt in a number of ways. First, it broadcast a series of ads supporting Holt. These ads, which began airing August 28, urged listeners to contact Rush Holt and thank him for standing up for environmental concerns. The ads were part of a nationwide campaign designed to generate support for politicians favorable to the Sierra Club's cause. The Sierra Club also gave the Holt campaign access to its member lists for the Twelfth District and mentioned Holt's candidacy in the Sierra Club newsletter in October, November, and December. There are approximately 1,500 Sierra Club members in the Twelfth District.[43]

New Jersey AFL-CIO

New Jersey AFL-CIO endorsed both Republican and Democratic candidates in New Jersey. To be effective advocates for its candidates, the union had organized a massive voter registration drive in the state. In spring 2000, over 26,000 union members were registered through a "worker-vote" registration program at work sites—and more than 107,000 union members were newly registered to vote since 1998 in New Jersey.[44] Comprehensive file maintenance of membership information paid off in the organization's ability to target an effective GOTV drive.

The AFL-CIO considered the Holt-Zimmer race an important battleground. To help reelect Rush Holt, 27,000 union members in the district were contacted through mail, phone calls, and, most effectively, by 1,000 union volunteers going door-to-door to talk face-to-face with union members. The AFL-CIO believed that this effort had an impact on the outcome of the race. "Union members [responded] more favorably to direct contact from a fellow member than to slick mail," noted John Shea.[45] Although it doesn't have exit polls for the Twelfth District, the AFL-CIO knows that, statewide, one-third of all votes in New Jersey were union votes. The organization was satisfied with the GOTV effort.

The National Education Association

The Twelfth District has more than 12,000 NEA members, an unusually high number. The NEA recognized the race's importance for education and undertook a strong pro-Holt campaign. It sent four mailings that supported Holt's education policy. These mailings mentioned Holt's desire to create smaller classrooms, improve Head Start programs, and make higher education more affordable. Two of the mailings also made anti-Zimmer statements, criticizing the candidate's unwillingness to allocate funds for education. The NEA put forth a total of $128,499 on independent expenditures and $36,000 on internal communications with NEA members.[46]

Other Groups

Ceasefire New Jersey sent a single mailing endorsing Rush Holt to 3,000 residents in the district, at a cost of about $700. The mailing said, "We need Rush Holt's voice in Congress to continue to speak out for common-sense gun safety laws." Ceasefire New Jersey regularly holds events across the state in support of New Jersey anti-handgun legislation. It created the mailing list by supplementing the names of those who attended these events with names from the mailing list of Handgun Control in Washington.[47]

CONCLUSION

The vote counting to determine the victor in this competitive race seemed almost as contentious and unsettled as the 2000 race for president. For over two weeks after the election, it was a "race too close to call,"[48] with Zimmer contesting absentee ballots and complaining that Middlesex and Mercer county officials engaged in ballot tampering. After the final vote tally on November 22, which showed Rush Holt as the victor by about 550 votes, Zimmer demanded a recount but finally conceded on November 30, when the recount increased Holt's margin of victory. Complaining of irregularities by Democratic officials and election workers, Zimmer asserted that "these irregularities are a cause of concern but not grounds for lengthy litigation or a divisive showdown in the House of Representatives."[49]

It is difficult to assess the exact impact of spending in this race, but it is clear that money played a large role in determining the final outcome. Given the closeness of the race, the GOTV effort was critical to both the Holt and Zimmer campaigns. Interviews with both campaigns revealed that campaign insiders believed that their direct mailings to constituents made the largest impact in stimulating turnout. But in light of the closeness of the race, even campaigns that might have only had a marginal effect on turnout—such as that undertaken by the Sierra Club—were almost certainly important.

There were several significant trends concerning outside money in this race. First, it is clear that a number of interest groups used internal communications to support their favored candidates. This was evident in the NEA's extensive communications with its members, the "foldout" posters sent out by the NFIB, and

NARAL's e-mails targeted at mobilizing its supporters. A second trend was the tendency of inaccurate advertising, paid for by the parties; these ads occasionally backfired on the candidate they were designed to help. It is often asserted that when advertising is paid for by outside organizations, inaccurate claims can be made without the candidates being held accountable. This race does not provide evidence of who was held accountable for the inaccurate ads sponsored by the DCCC and the NFIB, but it is clear from this race and Kentucky's Sixth District race that when a candidate's party sponsors an inaccurate ad, that candidate may be held responsible.

The final trend evident in this race is the central importance of party money. In this race, money from state and national party organizations sponsored a large number of mailings and media advertisements for both candidates. In comparison to the influence of party money, the role of interest-group spending was quite small. If this is the case in other congressional races, it is a significant finding that merits further attention.

Given the closeness of Holt's margin of victory in this election, he surely cannot consider his to be a safe seat, unless the state's redistricting redefines the district sufficiently to make it less of a swing district. Until then, the money chase continues in the New Jersey Twelfth Congressional District.

NOTES

For invaluable help in the collection of data and preparation of this manuscript, I would like to thank Theodore Brassfield, Frank Cesario, Andrew Ferrer, Alison Franklin, David Gail, Paul Gerber, Kacey Guy, Jonathan Ladd, Susan Lederman, Deborah Mohammed, and Rebecca Wein.

1. Michael Barone and Grant Ujifusa, *The Almanac of American Politics 2000* (Washington, D.C.: National Journal Group, 1999), 1008.

2. Sandra Basu, "Holt-Zimmer House Race: No Holds Barred," *Congressional Quarterly* (5 November 2000): 2583.

3. Michael Barone and Grant Ujifusa, *The Almanac of American Politics 1996*, (Washington, D.C.: National Journal Group, 1995), 874.

4. Ibid.

5. Barrone and Ujifusa, *Almanac of American Politics 2000*, 1059.

6. Mark. J. Magyar, "High Stakes," *New Jersey Reporter* (October 2000): 19.

7. "In 12th District, Rep. Rush Holt for Congress, Packet Editorial," *Congressman Rush Holt*, <www.rushholt.com/press/packet_endorsement.htm>, 18 October 2000 [accessed 19 December 2000].

8. Ibid.

9. "1999–2000 U.S. House and U.S. Senate Candidate Info for State of New Jersey," *FECInfo*, <www.fecinfo.com/cgi-win/x_statedis.exe>, 2000 [accessed 14 June 2001].

10. Neil Upmeyer, director, Rush Holt for Congress Finance Committee, telephone interview by Susan Lederman, 19 December 2000.

11. Brad Lawrence, Message and Media, Inc., telephone interview by Alison Franklin, 22 November 2000.

12. Our media tracking efforts were largely unable to confirm these figures. But given the large Republican presence in the district, such expenditures are not surprising.

13. The New Jersey Republican State Committee refused to comment on their involvement in the race. All the information reported here has been obtained from other sources.

14. John Holub, Zimmer campaign manager, telephone interview by Paul Gerber, 18 January 2001.

15. Holub said that he thought that this fund was pure soft money, but he was not sure. Holub, interview by Gerber.

16. Lawrence, interview by Franklin.

17. Tom Blakely, vice president, Jamestown Associates, telephone interview by Adam Berinsky, 15 November 2000.

18. John Holub, telephone interview by Paul Gerber, 21 November 2000.

19. Ibid.

20. See table 10.1.

21. Holub, interview by Gerber, 21 November 2000.

22. Federal Election Commission (FEC), "Party Fundraising Escalates," press release,<fecweb1.fec.gov/press/011201partyfunds.htm>, 12 January 2001 [accessed 15 January 2001].

23. Karin Johanson, political director, DCCC, telephone interview by David B. Magleby, 16 November 2000.

24. Karin Johanson, political director, DCCC, telephone interview by Jason Beal, 10 January 2001.

25. "New Jersey 12: DCCC Has a Soft Spot for Holt," *Hotline Weekly*, <nationaljournal.com/members/hotlineweekly/2000/092100.htm#26>, 21 September 2000 [accessed 19 December 2000].

26. Upmeyer, telephone interview.

27. "Attack on Zimmer In Very Bad Taste," *Courier News*, 3 October 2000, at <www.zimmer2000.com/news/news1003.html>, 18 January 2001.

28. "Holt Attacks Zimmer's Record," *Trentonian*, 25 October 2000, at <www.zwire.com/site/news.cfm?newsid=1002831&BRD=1697&PAG=461&dept_id=44551&rfi=8>, 18 January 2001.

29. Upmeyer, interview by Lederman.

30. Matt Garth, Northeast regional political director, NFIB, telephone interview by Jonathan Ladd, 24 November 2000.

31. Ibid.

32. Ibid.

33. Sharon Wolff, NEA, interview by David B. Magelby, Washington, D.C., 14 November 2000.

34. Matt Garth, telephone interview by Jonathan Ladd, 30 November 2000.

35. Sharon Wolff, telephone interview by Adam Berinsky, 20 December 2000.

36. Democratic Congressional Campaign Committee, "NJ-12 Liars For Zimmer," <www.dccc.org/news/rapidresponse/rapid.cfm?rid=173>, 26 October 2000 [accessed 18 January 2001].

37. Dan Craig, executive director, Eastern Regional Conference, U.S. Chamber of Commerce, telephone interview by Kacey Guy, 18 December 2000.

38. FEC, "Disclosure Database," <ftp.fec.gov> [accessed 15 January 2001].

39. "1999–00 Election Cycle Info for: HOLT, RUSH DEW," *FECInfo*, <www.fecinfo.com/cgi-win/x_candpg.exe?DoFn=H6NJ12144*2000>, 2000 [accessed 14 June 2001].

40. Chris Mather, deputy political director, NARAL, telephone interview by Jonathan Ladd, 5 December 2000.

41. Ibid.

42. "Issues," *Zimmer2000*, <www.zimmer2000.com/issues.html>, 2000 [accessed 18 January 2001].

43. Richard Issac, political director, New Jersey Sierra Club, telephone interview by Kacey Guy, 18 December 2000.

44. John Shea, director, New Jersey AFL-CIO Committee on Political Education, telephone interview by Susan Lederman, 3 January 2001.

45. Ibid.

46. "Independent Expenditures—HOLT, RUSH DEW for '00," *FECInfo*, <www.fecinfo.com/cgi-win/_indepexp.exe?00H6NJ12144>, 2000 [accessed 18 January 2001] and <www.fecinfo.com/cgi-win/x_indepexp.exe?DoFn=00H6NJ12144> [accessed 14 June 2001].

47. Nancy Axelrod, assistant director, Ceasefire New Jersey, telephone interview by Kacey Guy, 18 December 2000.

48. Michael Grunwald, "In N.J., Role Reversal in Race Too Close to Call," *The Washington Post*, <www.washingtonpost.com>, 15 November 2000 [accessed 20 December 2000].

49. Juliet Eilperin, "Zimmer Concedes to Democratic Rep. Holt," *Washington Post*, <www. washingtonpost.com>, 30 November 2000 [accessed 20 December 2000].

11

The 2000 Pennsylvania Fourth Congressional District Race

Christopher Jan Carman and David C. Barker

This chapter examines the 2000 Pennsylvania Fourth District contest in which Melissa Hart, a conservative Republican candidate for an open congressional seat, defeated Democrat Terry Van Horne in a Democratic district known as a union stronghold. How did this happen? We contend that this race boiled down to the national and state party organizations' soft money support of their candidates: Hart had it; Van Horne did not. Thus, while the main aggregate fundraising story of 2000 may have been the growth in soft money fundraising and targeting on the part of House Democrats (as many of our colleagues have pointed out in other chapters of this book), the Fourth District race in Pennsylvania paints a portrait of a struggling Democratic campaign, essentially "fighting with one arm" due to a considerable shortfall in Democratic Congressional Campaign Committee (DCCC) support. Further, although interest group activity was felt in this contest, that activity paled in comparison to that of the national parties, particularly the National Republican Campaign Committee (NRCC), both in terms of spending and apparent influence. Finally, our analysis of the Fourth District contest indicates that soft money support is often contingent upon candidate quality. While candidates may find it nearly impossible to compete without the ardent support of their national congressional party organizations, that support may often be lacking because of a perceived lack of candidate viability. In short, candidates (and campaigns) still matter.

INSIDE THE FOURTH DISTRICT RACE

In a victory noteworthy for its sheer size, Hart won this open-seat race by capturing every county in this heavily Democratic district. In short, Hart trounced Van

Horne by nearly 45,000 votes, or 59 percent to 41 percent, roughly the same margin garnered by her two neighboring incumbent representatives in defeating their unknown challengers.

It was not supposed to happen this way. In the previous three elections, Ron Klink (a popular Democrat who vacated the seat in to run for the U.S. Senate against Rick Santorum) had crushed his Republican opponents, winning with an average of 64 percent of the vote. Moreover, the district of old steel towns along the Ohio and Allegheny rivers boasts the highest concentration of union members in the commonwealth of Pennsylvania—some 64,000 in all (constituting approximately 12 percent of the district). As might be expected with such demographics, Democrats outnumber Republicans by approximately 84,000 voters.

THE CANDIDATES AND THEIR CAMPAIGNS

At first glance, Melissa Hart's profile does not appear to be particularly suited to the heavily unionized and strongly Democratic Fourth District. A single, thirty-eight-year-old state senator with a consistently conservative, probusiness/anti-union voting record, Hart did not even live in the Fourth District prior to running for its congressional seat.

By comparison, Van Horne seemed like a perfect fit for the district. A state representative from Westmoreland County (partially located within the Fourth District), with working-class roots and a speaking style immediately recognizable to locals as "quintessentially Pittsburgh," Van Horne had developed a solid reputation for constituent service. Further, based on this reputation, Van Horne had been reelected to the state house ten times. It is a substantial understatement to say that Van Horne was, *a priori*, expected to have a much stronger showing than he did.

However, in terms of hard money contributions, Hart outraised Van Horne by a considerable margin.[1] Van Horne claims that this monetary imbalance was one of the turning points of the campaign: "It's incredible the sheer amount of money raised on the other side by her campaign, and all the associated campaigns, to define me in a way that I'm not to people who don't know me. Her $1.5 million to my $600,000, and that's not counting all the soft money and independent expenditures she had."[2]

Indeed, by the end of June Hart's fundraising had surpassed the $500,000 mark, while Van Horne was still trying to amass $100,000. By the end of November, Hart's fundraising efforts surpassed Van Horne's by more than 100 percent. The Hart campaign raised $1,729,673 (spending $1,724,048) to Van Horne's $694,704 (spending $694,846).[3]

POLITICAL PARTY ACTIVITY

The greatest discrepancy in expenditures on behalf of the candidates can be found by examining the relative roles played by the national party campaign committees, both in the form of activities coordinated with the candidates' campaigns and in soft money spending. The high profile and importance of the race, in particular to the Republicans, reflected the importance that the Fourth District could (and would) play in the partisan distribution of congressional seats.

Melissa Hart: Life of the Party

Hart had been the Republican Party's choice for this race from the beginning, with encouraging calls from the NRCC in Washington, D.C., and promises of support from several former colleagues.[4] Both Majority Leader Dick Armey and Majority Whip Tom Delay contributed the maximum $10,000 apiece to Hart's campaign, and the NRCC introduced her to scores of Washingtonians with deep pockets. This helped Hart raise more money from outside the Fourth District than from within it.[5] Moreover, the NRCC purchased television time to run four anti-Van Horne ads and nearly tripled the number of mailings sent by Hart's campaign.[6]

Much of the Republican Party activity was well coordinated with Hart's campaign;[7] the NRCC spent $66,500 in coordinated expenditures alone.[8] These expenditures can be seen most clearly in the blitzkrieg of mailings sent to encourage Hart votes. The coordinated strategy of the NRCC and Hart campaign from the beginning was to target Democrats, converting one-third of them to Hart voters. To that end, registered Republicans were sent only one piece of literature on Hart's behalf, whereas Democrats were saturated.[9]

The Hart campaign's demographic targeting was remarkably specific. Knowing that their candidate was to the right of the median voter in the district on most issues, the Republican campaign focused its efforts on persuading 60,000–64,000 moderate Democratic voters. Within this target group, male Democrats received literature focused on taxes, military spending, and "sportsman's" (or gun) rights. Female Democrats within the target group, on the other hand, received information about Hart's efforts to aid senior citizens and fight domestic abuse. Senior citizens learned about Hart's commitment to expanding drug benefits and protecting Social Security.[10]

Of course, a significant portion of the money spent by the Republican party on Hart's behalf was uncoordinated with the Hart campaign. However, some of the advertisements funded by these uncoordinated expenditures raised a fair amount of controversy during the campaign season. Watching the Fourth District race in anticipation of the first soft money ads was much like watching a staring match: Everyone was waiting to see who would blink first. Somewhat predictably, it was the DCCC. In an attempt to prop up their lagging candidate, on September 17 the DCCC ran an ad attacking Hart on education, claiming that she voted against reducing classroom sizes and tightened school security and that she favors abolishing the Department of Education.[11] Hart quickly responded by holding a press conference in which she called for a ban on soft money funded ads in the race.[12] In another press conference, Hart stated, "I invite Representative Van Horne to attend a joint press conference with me to call on both parties, and any other sympathetic supporters, to participate in a Joint Soft Money Ceasefire for the duration of the campaign. It is time we worked to end the cynicism that is rampant among Americans."[13]

In a debate on September 19, Van Horne responded that the ads were out of his control—that they were being funded by the DCCC. Hart responded by arguing that if Van Horne could not control the ads run on his behalf, he lacked the political weight within his party to be an effective member of Congress.[14] Yet even the chairman of the NRCC, Tom Davis (R-Va.), said that Hart also would not be allowed to influence outside activity in the contest. Davis stated that, "She doesn't have any say about what we do in her race. . . . We have to protect our candidate whether she likes it or not."[15] Given the size of the ad campaign that followed, the NRCC was clearly willing to go to a great expense to protect and support its candidate.

The NRCC's ads started September 20, attacking Van Horne and accusing him of voting to raise state income, sales, and even pizza taxes.[16] The Van Horne campaign quickly accused Hart of hypocrisy, which, not surprisingly, the Hart campaign denied.

Terry Van Horne: Not Invited to the Party

Welcome or not, Hart's party support starkly contrasts the paucity of help that the Democratic Party provided Van Horne. The DCCC had supported one of Van Horne's rivals, Matt Mangino, during the primary and was therefore less enthusiastic toward its second choice during the fall campaign.[17]

Van Horne has never been a party favorite. A self-described independent, he has a history of being a maverick as a state representative in Harrisburg. He has gone against the Democratic grain several times on high-profile issues, such as abortion, and he has defied his leadership on a number of issues including support for house speaker candidates. As a result, the state house Democratic leaders stripped Van Horne of his membership on the prestigious Appropriations Committee.

The Pennsylvania Democrats' lack of enthusiasm for Van Horne may have led to the national party's weak involvement. For example, while the NRCC supplemented the Hart campaign with $66,500 in coordinated expenditures, the DCCC provided less than half that amount ($27,305), even knowing its candidate was clearly losing the hard money race.[18] Indeed, Van Horne complained that, "the national party never really kicked in any hard cash. With the Democratic Congressional Campaign Committee, you have to prove yourself all the time to them. You do what they say, and then they put more hoops in front of you."[19]

Another reason for Van Horne's lackluster support and uninspiring fundraising capacity can be traced to the NRCC. Early in April 2000, just after Van Horne became the official Democratic nominee, the NRCC issued a press release that resurrected an old story about Van Horne using a racial slur to describe a colleague, state representative Dwight Evans.[20] Van Horne argued that he was merely repeating another's comment when the word was used. Indeed, Van Horne publicly apologized at the time and was forgiven by Evans. Yet J. J. Balaban, Van Horne's campaign manager, stated that the NRCC's press release "became a big deal in Washington."[21] Certainly it seems that the practical effect of the NRCC's "reminder" was to dehydrate fundraising from traditional liberal sources outside the district.[22] "The ballots weren't even dry, and they attacked me as something I am not," Van Horne protested. "They used this issue in Washington to poison fundraising for me."[23] Fair or not, the story gave most political observers outside western Pennsylvania a powerfully negative first impression of Van Horne. Although the early press release may not have been the GOP's most consequential action in the Fourth District race, it was a harbinger of the television advertising deluge to come.

GETTING YOUR MONEY'S WORTH? CAMPAIGN ADVERTISING IN THE FOURTH DISTRICT

Buying television time has become the great money pit in modern American politics.[24] Accordingly, a great deal of scholarly controversy has surrounded the nature of political television advertising, particularly negative political ads. Although virtually all candidates express distaste for attack advertising, particularly their opposition's, conventional wisdom among pundits and political professionals holds that negative ads work. However, the extant research on political communication points to a different conclusion: On balance, negative ads are no more effective than positive ads.[25] The evidence suggests that an attack ad may succeed in raising voter concerns about the ad's target, but the effect often "boomerangs," engendering aversion toward the sponsor of the ad as well.[26] There is also evidence that voters are much more turned off by ads that attack an opponent's personal character than by ads designed to contrast elements of the candidates' voting records or policy preferences.[27] Of course, candidates increasingly attempt to avoid the brunt of the boomerang by only sponsoring positive ads, leaving parties and interest groups to do the dirty work.

As discussed previously, parties and interest groups are often eager to "take up their hatchets," even when the official campaign organization asks them not to. In the Fourth District, whether the efforts were coordinated or not, this pattern of positive campaigning on the part of the official campaign organizations, coupled with negative attacks by party organizations and others, held during the 2000 contest, with the Democrat being under attack far more than the Republican.

Considering first the ads sponsored by the candidates themselves, we found that Hart aired six ads, or twice as many as Van Horne.[28] Hart aired both the first and last ads of the campaign. Importantly, all of Hart's ads were positive, focusing on her background, achievements, and proposals.[29] By contrast, Van Horne only issued three ads during the course of the campaign. All three of his ads were in response to earlier Hart ads and seemed defensive, and two of the three (the first and the last) directly attacked Hart.[30]

When taking into account the ads that were not directly sponsored by the Hart or Van Horne campaigns, the picture changes dramatically. Whereas the DCCC issued two ads contrasting Hart's and Van Horne's voting records on education and health care issues, the NRCC ran four negative ads, three of them personal and sardonic. One NRCC ad, which accused Van Horne of defaulting on a small business loan, was pulled by some stations for its harsh tone and questionable validity.[31] Furthermore, in the last weeks of the campaign, the Chamber of Commerce also began running decidedly negative ads opposing Van Horne.

This disparity between the two candidates in television ads was duplicated in the mailings sent on behalf of the candidates. The NRCC's full-color, glossy, printed, mailed ads may have been quite effective. For example, the Republicans distributed a brochure calling attention to the fact that the executive director of the DCCC declared that the Democrats would "rip [Hart's] head off on television." In other mailed brochures, the Republicans addressed what they presented as Van Horne's questionable business practices as well as the fact that as a state representative, Van Horne voted to "tax the pizza man." After totaling all the mail in this race from the national and state parties, as well as outside groups, twenty-two pieces of literature were distributed on Hart's behalf; only eight pieces of literature supported Van Horne.

Tables 11.1 and 11.2, examined jointly, provide a sense of outside group participation in the Fourth District.[32]

Table 11.1. The Air War: Most Active Organizations' Collected Ad Buy Data in the Pennsylvania Fourth Congressional District Race

Type	*Organization*	*TV*	*Radio*	*Total Ad Buy $*	*CMAG TV*
Democratic Allies					
Candidates	Van Horne for Congress	N/A	$0	**$0**	$214,772
Political Parties	Pennsylvania Democratic Party	$471,875	$0	**$471,875**	$950,646
Interest Groups	AFL-CIO	$0	$0	**$0**	$ 23,835
Republican Allies					
Candidates	Hart for Congress	N/A	$0	**$0**	$641,122
Political Parties	Republican State Committee of Pennsylvania	$123,550	$0	**$123,550**	$0
	NRCC	$110,315	$0	**$110,315**	$258,192
	NRSC	$0	$0	**$0**	$263,936

Source: Election Advocacy and *Campaign Media Analysis Group* databases.
Notes: See appendix B for a more detailed explanation of the data. This table is not intended to portray comprehensive organization spending in the PA 4 race. A more complete picture can be obtained by examining this table together with table 11.2

Table 11.2. The Ground War: Most Active Organizations Observed Mail Activity in the Pennsylvania Fourth Congressional District Race

Type	*Organization*	*Total Unique Mail Pieces*
Democratic Allies		
Candidates	Van Horne for Congress	1
Interest Groups	AFL-CIO	2
	Pennsylvania State Education Association	1
	United Food and Commercial Workers International Union	1
	United Steelworkers of America	1
	Western Pennsylvania Laborers' Political Action Fund	1
Republican Allies		
Candidates	People with Hart	1
Political Parties	Republican Federal Committee of PA–Victory 2000	8
	National Republican Congressional Committee	3
	Republican State Committee of Pennsylvania	2
Interest Groups	National Federation of Independent Business	3
	National Rifle Association	2
	Christian Coalition	1
	National Right to Life PAC	1
	Republican Majority Issues Committee	1
	SBA List Candidate Fund	1
Nonpartisan		
Interest Groups	AARP	1

Source: Election Advocacy database.
Notes: See appendix B for a more detailed explanation of the data. Totals exclude all presidential data. Data include all ad campaigns that mentioned any PA 4 candidate, including those ads that simultaneously mentioned any presidential candidate. This table is not intended to represent comprehensive organization activity in the PA 4 race. A more complete picture can be obtained by examining this table and table 11.1 together.

CONCLUSION

One thing is clear from observing Pennsylvania's Fourth District race in 2000: Outside money greatly expanded the funding gulf between the two candidates. Melissa Hart was much more successful in attracting hard money contributions than Terry Van Horne was. In fact, the disparity in outside support meant that the Hart campaign could use both print and broadcast media to define its candidate in a manner consistent with the desires of Fourth District voters (i.e., more to the center than her voting record in the Pennsylvania senate would otherwise indicate)[33] instead of devoting its resources to attacking the opposition. The task of defining the opposition was left to the NRCC, the Chamber of Commerce, and a number of other groups. These groups used their extensive resources to attack Van Horne and cast a dark shadow over both voters' and donors' perceptions of the Democratic candidate.

Given its relative lack of party and interest group support, the Van Horne campaign, on the other hand, found itself in the position of trying to define its candidate as well as the opposing candidate. In so doing, the campaign validated the old cliché "jack of all trades, but master of none." Public opinion data demonstrate that the Van Horne campaign was not successful at positively defining its candidate or at negatively defining Hart. Although the DCCC offered Van Horne some support, it was too minimal to bridge the funding gulf. Furthermore, the vast majority of the traditional Democratic interest groups that were active in other races (e.g., Planned Parenthood, Handgun Control Inc., Emily's List, League of Conservation Voters, Sierra Club) stayed out of the Fourth District contest, and new groups, such as the NAACP National Voter Fund, which had been influential in helping Democrats in other contests, stayed away from Van Horne as well.

What impact did the ad war have on the campaign? Given the advantages Hart enjoyed in fundraising and media attention, it is impossible to determine whether Van Horne could have won this race with different ads. But the scholarly findings on ad effectiveness lead us to believe that Van Horne did not help himself with his "too little, too late, too negative" ad strategy—especially given the DCCC's failure to match the NRCC advertising and the paucity of television advertising by labor unions, teachers' organizations, or other Democrat-friendly groups that were expected to show much stronger support for Van Horne than they did.

Public opinion tracking polls point to a similar conclusion.[34] One week prior to the election, three times as many voters had heard of Hart as had heard of Van Horne.[35] This discrepancy indicates the difference in visibility between the two candidates. "This race was lost on television," said J. J. Balaban, Van Horne's communications director. "Hart ran well everywhere because TV communicates everywhere, and she was on TV far more than Van Horne."[36]

More strikingly, as the trend lines in figures 11.1 and 11.2 display, the percentage of voters who expressed a favorable impression of Hart became greater as the campaign progressed, with Hart's strongest showing coming as the campaign was winding to a close: 55 percent favorable to 25 percent unfavorable. By contrast, Van Horne began the campaign with more voters expressing a favorable impression of him than an unfavorable one, but that ratio reversed itself in the second week of October, and Van Horne's "favorables" never exceeded his "unfavorables" again.

Again, we cannot directly attribute these poll numbers or Van Horne's poor showing on November 7 to his less-sophisticated and under-armed ad war. But at least some of Hart's overwhelming victory can be ascribed to her ad war advantages in both strategy and artillery. Voters seemed to respond positively to Hart's positive ads, while Van Horne's negative ads may have boomeranged. Moreover, voters did not seem to punish Hart for the NRCC and Chamber of Commerce air raids on Van Horne. This negativity appears to have taken its toll on attitudes toward Van Horne because more voters felt unfavorable toward him as the campaign progressed.

Figure 11.1. Public Perceptions of Hart in the 2000 Pennsylvania Fourth District Campaign

Percent of Respondents

60
50
40
30
20
10
0

Hart Favorable
Hart Unfavorable

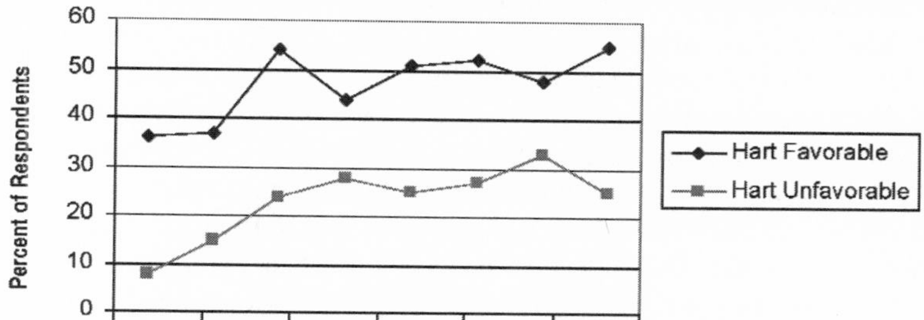

	Oct 99	May 00	27 Sep	11 Oct	16 Oct	29 Oct
Hart Favorable	36	37	44	51	52	55
Hart Unfavorable	8	15	28	25	27	25

Poll Dates, 1999-2000

Source: Neil Newhouse, Public Opinion Strategies, data provided to Christian Marchant, People with Hart, 29 October 2000.
Note: N = 350 (Likely Voters in PA-4).

Figure 11.2. Public Perceptions of Van Horne in the 2000 Pennsylvania Fourth District Campaign

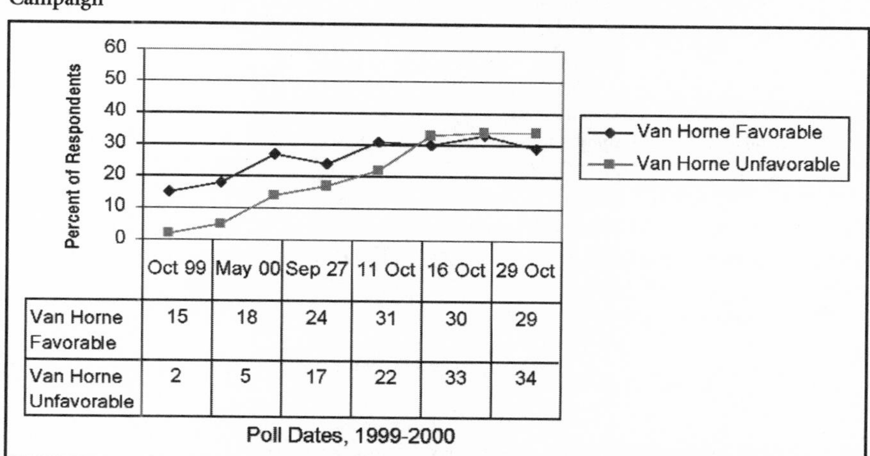

	Oct 99	May 00	Sep 27	11 Oct	16 Oct	29 Oct
Van Horne Favorable	15	18	24	31	30	29
Van Horne Unfavorable	2	5	17	22	33	34

Source: Neil Newhouse, Public Opinion Strategies, data provided to Christian Marchant, People with Hart, 29 October 2000.
Note: N = 350 (Likely Voters in PA-4).

Finally, Hart probably benefited from the targeted postal war. The Hart campaign and its allies attempted to deliver a specific message to a specific group of voters to convince them that Hart, if elected, would address their concerns in Washington, D.C. On the other hand, the Van Horne campaign strategy, to "simply hold on to the Democrats," did not have the resources to counter effectively with a sophisticated, targeted mail campaign of their own.[37]

How did a conservative "carpetbagger" handily defeat a hometown boy with solid pro-union credentials in a Democratic district? Simply, Hart raised and spent much more money than her Democratic opponent.[38] Further, the national parties grossly accentuated this funding gap: The NRCC threw its full support behind Hart, while the DCCC was, for a variety of reasons, much less resounding in its support of Van Horne.[39] This disparity in both hard and soft money expenditures allowed the Hart campaign to "get out in front" with its message early on and effectively negate the Democrat's message before it was even delivered.[40] Outside support also allowed the Hart campaign to run a positive, candidate-centered race, leaving the mudslinging to its outside supporters while the Van Horne campaign was left to pursue both of these tasks itself.

NOTES

1. "Total Raised and Spent: 2000 Pennsylvania District 4," *Center for Responsible Politics*, <www.opensecrets.org/2000elect/dist_total/PA04.html>, 2000 [accessed 18 December 2000].

2. According to Jon Delano, Van Horne's "'stream of consciousness' manner of talking can leave some listeners liking the guy for his openness but wondering exactly what he said," Jon Delano, "Game, Set, Match," *Pittsburgh* (December 2000): 52–56, 187.

3. "Total Raised and Spent: 2000 Pennsylvania District 4."

4. Christian Marchant, People with Hart, interview by Christopher Carman, Pittsburgh, Pennsylvania, 14 December 2000.

5. "Total Raised and Spent: 2000 Pennsylvania District 4."

6. Marchant, interview by Carman.

7. Ibid.

8. Federal Election Commission (FEC), "Committees Who Gave to This Candidate," <herndon1.sdrdc.com/cgi-bin/can_give/1999_HOPA04154>, 2000 [accessed 22 December 2000].

9. Marchant, interview by Carman.

10. Ibid.

11. Dennis B. Roddy, "Hart, Van Horne Debate 'Soft Money,'" *Pittsburgh Post-Gazette*, 20 September 2000, final edition.

12. Dennis B. Roddy, "Hart Pounds Van Horne's 'Soft' Spots," *Pittsburgh Post-Gazette*, 19 September 2000, final edition; Sandra Basu, "Parties Ratchet Up Pressure in Pa.'s 4th District," *Washington Post Online*, <www.washingtonpost.com>, 1 November 2000 [accessed 2 November 2000].

13. Rachel Van Dongen, "The Reform Network: McCain on the Air," *Roll Call Online*, <www.rollcall.com/pages/politics/00/09/pol0928a.html>, 28 September 2000 [accessed 29 September 2000].

14. Ibid.

15. Ibid.

16. Dennis B. Roddy, "Anti-Van Horne Spot Follows Soft Money Debate with Hart," *Pittsburgh Post-Gazette*, 21 September 2000, final edition.

17. Karin Johanson, DCCC, interview by David B. Magleby, Washington, D.C., 20 November 2000; see also Tom Squitieri, "House Race 'The Only One That Has People Excited," *USA Today*, 3 April 2000, first edition.

18. FEC, "Committees Who Gave to This Candidate."

19. Van Horne, quoted in Delano, "Game, Set, Match," 54.

20. Robert Schlesinger, "Both Parties Home in on Western Pennsylvania District," *Voter.com*, <www.voter.com/news/article/0,1175,2-15161.html>, 1 November 2000 [accessed 2 November 2000].

21. J. J. Balaban, Van Horne for Congress, telephone interview by Christopher Carman, 16 May 2001.

22. Tony Norman, "A Race to Play the Race Card," *Pittsburgh Post-Gazette*, 11 April 2000, sooner edition.

23. Van Horne, quoted in Delano, "Game, Set, Match," 56.

24. Gary C. Jacobson, *The Politics of Congressional Elections*, 4th ed. (New York: Longman, 1997).

25. E.g., Richard R. Lau, Lee Sigelman, Caroline Heldman, and Paul Babbitt, "The Effects of Negative Political Advertisements: A Meta-Analytic Assessment," *American Political Science Review* 93, no. 4 (1999): 851–76.

26. Ibid.

27. For example, see Kathleen Hall Jamieson, *Everything You Think You Know About Politics . . . and Why You're Wrong* (New York: Basic Books, 2000).

28. Unfortunately, due to the overall lack of cooperation by Pittsburgh media outlets, we are forced to frame our discussion in terms of overall numbers of ads, as opposed to the preferred "ad buy" data.

29. Hart's first ad focused on her familial coal-mining roots; the rest of the ads discussed Hart's record of achievement and support for tax reduction, a prescription drug benefit, an anti-pornography bill, Social Security, and education.

30. Van Horne's first ad accused Hart of taking money from drug companies, and his final ad complained about her distorting his record.

31. "Two TV Stations Pull GOP Ad," *Pittsburgh Post-Gazette*, 14 October 2000, sooner edition.

32. Table 11.2 provides a clearer picture of the range, magnitude, and skewness of outside participation in the Fourth District race. In table 11.1 it appears that, for unclear reasons, media outlets in Pittsburgh were less cooperative than outlets in their media markets in providing ad but data. The little information we did gather was quite difficult to come by. Further, our guess is that the CMAG data do not reflect fully the magnitude of the as buys in the Fourth District race. For example, the CMAG data do not show the Chamber of Commerce's television ad buys made to support Hart.

33. Schlesinger, "Both Parties Home in on Western Pennsylvania District."

34. The bulk of our public opinion data was supplied by the Hart campaign's internal polls, but these polls were conducted by a reputable national polling firm and utilized districtwide random samples of the voting population.

35. Data collected by Neil Newhouse, Public Opinion Strategies, data provided to Christian Marchant, People with Hart, 29 October 2000.

36. Quoted in Delano, "Game, Set, Match," 52–56, 187.

37. Balaban, telephone interview by Carman.

38. Bernadette Budde, Business-Industry Political Action Committee (BIPAC), interview by David B. Magleby, Washington, D.C., 10 November 2000.

39. See Van Dongen, "Reform Network: McCain on the Air"; Marchant, interview by Carman; and Johanson, interview by Magleby.

40. Marchant, interview by Carman.

12

The 2000 Washington Second Congressional District Race

Todd Donovan and Charles Morrow

Washington's Second Congressional District lies between the North Cascade mountain range and the Puget Sound. The Canadian border defines the northern end of the district. In 2000, Democrat Rick Larsen defeated Republican John Koster, with 50 percent of the vote compared to Koster's 46 percent. All totaled, the two candidates were outspent by parties and interest groups, with total spending reaching an estimated $6 million.

Because it was an open seat with a recent history of close races, both parties believed they had an opportunity to win in 2000. Democrats had held the district for forty years, but Jack Metcalf (R) won with 55 percent of the vote when it became an open seat in 1994. He was narrowly reelected in 1996 (48.5 percent to 47.8 percent), won again in 1998 with 55 percent, and then announced that he would not seek reelection in 2000.[1]

What made this a $6 million seat in 2000? Spending was driven by the competitiveness of the district, competition in the Seattle media market for scarce television time, candidates with polarized positions on "hot-button" issues, and a nationwide dearth of close House races that parties and outside groups could expect to influence. These four factors rarely intersect as they did here in 2000. This chapter documents where the "outside" money came from and how it was spent and discusses the potential impact of outside spending.

INSIDE THE SECOND DISTRICT

The Second District is 94 percent white and has a median income of $31,500. Almost 60 percent of its residents live in urban places.[2] Its major metropolitan areas, Bellingham and Everett, are among the fastest growing in the United States.

Bellingham and the San Juan Islands contain the district's most left-of-center voters; Nader received 11 percent of the vote in San Juan County and 7 percent in the city of Bellingham. Nearly half of the district's voters live in Everett and the north Snohomish County area. A strong labor presence makes Snohomish the most solidly Democratic part of the Second District.

The balance of the district includes several small and midsized towns. Some of these places still depend on agriculture and timber, but many are growing as they house commuters working in the Seattle area. These outlying communities—and the military personnel and retirees concentrated in Island County—typically provide solid support for Republicans.

These demographics create a district in which the major parties are virtually at parity. Conservative Republicans and liberal Democrats are elected from the same state house district in the same election (two members are elected per district).[3] The balance between parties also makes the district competitive for candidates who can paint themselves as being near the political center. A candidate from the more extreme wing of either party might also be competitive if he or she could out-mobilize an opponent. In federal elections, the Second District voted pluralities of 47 to 39 percent for Clinton in 1996, and 39 to 33 percent for Clinton in 1992. Although the previous incumbent, Metcalf, maintained a fairly conservative voting record, he broke ranks with his party on enough labor, environmental, and social issues to win reelection twice. In 1996 he squeaked back in with an 1,800-vote margin.

THE CANDIDATES AND THEIR CAMPAIGNS

Given the 1996 margin and Metcalf's early announcement of his retirement,[4] it is surprising that there was no competition in the 2000 primary. This belies the fact that multiple challengers came forward in each party. Fundraising success, rather than the voter primary, narrowed the field to one candidate in each party; the only candidates remaining by the time of the September primary were Larsen and Koster. They both secured early backing from their parties' key contributors and national congressional campaign committees.

On the Republican side, both John Koster and Barry Sehlin established finance committees, but contributions to both were constrained by fear that a divisive GOP primary would leave the eventual nominee weakened.[5] Sehlin made his candidacy known early in 1999, and handicappers in both parties thought he would be a formidable candidate. A former base commander of Whidbey Naval Air Station and an influential state house Budget Committee chair, he was in the moderate wing of the state GOP. He served on the same aircraft carrier as John McCain, and McCain appeared at a fundraiser for Sehlin in late 1999.[6] Sehlin had raised more than Koster by the end of 1999 and had collected $140,000 by April 2000. Neither candidate had much in the bank at this point, however.[7] Sehlin concluded that he could not raise enough money from outside the district to remain a viable candidate.[8] After "having conversations with various people," he decided that Koster would not withdraw and that neither candidate could raise sufficient money for the general election if they fought each other through the primary.[9] Sehlin withdrew in late April.

Koster, a three-term state representative and dairy farmer, had positions on some social issues that were probably more conservative than the median voter's preference. Koster declared his candidacy in December 1999 and secured endorsements from GOP conservatives, including Tom Delay and Steve Largent.[10] In March 2000 he distinguished himself with an anti-abortion fundraising appeal. Comments from these letters later became content for ads used against him by Larsen and the Democratic Party.[11] Delay traveled to the district to raise money for Koster in April and gave him a $10,000 check from the National Republican Congressional Committee (NRCC).[12] Even with Sehlin gone, Koster had raised only $300,000 by July 2000.[13] He eventually raised $1,118,046.[14]

A Snohomish County council president, Larsen announced his candidacy in May 1999 and had raised $280,000 by the end of 1999. He had collected over $700,000 by July 2000.[15] In mid-1999, other Democrats (state Representative Jeff Morris and sportscaster Tony Ventrella) suggested themselves as possible candidates, but neither could raise much money from outside the district. Morris and Larsen each secured endorsements from different labor groups in 1999. These local and trade-based groups meet as a single statewide group (the State Labor Council, AFL-CIO) to endorse candidates. Morris withdrew after Larsen secured enough votes to ensure that he would win the Council's endorsement. Morris noted that "labor money flows as a block to the [state Council] endorsed candidate . . . since federal labor PACs follow [the state Council endorsement], it's worth over $200,000."[16] Larsen's early fundraising prowess was also enhanced when the Democratic Congressional Campaign Committee (DCCC) threw its support his way. He traveled to Washington, D.C., to meet with DCCC officials in April 1999 and had what he described as "a very encouraging meeting."[17] The DCCC featured Larsen at a television news conference in December, and Patrick Kennedy and Dick Gephart visited Seattle to raise money for Larsen and other Democrats in February 2000.[18] Kennedy visited the Second District again on another fundraising trip for Larsen in April.[19] In the end, Larsen had raised nearly $1.6 million.[20]

Although the real competition was between the two major-party candidates, the Second District's Libertarian and Natural Law candidates drew 12,000 votes in 2000 (4 percent), nearly the same amount as Larsen's victory margin. Neither minor candidate conducted any visible campaign, and there is no record that either raised or spent money.[21] Given their record of support in the district, minor candidates add an additional element of uncertainty to many Second District contests.

Neither Larsen nor Koster began serious advertising until after the September primary. Koster mailed one pre-primary piece and ran one radio ad. Other than this, each campaign was largely silent until mid-October, when the "air wars" heated up. Table 12.1 provides an estimate of media spending in this race. Data are from public records we obtained at television and radio stations in the area and from interviews with campaign staff.[22] We found that Larsen spent about $573,000 of the $1,584,392 he raised (36 percent) on television, while Koster spent about 40 percent of his $1,118,046 on television (these figures are purchases at the station and do not include production costs and other fees).

Table 12.1 also compares candidate spending to party and interest group spending. Both candidates were outspent on television by large margins by their respective parties. We must stress that our data for noncandidate media spending in table 12.1 probably underestimate party purchases. Station

Table 12.1. The Air War: Estimated Media Spending in Washington's Second Congressional District, 2000

Type	*Organization*	*TV*	*Radio*	*Total Ad Buy $*
Democratic Allies				
Candidate	Citizens to Elect Rick Larsen	$ 573,000	$ 20,000	$ 593,000
Political Party	Dem. Congressional Campaign Committee	$ 70,000	$0	$ 70,000
	Washington State Dem. Party	$1,500,000	$ 20,000	$1,520,000
Interest Groups	Sierra Club	$ 43,000	$0	$ 43,000
	National Education Assoc.	$0	$ 30,000	$ 30,000
	Natl. Committee to Protect Social Security	$0	$ 2,000	$ 2,000
Republican Allies				
Candidate	Koster for Congress	$ 441,000	$ 12,000	$ 453,000
Political Party	Natl. Republican Campaign Committee	$ 66,000	$ 10,000	$ 76,000
	Republican State Committee of Washington	$ 700,000	$0	$ 700,000
Interest Groups	US Chamber of Commerce	$ 250,000	$0	$ 250,000
	Building Assoc. of Washington	$0	$ 40,000	$ 40,000
	National Right to Life PAC	$0	$ 5,000	$ 5,000
	National Rifle Assoc. PVF	$ 2,500	$ 2,500	
	Traditional Values Coalition	$ 1,500	$ 1,500	
Totals		**$3,643,000**	**$ 143,000**	**$3,786,000**

Source: Public files of purchase records in offices of all U.S. cable, all U.S. broadcast television, and selected U.S. radio stations that reach the Second Congressional District in Washington.

Notes: Table lists spending by groups airing Larsen or Koster ads. State party television money went to many races, but purchase records do not always indicate which candidates will benefit from the ad purchase. We estimate the proportion spent on this race from interviews and observations of ad frequency.

KOMO, which sold $9.2 million in political ads in 2000, would not provide us with information about the value of purchases made by parties and groups.[23]

Although we have no evidence of direct coordination between candidate, party, and/or groups, we found substantial overlap in the content and appearance of ads purchased by these different actors. Whether coordinated or not, candidate, party, and group campaigns were often structured on identical themes and issues. In one of Larsen's more heavily played television ads, for example, a narrator attacked Koster's record on abortion rights and suggested that Koster would limit access to birth control. Images from that ad also appeared in a Democratic Party mailer and in one of Larsen's mass-mailed advertisements attacking Koster on reproductive choice. As we note below, parts of Democratic Party mailings and Larsen campaign mailers attacking Koster on abortion were identical.

Koster's first television ad was biographical, and his second characterized Larsen as a professional lobbyist. The lobbyist attack was seen as a response to Larsen's abortion attack and was echoed in another anti-Larsen television ad funded by the Republican Party.[24] Like Larsen, Koster benefited from substantial party-funded purchases that bolstered the candidate's presence on television.

Larsen's fundraising advantage meant that he could outspend Koster in all forms of communication. Figure 12.1 displays campaign activity funded directly by the candidates' campaign committees. Larsen's campaign was more active in all media, producing more radio ads (4–3), television ads (3–2), and mailings (14–8) than Koster. Information collected at radio stations also showed that Larsen outspent Koster in radio ads. Figure 12.2 illustrates that each candidates' combined ad production in television and mail was exceeded by party organizations and/or interest groups. Figure 12.2 masks the fact that the majority of party and group campaign activity benefited the eventual winner, Larsen. We discuss this below.

Figure 12.1. Candidate Campaign Activity, Washington Second Congressional District, 2000

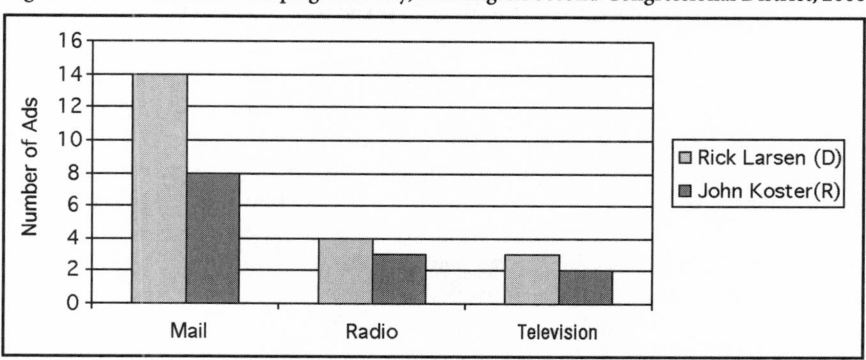

Source: Election Advocacy database.

Figure 12.2. Group, Party, and Candidate Campaign Activity, Washington Second Congressional District, 2000

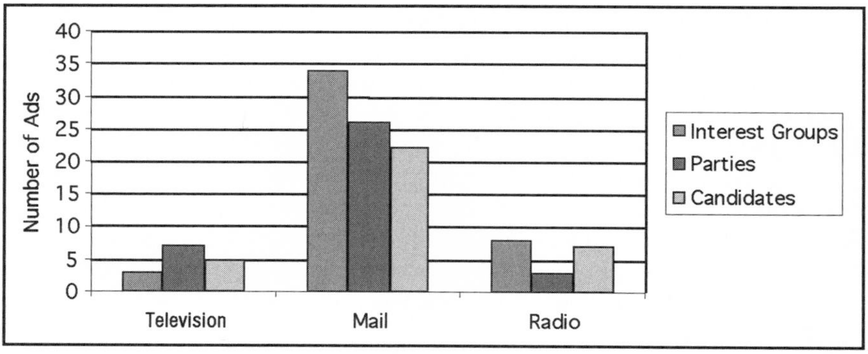

Number of Ads
40
35
30
25
20
15
10
5
0
Television
Mail
Radio
Interest Groups
Parties
Candidates

Source: Election Advocacy database.

POLITICAL PARTY CONTRIBUTIONS

The Air War

In the 2000 election cycle, the Republican and Democratic national committees transferred over $22 million to Washington State, about 72 percent of which was soft money.[25] These transfers, listed in table 12.2, reflect that both parties perceived the outcome of the state's presidential and Senate contests to be uncertain.[26]

Most of this money was probably directed at the presidential election, but the Second District race also generated substantial party spending on television. A DCCC official reported that nearly all of its $2.8 million in federal and nonfederal transfers to Washington went toward the Second.[27] Democrats used two in-state bank accounts to spend this money (the Washington State Democratic Central Committee, WSDCC, and Washington State Democratic Party, WSDP), as did Republicans (the Republican State Committee of Washington, RSCW, and Washington State Republican Party, WSRP).

Party spending boosted two Seattle stations into the top ten in political ad dollars received nationally. The top Seattle stations collected nearly $30 million in revenue from political ads during the 2000 campaign, with over 30,000 political spots broadcast.[28] Some stations quadrupled their charges for political ads between August and late October, charging as much as $4,000 per thirty-second spot as many groups, party committees, and candidates competed for airtime.[29]

The RSCW ran three Second Congressional District television ads: two attacking Larsen and one promoting Koster. The attacks emphasized that Larsen had served as a lobbyist and had voted to increase his salary.[30] They also claimed Larsen would raise taxes. The RSCW bought $2.2 million of time in the area to pay for these attacks and to fund two presidential election ads and other GOP ads.

Table 12.2. Party Committee Transfers to Washington State as of 27 November 2000

Committee	*Amount*
Democratic	
Democratic National Committee (federal)	$ 1,707,968
Democratic National Committee (nonfederal)	$ 4,550,121
Democratic National Senatorial Committee (federal)	$ 359,730
Democratic National Senatorial Committee (nonfederal)	$ 828,740
Democratic National Congressional Committee (federal)	$ 833,970
Democratic National Congressional Committee (nonfederal)	$ 1,945,930
Democratic transfers	**$10,226,459**
Republican	
Republican National Committee (federal)	$ 1,746,816
Republican National Committee (nonfederal)	$ 4,874,832
Republican National Senatorial Committee (federal)	$ 782,200
Republican National Senatorial Committee (nonfederal)	$ 1,742,900
Republican National Congressional Committee (federal)	$ 850,560
Republican National Congressional Committee (nonfederal)	$ 1,781,401
Republican transfers	**$11,778,709**
Total transferred to Washington State	**$22,005,168**

Source: Federal Election Commission, press release, <www.fec.gov/press/pty00text.htm>, 3 November 2000 and <fecweb1.fec.gov/press/nattostate20-00.htm> [accessed 28 January 2001].

At stations that provided access to records, we found that the WSDP bought $1.5 million in ads, running three ads against Koster: one attacking his positions on reproductive rights, one attacking his positions on education, and one comparing Larsen and Koster. All of the ads echoed the main themes of Larsen's television ads.

Although most television time was bought via the party's state-based checking accounts, national committees made some smaller direct purchases of air time. The DCCC paid for one ad against Koster that stressed reproductive rights, and the NRCC ran two ads against Larsen.[31]

Given the uncertainty about how bulk-purchase party ad buys are linked to ads for specific candidates and the fact that we did not have access to KOMO's records, it is difficult to know precisely how much the parties spent on television in this race. Given interviews and our observations of spending records, we estimate that Republicans spent at least $700,000, and Democrats at least twice that, for their respective candidates. Most of this was paid for with soft money transferred to the state parties from the DCCC and NRCC. These are conservative estimates and are probably low. A DCCC official reported that it spent $2.4 million on media for the Second District, and $165,000 on mail.[32] We were unable to have an NRCC official confirm how much of the $2.6 million it transferred to the state was directed at the Second District. Logic would dictate that much of this money would follow Democratic cash to the state's most competitive seat. Whatever the actual total may have been, it appears that spending on television by both candidates was eclipsed by purchases made by parties and that Larsen benefited from more party soft money television spending than Koster did. Spending on television by both candidates was eclipsed by purchases made by their respective parties.

Compared to the resources the parties dedicated to television, relatively little was spent on radio. The WSDP made a small purchase on at least one station broadcasting to the district, but the ad could have been for another race. The NRCC bought $10,000 of radio time and ran ads attacking Larsen on taxes (one ad warned voters that Larsen was "a pickpocket," loose in the Second District).[33]

The Ground War

Again, candidate activity through the mail was rivaled, if not subsumed, by the combined totals of outside groups and parties. As with television, the parties also sent more unique mass-mailed ads than the candidates did (see figure 12.2); however, it is more difficult to estimate spending in this area. Table 12.3 lists the organizations funding mailings that either promoted or attacked a Second Congressional District candidate, the number of unique ads each sent, conservative estimates of the total volume of mail sent, and, when we could determine, the total amount spent. Mailings counted here include ads discussing campaign issues and candidates, get-out-the-vote (GOTV) mailings, and party and candidate fundraising appeals. Many of the ads showed definite thematic similarities between candidates and parties.

On the Republican side, the NRCC mass-mailed five glossy color brochures attacking Larsen's record on taxation, and the WSRP sent two promoting Koster in the Second Congressional District.[34] The NRCC's mailers attacking Larsen's tax votes were similar to Koster's own ads. Koster's campaign sent four mass-mailings, three on low-cost newsprint and one postcard. They also sent four fundraising letters that doubled as campaign material. Given the production quality of the ads we observed, the NRCC likely outspent its candidate in mailing ads.

Larsen sent nearly as many unique mailings (fourteen) as his party did (nineteen), although a number of party and candidate mailings were relatively low-volume fundraising appeals. The WSDCC funded four glossy mass mailings that attacked Koster or promoted Larsen. The WSDCC mail also echoed themes from Larsen's television, radio, and mail campaigns by praising Larsen's position on petroleum pipeline safety. These WSDCC ads (and similar Larsen radio ads) arrived five days after Koster ran a radio ad criticizing Larsen's position on pipeline regulation.[35] The WSDCC, Larsen's campaign, and interest groups also sent mass mailings attacking Koster's position on abortion. Large parts of two WSDCC mailings were indistinguishable from two ads sent by Larsen. One particular WSDCC mailer used photos, font, layout, and text that were identical to the content of an ad mailed by Larsen. The party ad and the candidate's ad both also contained

Table 12.3. The Ground War: Most Active Organizations' Observed Mail Activity in Washington's Second District Race, 2000

Type	*Organization*	*Unique ads*	*Spending*	*Total pieces mailed*
Democratic Allies				
Candidate	Citizens to Elect Rick Larsen	14		200,000
Political Party	WA State Dem. Central Committee	10	$165,000	100,000
	Dem. Cong. Campaign Committee	5		
	Natl. Com. for an Effective Congress	2		
	Local party organizations	2		1,000
Interest Groups	National Education Association	8	$218,000	125,000
	WA Labor Council/AFL-CIO	3		51,000
	NARAL	3	$ 57,478	100,000
	Planned Parenthood	3	$ 5,000	30,000
	Sierra Club	2		30,000
	Committee for a Progressive Future	2		5,000
	Others	4		
Republican Allies				
Candidate	Koster for Congress	8		120,000
Political Party	Natl. Republican Campaign Com.	6		100,000
	WA State Republican Party	2		30,000
	Local Party Organizations	1		1,000
Interest Groups	National Rifle Association	3		44,000
	Citizens for a Sound Economy	1		35,000
	National Right to Life PAC	1	$ 10,222	15,000
	Business Industry PAC	1		
	National Federation of Ind. Business	1		
	Others	1		500
Total for Both Candidates		**83**		

Source: Election Advocacy database.

identical images of a Koster fundraising letter and identical quotes from the letter stressing Koster's tough stance against abortion.

Overall, we estimate that for the Second District the parties combined spent between $2.5 and $3.7 million on television, radio, and direct mail.

INTEREST GROUP CONTRIBUTIONS

The Air War

Although parties dominated television, interest groups also made large purchases. Two interest groups made major television ad buys that attacked the candidates. The U.S. Chamber of Commerce spent $250,000 for two ads that attacked Larsen for "scaring seniors" and promoting a "big government" prescription drug plan.[36]

The Sierra Club initiated its campaign with a $250,000 buy two days after announcing that it would attack Koster.[37] Clearly, much of this went to other races. A Sierra Club official indicated that its anti-Koster ad ran primarily on cable during shows directed at "independent women voters aged 25–50 . . . in Snohomish and Whatcom County."[38] Records show that in late October the Sierra Club spent about $45,000 on cable television in the area. The National Education Association (NEA) also ran radio ads as part of its $221,568 independent expenditure campaign supporting Larsen.[39]

Only one interest group ad, from the National Committee to Protect Social Security, promoted Larsen on radio. In contrast, the largest radio buy for any party, group, or candidate was made by the Building Industry Association of Washington (BIAW) on Koster's behalf. The BIAW publicized the plight of Vicki Klein, a previously anonymous homeowner whose flood-plain zoning problem had been "ignored" by Larsen and the Snohomish Council. The BIAW also bought "tens of thousands of dollars" of airtime for two "voter education" ads and paid with corporate funds since they avoided express advocacy.[40] Some of Koster's ads also seemed to show coordination between candidate and noncandidate campaigns; just one week after the BIAW ads aired, Koster's campaign sent out a mailer featuring a quote about flood regulations from "Vicki Klein, homeowner." The National Rifle Association (NRA) and two anti-abortion groups also made small radio purchases to help Koster.

The Ground War

Interest groups dominated the mail campaign even more than parties, at least in terms of the quantity of unique communications, with Larsen being the main beneficiary. Fundraising letters discounted, ads sent by Larsen and Koster were only a fraction of what interest groups mailed. Groups sent twenty-five different ads benefiting Larsen and eight benefiting Koster (see table 12.3). The groups listed in table 12.3 are those that produced ads that made explicit reference to the candidates. Although some of these mailings were low volume, many went to at least 10,000 households.

On Larsen's side, unions sent a large volume of mail into the district. The state Labor Council/AFL-CIO and the NEA each sent its members multiple color brochures attacking Koster. Labor reported that three distinct ads (51,000 pieces) associated with the race were sent to 17,000 labor households. By mailing exclusively to union members, labor was exempt from independent expenditure disclosure requirements.[41]

The 7,000 NEA/WEA members in the Second Congressional District also received four internal communication issue mailers that noted, "Larsen is the better choice" (28,000 pieces of mail), and WEA promoted Larsen by sending members a postcard that used his campaign logo. The NEA Fund for Children and Public Education used independent expenditures to send three mailings (an estimated 40,000 pieces) to NEA members as well as a larger number of voters targeted as "education-affiliated." The NEA spent $221,568 on its independent expenditure campaign and an additional $26,540 on internal communications supporting Larsen.[42] Before sending mailings, the NEA, like other groups, conducted surveys to determine "if they could make a difference" with the spending.[43]

The Sierra Club sent mail to its members and other targeted voters. The regional political director reported that two pieces were mailed to 15,000 homes in the target audience (30,000 pieces of mail) identified in advance by telephone.[44]The League of Conservation Voters (LCV) also sent its members a voter guide recommending Larsen. The LCV sold the Sierra Club a list of thousands of local "green voters," which they had assembled from numerous environmental groups.[45]

Washington State NARAL and Planned Parenthood's state affiliate sent ads promoting Larsen and attacking Koster in relatively large volumes. NARAL mailed three multi-fold, glossy ads discussing the candidates (including an explicit "Vote for Rick Larsen" plea), as well as four other ads for higher federal offices; it reported $57,485 in independent expenditures for Larsen.[46] NARAL's 35,000–40,000 member target audience in the Second District included "women 25–49 who might vote for Nader" and "pro-choice voters." This audience was identified from phone canvasses done in the district since 1996.[47]NARAL sent about 100,000 pieces of mail dealing with the Second Congressional District race.[48] Planned Parenthood sent out three mailings to 10,000 homes, including two anti-Koster ads with explicit "Rick Larsen for Congress" pleas.[49]

Campaign for a Progressive Future sent two antigun ads against Koster, and Handgun Control sent a postcard urging a vote for Larsen.[50]

Koster's campaign also benefited from anti-Larsen mail ads sent by groups, but we observed much less activity on his behalf; few pieces were sent in large numbers. Citizens for a Sound Economy (CSE), a probusiness issue advocacy group, mailed one ad comparing Larsen's and Koster's tax records to about 35,000 homes in the Second Congressional District, targeting independent voters.[51] The National Right to Life PAC also spent $10,222 mailing a large card that urged a vote for John Koster.[52]

Other pro-Koster mailings from groups such as the National Federation of Independent Business (NFIB) and the NRA went mostly to group members. The local NRA election coordinator reported that the NRA attempted to contact "22,000 pro-gun households" by phone and doorbell.[53] It also sent out mailers, and at least two of three NRA mailings (both small postcards) were internal communications directed to members only. A third NRA letter with a brochure and "Sportsmen for Koster" bumper-stickers was addressed to "Dear Washington Hunter" and sent in larger volumes. The Christian Coalition also claimed to have mailed "thousands" of voter's guides endorsing Koster and to have distributed 125,000 guides in the district via Christian bookstores, businesses, and schools.[54]

Given the data we have from television stations, interviews, and FEC reports, we estimate that interest groups spent at least $800,000 to $1 million on this race.

CONCLUSION

It is difficult to establish how outside money affected the outcome of the Second District general election contest. Some effects of outside money are clear: Both major party nominees cultivated early, pre-primary money from their respective national party congressional campaign committees and from key party donors. The money chase, rather than a voter primary, determined who each party's nominee would be. After this, their own campaigns were eclipsed by the combined efforts of parties and interest groups who worked on their behalf. At times, "outside" money ads became nearly indistinguishable from the candidates' own ads.

Outside money was also clearly evident in pumping up the volume of the campaign generally. Households in the district were overwhelmed with mail, television, and radio ads. We found eighty-three mailings associated with the Koster-Larsen race, seventy-six additional mailings advocating presidential candidates, and another twelve GOTV mailings for these two contests: 171 distinct pieces of mail for congressional and presidential races alone. We estimate that at least 1 million pieces of mail were sent targeting the Second District race itself. Households also received large volumes of mail for other state and federal races. In the last week, some received over twelve pieces of mail per day. Letter carriers were running two-hours behind their regular schedule due to the heavy volume of campaign mail.

Based on data in table 12.1, we estimate that over $3.6 million was spent on at least fifteen different television ads for the 2000 Second District race. In contrast, we know that the parties and the Bush and Gore campaigns spent well over $17 million to show another twenty-five television ads just for the presidential contest in the Seattle area. Ten million dollars' worth of additional ads aired for Senate, governor, initiatives, and other races. Given the volume of ads in this election context, it would probably take several million dollars for a U.S. House race to register above the din of these other campaigns.

Unlike other cases discussed in this volume, there was no well-funded incumbent here, nor a candidate with an overwhelming advantage in fundraising. Thus, outside money did not necessarily bring competitiveness to the race by vastly improving either candidate's prospects. The competitiveness of the race, rather, probably attracted the money. Given the volume of campaign activity, it is difficult to assess the efficacy of outside spending efforts directed at the Second Congressional District. However, it is clear that advantages in campaign spending matter in U.S. elections, so it should not be surprising that the side with the most outside resources won a competitive open seat. But Larsen's own campaign had a financial advantage without party soft money and interest group spending, and may have won anyway. Larsen outspent Koster on television, and outside spending for Koster never erased Larsen's advantage. Pro-Larsen outside groups also seem to have outspent pro-Koster groups in mail advertisements.

Of course, this does not mean that this spending did not matter. Interviews with consultants suggest that several interest groups (NARAL, Planned Parenthood, Sierra Club, and NEA) had target audiences (independent voting women and new voters) that overlapped substantially. The cumulative effect of their messages might have assisted Larsen by mobilizing these voters. A Labor official also noted that previous post-election studies found person-to-person contacts (from coworkers) more efficacious than other campaign activities. Local labor groups made substantial efforts leafleting near work sites and believed that this was more effective than television or mail. On Koster's side, voter mobilization may have been weaker. The Christian Coalition director, for example, claimed to be disappointed by the inability to mobilize voters.

Beyond these questions of the marginal advantages that outside money might have provided either candidate, there are larger questions about the effects of this spending. There is no smoking gun to show that outside money determined who won this race, but it clearly affected what the campaign looked like. Voters heard a message that was transmitted more by parties and groups than by candidates. This raises questions about who ultimately shaped the messages that voters heard. We observed candidates employing campaign messages only after they were first broadcast in outside-group or party ads, and we also observed groups and parties using themes first broadcast in candidate ads. It is not at all clear that the candidates generally led in this game of setting campaign messages. It may be that one of the larger but subtle effects of outside spending is that candidate control over messages is diminished. We leave it to others to test for this effect and to establish if such an effect is good or bad.

NOTES

1. Before 1994 the District had been Democratic since 1940, when future U.S. Senator Henry "Scoop" Jackson won the seat.

2. Michael Barone and Grant Ujifusa, *Almanac of American Politics* (Washington, D.C.: National Journal, 2000).

3. John Koster (Thirty-ninth District, Snohomish County) was one of the more conservative Republicans in the state house, while Hans Dunshee (Thirty-ninth District, Snohomish County) is one of the state's more liberal Democrats. They were elected at the same time. Barry Sehlin is considered a moderate house Republican (Tenth District Island County). Kelli Linville (Forty-second District, Whatcom County) is one of the more conservative Democrats in the legislature, while her Forty-second District counterpart Doug Erikson is seen by some as being a relatively moderate Republican. State house winners

from inside the Second Congressional District in 2000, including incumbents such as Linville (D), Sehlin (R), and Dunshee (D), were elected with only 50 percent of the vote or less.

4. Before the 1998 campaign, Metcalf announced that he would only seek three terms in the U.S. House, thus setting 2000 as a retirement date.

5. David Postman, "One Drops Out of Race to Replace Metcalf," *Seattle Times*, 21 April 2000, local section.

6. Joel Connelly, "Koster Joins Race to Succeed Jack Metcalf," *Seattle Post-Intelligencer*, 7 December 1999, local section.

7. "Federal Candidates Information Page," *FEC Info.com*, <www.fecinfo.com/fecinfo/_states.htm>, [accessed 10 December 2000].

8. Joel Connelly, "Potomac Watch: Campaign Donors Play Big Role in Picking Candidates," *Seattle Post-Intelligencer*, 3 July 2000, local section.

9. Barry Sehlin, telephone interview by Todd Donovan, 18 January 2001.

10. Joel Connelly, "Potomac Watch: In Koster, GOP Has Uncompromising Candidate," *Seattle Post-Intelligencer*, 15 May 2000, national section; and Manny Gonzales, "Delay Is Here for Koster," *Seattle Times*, 26 April 2000, local section.

11. For example, Koster linked those resisting "the abortion industry" to "the Allied soldiers fighting in World War II." He claimed that he would "not defend the abortion industry" and supply "not one dime for Planned Parenthood. Not one dime for the United Nations Population Fund" if elected. Copy of letter on file with authors. Connelly, "Potomoc Watch: In Koster, GOP Has Uncompromising Candidate." Planned Parenthood responded in kind, along with NARAL, directing several anti-Koster mailings and phone calls to Second District voters before the general election. National Right to Life PAC aired some radio ads on Koster's behalf but spent far less than pro-choice groups did.

12. Gonzales, "Delay Is Here for Koster."

13. Ironically, some outside groups that spent money on behalf of GOP candidates in other competitive districts may have avoided Washington Second because Koster was perceived as being too conservative, and, hence, unelectable. As a campaign consultant who organized congressional campaign activity for one business group said, "it was a miracle that Koster came as close as he did." This consultant's group offered Koster minimal help, and we have no way of knowing if Sehlin would have attracted more interest from this group. (Bernadette Buddle, BIPAC, interview by David B. Magleby, Washington, D.C., 10 November 2000).

14. Federal Election Commission (FEC), "Summary Reports Search," <herndon1.sdrdc.com/fecimg/srssea.html>, 31 December 2000 [accessed 14 August 2001].

15. See Federal Election Commission (FEC), "Financial Activity of House Campaigns in the State of Washington," <www.fec.gov/2000/wahse99.htmfec.gov>, 18 October 2000 [accessed 10 December 2000] and Cathleen, Tarpley, "Key Races May Get Cash That's Over Cap," *Seattle Times*, 12 July 2000.

16. Jeff Morris, telephone interview by Todd Donovan, 24 January 2001.

17. Joel Connelly, "Metcalf's Departure Leaves Many Coveting Congressional Seat," *Seattle Post-Intelligencer*, 26 April 2000, national section.

18. See Joel Connelly, "Potomac Watch: Now that the Battle Is Over, Sparring for Congress Starts," *Seattle Post-Intelligencer*, 6 December 1999, national section, and Joel Connelly, "State Districts Key for Democrats," *Seattle Post Intelligencer*, 23 February 2000, local section.

19. Connelly, "Potomoc Watch: Now the Battle Is Over."

20. FEC, "Summary Reports Search."

21. *FEC Info.com*, <www.fecinfo.com/fecinfo/_states.htm> [accessed 28 January 2001].

22. The Second District has no major network-affiliate broadcast television station located in the District. Without cable, residents in the north receive only Canadian broadcast television. Some residents in the south can receive Seattle television without cable. Nearly all television ads targeting the Second Congressional District were thus purchased in the Seattle market, on cable (via Seattle offices), or on one small independent station in Bellingham.

23. Alliance for Better Campaigns, *Gouging Democracy: How the Televisions Industry Profiteered on Campaign 2000* (Washington, D.C.: Alliance for Better Campaigns, 2001).

24. Kevin Galvin, "Campaign Notebook," *Seattle Times*, 31 October 2000, local section.

25. Federal Election Commission (FEC), "Party Fundraising Escalates," press release, <fecweb1.fec.gov/press/011201partyfunds.htm> [accessed 12 January 2001].

26. In the Cantwell versus Gorton Senate race, the Democratic candidate Cantwell refused party soft money.

27. Karin Johanson, political director, DCCC, telephone interview by Jason Beal, 10 January 2001.

28. Alliance for Better Campaigns, *Gouging Democracy*.

29. David Postman, "TV Ad Costs Zoom as Election Nears," *Seattle Times*, 31 October 2000.

30. Joel Connelly reported that Democrats insisted the state GOP rework one of these ads, since they claimed it stated falsely that Larsen increased his salary. Joel Connelly, "2nd District Candidate Is Subject of Phone Slurs," *Seattle Post-Intelligencer*, 27 October 2000, Northwest section.

31. A press report noted that the NRCC "shelled out more than $66,000 [in October] to help Koster underwrite TV ads"; see Kevin Galvin, "Campaign Notebook," *Seattle Times*, 31 October 2000, local section. We found records of $28,000 in television buys by the NRCC (this omits purchases that KOMO would not reveal). However, our observers in the District had no clear record of the content of the NRCC ads.

32. Johanson, interview by Beal.

33. The voiceover on the "pickpocket" ad may have said, "paid for by the RCCC," a potential error in production. We have no record that any radio time was sold to the RCCC, and assume it was an NRCC ad.

34. The NRCC ads repeated Koster themes of Larsen committing "three strikes" on taxes, hitting his tax target "three times," getting his taxation wishes "three times," and something having to do with "three bears." A fourth ad ridiculed Larsen as having a tax habit "like a kid in a candy store."

35. In 1998, an Olympic Pipeline Company gas pipeline ruptured and exploded in Bellingham, killing three boys near a city park. Koster had voted against funding some new safety standards that Larsen endorsed. His campaign may have attacked on the issue to protect itself.

36. Press reports indicated that the U.S. Chamber of Commerce had planned a $100,000 purchase to help Koster; see John Hendron, "Washington Races to Reap Outside Cash," *Seattle Times*, 26 March 2000, local news. We did not observe Chamber ads on behalf of any other candidate.

37. Postman, "TV Ad Costs Zoom as Election Nears." *National Journal's Hotline* reported that the Sierra Club would buy $300,000 in television time in three House races,

including the Second District in Washington. The others announced were the Utah Second and Ohio Twelfth.

38. Bill Arthur, political director, Sierra Club Northwest Seattle, telephone interview by Todd Donovan, December 2000.

39. Data for independent expenditures, internal communication, and party coordinated expenditures were obtained from the FEC, "Disclosure Database," <ftp.fec.gov> [accessed 22 January 2001].

40. Sweeney offered this as a "ballpark estimate" and stated that the group spent less than $100,000. Elliot Sweeny, Building Industry Association of Washington Political Affairs, telephone interview by Todd Donovan, November 2000.

41. David Groves, Washington Labor Council—AFL-CIO, telephone interview by Todd Donovan, December 2000.

42. FEC, "Disclosure Database."

43. Kris Hanselman, political director, Washington Education Association, e-mail correspondence with Todd Donovan, December 2000.

44. As noted previously, the Sierra Club targeted independent women voters aged twenty-five to fifty, "women voters in Snohomish and Whatcom County," and newly registered voters in Island County. Arthur, interview by Donovan.

45. Ed Zuckerman, Washington Conservation Voters, telephone interview by Todd Donovan, December 2000.

46. FEC, "Disclosure Database."

47. Karen Cooper, Washington NARAL, telephone interview by Todd Donovan, November 2000.

48. NARAL sent similar mailings on behalf of Jay Inslee, in the First District. Statewide, NARAL sent "4-7 mailings to about 150,000 people each," and spent "well over $1 million" on federal elections in the state. NARAL's anti-Nader, anti-Bush television ads were added to the Seattle market in the final week of the campaign, since the ads generated "$3 to $4 million" after being shown to "major donors." Cooper, interview by Donovan.

49. Planned Parenthood Washington, telephone interview by Charles Morrow, December 2000. Mailed ads on file with author. Planned Parenthood reported $5,044 in independent expenditures for Larsen. FEC, "Disclosure Database."

50. We found more Campaign for a Progressive Future ads than Handgun Control ads, but both were less common than the NARAL ads.

51. Heath Heikkila, grassroots manager, Citizens for a Sound Economy PAC, telephone interview by Charles Morrow, December 2000.

52. FEC, "Disclosure Database."

53. Greg Roberts, Second District election volunteer coordinator, National Rifle Association, e-mail correspondence with Todd Donovan, October 2000.

54. Rick Forcier, field director, Christian Coalition of Washington State, telephone interview by Charles Morrow, December 2000. Our observations suggest that fewer guides may have been distributed.

13

Conclusions and Implications for Future Elections

David B. Magleby

Competitive congressional elections are no longer only contests between the major party candidates. In addition to candidates, contestants in these races include political parties and interest groups, who mount their own candidate-specific campaigns. As we have observed in this book and in previous research on the 1998 elections, outside money approximately equals candidate spending in competitive contests. This increase in outside money means campaigning in these contests is now a team sport. The party and interest group communications are typically more negative in tone compared to the more positive candidate communications.

Party, interest group, and candidate themes were largely the same in 2000. Neither party was willing to cede to the other core issues like Social Security, senior citizens, or education, and health care was a common theme for both Republicans and Democrats and interest groups. Taxes were emphasized more in the Republican Party and by GOP-allied interest group communications, and the Democratic Party and its allied groups emphasized the environment more. The level of issue congruence in 2000 among the parties, interest groups, and candidates was a departure from 1998, when House Republican candidates complained about their party committee running ads on President Clinton's misconduct and character problems, while their ads focused on other issues like education, taxes, and Social Security. They felt at a disadvantage against Democrats whose party committees and interest groups allies stressed the issue agendas of the candidates: health care, Social Security, and education.[1]

The fact that the parties and interest groups largely converged in their issue agendas and reinforced the themes of the candidates suggests that the parties and interest groups found ways to effectively coordinate with each other. It also suggests that competitive congressional campaigns now basically encompass the candidates, parties, and interest groups.

However, as we have shown, the tone of the party and interest group communications was often more negative than that of the ads from the candidates. There is an implicit division of labor in competitive races, with the outside money delivering the attack while the candidate delivers a more positive message. Some party committee staff indicate that a reason for this division of labor is that party lawyers had advised that soft money can more clearly be spent on issue ads that attack one candidate rather than contrast the two candidates.

DEMISE OF THE FEDERAL ELECTION CAMPAIGN ACT

For a time the post-Watergate campaign laws successfully required disclosure of campaign activity related to federal contests, limited contributions made to candidates and political parties for candidate campaigning purposes, and provided public funding for presidential general election campaigns through a taxpayer check-off fund. However, as we have demonstrated, issue advocacy, especially by so-called Section 527 groups, provides a substantial escape from disclosure for individuals and groups. Although legislation mandating some disclosure for 527 groups was enacted and signed into law in July 2000, disclosure remains limited.

The soft money loophole permits large donors to give unlimited amounts of soft money to political parties, much of which goes to promote and especially attack particular candidates. The growth in joint fundraising committees, or "victory funds," illustrates the close connection donors perceive between their candidate and party giving. Not surprisingly, courting large donors has become an important element of both parties' fundraising efforts. This renewed influence of large donors circumvents the FECA's attempt to limit the effect wealthy individuals can have on elections.

The influence of wealthy individuals not only circumvented the FECA with soft money, it also directly eroded a central FECA provision: public financing. Although public financing is not a part of congressional elections and therefore is not part of the scope of this study, it is worth noting that the decision by George W. Bush to bypass federal matching funds in the 2000 presidential primaries was a significant departure from what all other front-running candidates had done since the FECA was enacted. Bush justified his rejection of matching funds and their concomitant spending limitations as necessary to compete against billionaire Steve Forbes, who also rejected matching funds. Presidential general elections offer candidates the best of both worlds: They may accept the federal grant with its spending limit while benefiting from the unlimited soft money fundraising and spending on their behalf by the political parties.

The net effect of the surge in soft money and issue advocacy is much more limited disclosure, the return to prominence of large contributors, and largely unconstrained campaign spending by parties and interest groups. Candidates, in this electoral free-for-all, fall under what is left of FECA: static contribution limits for individual and PAC contributors, required disclosure by candidates of their receipts and expenditures, and a growing importance placed on self-financing.

SOFT MONEY MORE IMPORTANT THAN EVER

The 2000 elections saw a surge in party soft money for all party committees, especially in the Democratic committees. As Jim Jordan of the DSCC said, "Soft money was key to this cycle."[2] When the party committees decided to deploy soft money resources, as they often did in our sample of competitive races, it was in substantial sums, sometimes matching or exceeding the candidate's hard money spending. In Montana and Delaware Senate races in 2000, for example, the party committee (DSCC) transfers exceeded the total spending by the Democratic candidates. When internal communications and independent expenditures in the Michigan Senate race for Debbie Stabenow (D) and against Spence Abraham (R) are added to the DSCC hard and soft money transfers, the noncandidate spending in the race is only $100,000 less than the candidate spending of $8.1 million. All of this is disclosed activity. When issue advocacy is added, the noncandidate spending clearly exceeded the candidate spending in this case as well.

The growth in soft money use in 2000 was truly remarkable. Soft money receipts rose by 146 percent for the DSCC from 1998 to 2000 and by 236 percent for the DCCC over the same two-year period.[3] The Democrats not only saw the greatest growth in soft money spending, they deployed the resource well. Without soft money spending, it is doubtful whether the Democrats would have achieved their net gain of four seats and a 50/50 party tie in the Senate. Joseph Pika concludes "non-candidate spending played a determinative role in the outcome of [the Delaware Senate] race,"[4] and Michael Traugott's view of the Michigan Senate race is similar: Stabenow would not have won without outside help.[5]

The fact that huge amounts of soft money practically became a necessity in competitive campaigns raises a series of questions. First, what changed in 2000 that explains this dramatic growth in soft money? Part of the answer is that the Democrats saw an opportunity to regain partisan control of the House, which early on in the cycle seemed more likely in the House than the Senate. However, Minority Leader Gephardt minimized retirements and departures from the House to run for other offices, resulting in the Democrats having fewer open seats to defend. Another part of the explanation for the Democratic surge is the leadership of DCCC chair Patrick Kennedy, who made fundraising a central priority.[6]

The Democrats' success with soft money leads to another question. Given the growth in hard money and the abundance of money in the 2000 elections generally, why did the NRSC not have the same growth in soft money as the DSCC? One possible explanation is that there was more competition for soft money contributions from George W. Bush and House candidates. Early in the election cycle, House Republicans seemed more likely to lose their majority than Senate

Republicans and therefore picked up more party contribution dollars than did Senate Republicans. Another explanation is that with more GOP Senate incumbents running, their fundraising reduced the available pool of soft money for the party. Whatever the explanation, the Democratic advantage in soft money is not likely to last, given historic patterns. Republican fundraisers are likely to find ways to reestablish their soft money advantage.

Given these positive developments for the House Democrats and the Democratic Senate victories, why didn't Democrats pick up more House seats? Smart counter-strategies by the Republicans are part of the answer. Learning a lesson from 1998, they abandoned any effort to nationalize the campaign, like the ill-fated Operation Breakout. Instead they concentrated on supporting the most electable candidate, even if it meant becoming involved in party primaries like those in Illinois Ten and Pennsylvania Four. Republicans also purchased television time for the last weeks of the campaign early, when it was less expensive and more available. In contrast, the Democrats saved more of their money until the end, and in some races they were not able to spend as effectively.

But soft money is not the only factor affecting the outcome of congressional races. One important lesson from the 2000 House races is that even in an era of substantial outside money spending, quality candidates are critically important. Professionals from both parties repeatedly pointed to the relative strengths of their candidates—Schweitzer (D-Mont. Senate), Hoeffel (D-Pa. 13), Hart (R-Pa. 4), Ross (D-Ark. 4), and Kirk (R-Ill. 10)—over their opponents. As Karin Johanson of the DCCC, said, "The better candidate almost always wins."[7] Others pointed to weakness in candidates Dickey (R-Ark. 4), Roth (R-Del. Senate), and Greenleaf (R-Pa. 13). In races where candidates were more evenly matched, this variable was not as important.

Because party soft money has come to be such an important part of competitive congressional contests, decisions about which races receive soft money allocations and which do not clearly elevate the power and importance of the party committee leadership. In 2000, as in 1998, the party committees "played it by the numbers," meaning they relied on polling data to determine which races remained the most competitive.[8]There were notable exceptions, such as the NRSC's modest investment in Roth's race in Delaware.

Given the magnitude of the amounts of money involved and the fact that many candidates desire help, there will no doubt be pressure over time to spread the soft money around more. But party committee leaders and staff will continue to point to the narrow margin of party control as an argument for retaining their discretion and concentrating resources in relatively few races. As noted in chapter 2, the 2000 House Democratic Campaign Committee chair, Patrick Kennedy, made soft money fundraising a major priority, as did his Senate Democratic counterpart, Robert Toricelli. Both parties are likely to make the ability to raise money an important prerequisite as they recruit campaign committee chairs. How future party committee chairs allocate soft money is an important issue to monitor.

GROWTH IN ELECTION ISSUE ADVOCACY

Although soft money spending is probably the most significant story in the 2000 elections, interest groups also invested heavily in the 2000 elections, spending an estimated $364 million on issue advocacy, independent expenditures, and internal communications.[9] Most pursued a mixed strategy, contributing hard money to candidates and political parties through their political action committees (PACs), donating to the parties through soft money, and "diversifying their portfolio" by investing in issue advocacy or independent expenditures. Although a few groups like the American Association of Retired Persons (AARP) communicated only through pure issue advocacy, with a generic GOTV reminder or a call to pay attention to an issue, such communications are rare.

As in 1998, most interest groups in 2000 (195), under the pretext of issue advocacy, mounted the equivalent of full-fledged campaigns for and against specific candidates. The campaigns were fully professional and included pollsters, media consultants, general strategists, mail consultants, and so forth. Decisions about where to deploy interest group resources were based on polling and, in some instances, regular tracking polls.

In some cases, not only *where* money was deployed, but *how* it was deployed was extremely important. New in 1999–2000 were "Section 527 organizations," which included the Republican Majority Issues Committee, Americans for Equality (part of the NAACP National Voter Fund), and the Republican Leadership Council. Some of these groups were involved in our contests, and all were unwilling to talk to us during and after the election.

Election issue advocacy helped set the agenda in several 2000 congressional races. For example, asbestos-related health problems became important in Montana due to issue advocacy. An anti-immigration group, Federation for American Immigration Reform (FAIR), ran ads making immigration an issue against Senator Spence Abraham in Michigan. Occasionally, as in these examples, issue advocacy revolved around an issue that only affected a specific race. More typically, however, issue advocacy reinforced the broad themes of the 2000 campaign: Social Security, prescription drugs, education, abortion, and guns. The congruence among candidate, party soft money, and election issue advocacy in issue agenda does not minimize the importance of the interest groups. The fact that to voters the campaign communications were indistinguishable meant candidates who were less well funded, like Debbie Stabenow, could benefit from the efforts of allied groups. During the summer of 2000 Stabenow could not afford to run ads and Abraham was advertising heavily, so groups ran ads on her behalf.

In the seventeen races we observed, 237 interest groups (and 93 national and state party organizations) communicated with voters. Broadcast advertising was an important element in competitive races in 2000. Even in the California Twenty-seventh Congressional District, where voters are only a fraction of the Los Angeles media market, both campaigns and their allied parties and interest groups ran broadcast ads. In Senate races, television and radio were also major components of the inside and outside money campaigns.

Perhaps the most significant issue advocacy campaigning came not in the air war but in the ground war. Election issue advocacy in 2000 again made extensive use of telephone contacts and targeted direct mail. Overall, 159 interest groups (and 81 national and state party organizations) sent out mail or mounted a telephone campaign. Unions, environmental groups, the NRA, pro- and anti-choice organizations, and businesses also mounted extensive internal communications with their members. Organizations like NARAL and the AFL-CIO conducted in-person contacts, through the mail and on the phone, and organized GOTV drives.[10] As Grover Norquist, a leader in the paycheck protection movement, observed, "Unions have learned they activate their opponents when they use TV/radio. By using grassroots and mail they mobilize their folks and not opponents."[11] Academics in several of our sample races report union successes in mobilizing their membership.[12] In Missouri, for example, in early 2000 the AFL-CIO updated its membership rosters, implemented a voter registration drive, and ultimately generated a list of nearly 600,000 active and retired members who could be contacted as the general election approached.[13] Internal communications are difficult to monitor and serve as a reminder that understanding the scope and impact of outside money requires the kind of monitoring methodology we utilized.

IMPORTANCE OF THE GROUND WAR

Our research demonstrates that in competitive contests, campaigns attempt to persuade voters not only through radio and television ads; more targeted communications are also important. Some groups, like the NEA and NRA, use mail to communicate with their membership but also to reach a broader audience. For example, in the Washington Second Congressional District the NRA sent a "Dear Washington Hunter" mailer, reaching beyond NRA members to Washington hunters. Political parties mounted large direct mail campaigns in competitive races in 2000. The volume of mail forced groups, parties, and candidates to find ways to get the attention of voters who received a dozen or more pieces of political mail each day. They did this by sending oversized, more colorful, and more attention-getting mail.

Telephones were another important tool in voter communication in 2000. In Missouri the AFL-CIO made available a purple traveling phone bank, jokingly referred to as the "Barney truck," which allowed unions to make hundreds of thousands of phone calls to their members, using each local group's own volunteers to deliver the message.[14] Groups and parties used recorded messages with the messenger selected to appeal to the demographic profile of the intended recipient. As Election Day approached the volume of telephoning increased.

Personal contact has been given greater emphasis by several groups in recent election cycles, most notably by organized labor. The AFL-CIO expanded its member-to-member efforts in 2000, taking advantage of the ongoing relationship union members have with their local leaders. In the Connecticut Fifth District race, for example, local union presidents signed letters to their members.[15] Business interests, while lacking the extensive network of relationships enjoyed by labor, put technology to work with Web sites and voter activation tools available on the Internet. A race in which the BIPAC Web site was effectively used to the benefit of a Republican candidate was the Kentucky Sixth Congressional District race in 2000.[16]

Ground war data will always be incomplete, and we recognize that our data are often only suggestive. This is due in part to the absence of disclosure requirements for issue advocacy paid for by interest groups and limited disclosure requirements for how party soft money is actually expended. Yet the data we collected and analyzed demonstrate the importance of including nonbroadcast communications in any assessment of candidate, party, or interest group campaigning in competitive races.

IMPLICATIONS

The two parties worked with slightly different campaign strategies in 2000. Overall Democrats had the advantage, with more active and visible interest group support. As noted, on issues like abortion and the environment, Democratic candidates typically received more support from their allies than did the Republicans. Organized labor, especially when school teachers are included, mounted large-scale voter persuasion and mobilization efforts, typically for Democrats. By most accounts, the most effective Republican ally was the NRA.[17] In terms of overall spending, Citizens for Better Medicare (CBM) was a major player assisting Republicans, even though the group insists its communications were about issues and not candidates.[18]

Republican candidates as a rule have benefited from access to more party resources, including soft money, but in 2000 the close party balance in soft money permitted Democrats to be more competitive. This was especially the case in competitive Senate races, where the DSCC outperformed the NRSC.

These differences, in the short run at least, have implications for campaign finance reform. The AFL-CIO was an outspoken opponent of the McCain-Feingold and Shayes-Meehan bills in 2001, as was the NRA and much of the business community.[19] Democrats had to assess whether their ascendancy in soft money fundraising was transitory, especially with Republicans back in control of the White House after the 2000 election. President Clinton, who made soft money fundraising a high priority for his own reelection in 1996, was also heavily involved in raising money for the party in 2000. Democratic leaders in both the

House and Senate stressed to their caucuses that their party could not keep up with Republicans in soft money, so a ban along the lines of McCain-Feingold was in their interest.[20] Anticipating the actual impact of reform is difficult because the real test will be in how the parties adapt to new rules.

IMPACT ON VOTERS

For voters in competitive races like the seventeen we monitored, an election like the 2000 election is much more intense than the typical congressional contest. It means more frequent political commercials on television and radio. For undecided voters it often means a deluge of mail and telephone calls. In Montana the deluge of mail was likened to the Christmas rush, with people complaining about late deliveries.[21] The sheer volume of communications through television, radio, mail, and telephone makes it difficult to sort through all the information. A voter's task is further complicated by election issue advocacy, which often masks a group's true identity behind innocuous names like Campaign for America's Children, Council for a Livable World, American Family Voices, and Committee for Good Common Sense. Most voters work from the assumption that the communications are from one or another of the candidates, although in several of our races most of the communications were not. In a separate research project in 2000, we demonstrated that voters could not differentiate the source of political communications (including mail), and, moreover, assume that communications come from the candidate.[22]As Jim Jordan of the DSCC observed, "What matters is tone, not the revenue source."[23]

So many different messengers in campaigns means that no one is really held accountable for the content or tone of the campaign. Voters may assume that it is the candidates who are responsible, but the candidates often disavow the interest group messages and even their own party's soft money funded communications, as happened in the New Jersey Twelfth Congressional District race. The DCCC sent a mailer attacking Zimmer's record on breast cancer votes, and the media decried Holt's attacks because Zimmer's mother had died of lymphoma and three sisters had survived breast cancer.[24]

Often candidates who benefit from outside money complain that it is a double-edged sword. Illinois Tenth Congressional District candidate Lauren Beth Gash said, "It is difficult to be the candidate when there is a message going out that you don't control."[25]

The news media have a difficult time helping voters sort out who is behind the numerous issue advocacy organizations, as well as the difference between party and candidate communications. Campaign reporting is typically limited to broadcast advertising and does not explore the mail and telephone campaigns or the GOTV efforts by candidates, parties, and interest groups. But even with these limitations, according to a Lexis-Nexis search, media coverage of issue advocacy and interest group participation in elections has tripled since the previous presidential election. Front-page stories on issue advocacy written by journalists who attended our reporter conferences appeared in the *San Francisco Examiner*, the *Richmond-Times Dispatch*, the *Kansas City Star*, the *Arkansas Democrat-Gazette*, and other newspapers.[26]

A LOOK AHEAD: 2002

Patrick Kennedy, with the strong encouragement of Minority Leader Gephardt, transformed the DCCC's soft money fundraising, partly with the expectation of a majority. Whether Nita Lowey (N.Y. 18), the new DCCC chair, will be able to retain that lead in 2001–2002 is uncertain. For the Republicans, Representative Tom Davis has won the praise of fellow partisans for holding off the Democratic push in 2000 and again has the advantage of incumbency and the ability of the majority to set the legislative agenda for the 2001–2002 election cycle.

A major difference between the House and Senate and between 2000 and 2002 will be the number of competitive races. In 1998 and 2000 there were a dozen or fewer competitive Senate races and fewer than thirty competitive House races. The number of competitive Senate races in 2002 will remain at a dozen or fewer, while the number of competitive House races after redistricting could grow by a factor of three or four.

The very narrow margins in both houses remain an open invitation to a continuation of the soft money chase of recent cycles. Democrats seem to have found new donors or convinced old donors to give a lot more. Republicans will no doubt refer to the surge in Democratic money in their appeals to their donors in the future. Going into the 2002 election, Republicans will have the added assistance of a sitting president. All of this points to an expansion of soft money and issue advocacy in 2002 and beyond.

The strategic environment of 2002 will be different from 2000, however. Because it will be a midterm election with lower voter turnout, more emphasis will be placed on voter identification and activation. Mobilizing voters through personal contact and targeted messages will be even more important. In that sense 2002 will more closely resemble 1998. In our research on that cycle the ground war was especially important.[27]

All the incentives for continued high levels of candidate, party, and interest group spending exist for 2002 and beyond. The close party balance in Congress, the enduring rancor from the 2000 presidential ballot-counting controversy in Florida, and a sitting president who is a proven fundraiser all point to a continued emphasis on soft money and election issue advocacy. As in the past, this will continue to affect the institution as a whole. Even relatively safe incumbents will feel added pressure to raise more money and to raise it early, and legislative leadership will press members to assist in party hard- and soft money fundraising. Linda

Lipson, political director of the Association of Trial Lawyers of America, reported "requests for money were more frequent this cycle."[28] Donors, especially soft money donors, will continue to be pressed for more and more assistance. The process is, in short, like an arms race, where no one knows how much money is enough and it is safest to assume you can never have too much money. As Lipson puts it, "If you don't do it, you will get buried."[29]

Perhaps the pressures to raise more money, the uncertainty posed to incumbents by the possibility of election issue advocacy, and the loss of candidate control over campaigns will prompt members of Congress to reform this system. When they do so, they must be sensitive to the variety of ways in which individuals and groups may circumvent their intent.

Campaign spending by candidates, parties, and interest groups has significantly expanded in recent years. This phenomenon occurs in competitive races where party control of Congress is likely to be determined. Barring changes in the rules of campaign finance, this trend will continue. The elevated importance of large donors who largely fund the party soft money spending and of interest groups with clear policy agendas raises important questions of money spent in these ways buying influence. The decline of effective disclosure is also a concern in terms of interest groups being accountable for their communications. Absent disclosure, voters face a deluge of information without the tools to effectively assess its reliability. At a minimum, restoring full disclosure, including issue advocacy sponsorship, would help voters perform their important role and permit the media to more effectively report on competitive campaigns.

NOTES

1. David Magleby, *Outside Money: Soft Money and Issue Advocacy in the 1998 Congressional Elections* (Lanham, Md.: Rowman & Littlefield, 2000), 218.
2. Jim Jordan, Democratic Senatorial Campaign Committee (DSCC), interview by David B. Magleby, Washington, D.C., 19 November 2000.
3. Federal Election Commission, "National Party Nonfederal Activity," press release, 15 May 2001.
4. Joseph Pika, "The 2000 Delaware Senate Race," in "Outside Money," ed. David B. Magleby, *PS: eSymposium*, <www.apsa.com/PS/june01/pika.cfm>, June 2001 [accessed 15 September 2001].
5. See chapter 5.
6. David Espo, "For Gephardt, the Goal Is a Democratic Majority in the House," *Los Angeles Times*, 4 November 2000.
7. Karin Johansen, Democratic Congressional Campaign Committee (DCCC), interview by David B. Magleby, Washington, D.C., 20 November 2000.
8. Magleby, *Outside Money*, 219.
9. Information derived from interviews, *CMAG* data, *Election Advocacy* database, and Erika Falk, Annenberg Public Policy Center, "Issue Advocacy Advertising through the Presidential Primary: 1999–2000 Election Cycle" press release, 20 September 2000.

10. Dan Balz, "NARAL Targets Voters in Fifteen States," *Washington Post*, 26 September 2000, final edition.

11. Grover Norquist, Americans for Tax Reform, telephone interview by David B. Magleby, 11 January 2001.

12. See Michael Traugott, "Soft Money and Challenger Viability: The 2000 Michigan Senate Race," in "Outside Money," ed. Magleby; Scott Keeter, Harry Wilson, Robert Holsworth, Stephen Medvic, and Robert Dudley, "The 2000 Virginia Senate Race," in "Outside Money," ed. Magleby; Drew Linzer and David Menefee-Libey, "The 2000 California Twenty-seventh Congressional District Race," in "Outside Money," ed. Magleby; Robin Kolodny and Sandra Suarez, "The 2000 Connecticut Fifth Congressional District Race," in "Outside Money," ed. Magleby; Adam J. Berinsky and Sue S. Lederman, "The 2000 New Jersey Twelfth Congressional District Race," in "Outside Money," ed. Magleby; and Rebekah Herrick and Charles Peaden, "The 2000 Oklahoma Second Congressional District Race," in "Outside Money," ed. Magleby.

13. Martha Kropf, E. Terrance Jones, Dale Neuman, Maureen Gilbride Mears, Anthony Simones, and Allison Hayes, "The 2000 Missouri Senate Race," in "Outside Money," ed. Magleby.

14. Ibid.

15. Kolodny and Suarez, "The Connecticut Fifth Congressional District Race."

16. Penny Miller and Don A. Gross, "The 2000 Kentucky Sixth Congressional District Race," in "Outside Money," ed. Magleby.

17. See chapter 4.

18. Tim Ryan, executive director, Citizens for Better Medicare, telephone interview by David Magleby and Anna N. Baker, 14 May 2001.

19. Allison Mitchell and Adam Clymer, "Democrats Maneuver on Soft Money as Vote Nears," *New York Times*, 11 July 2001, A12; Daniel Kaufman, "Statement by AFSCME Director of Legislation Charles Loveless on H.R. 2356, the Bipartisan Campaign Reform Act of 2001," press release, *AFSCME News*, <www.afscme.org/press/pr010712.htm> [accessed 12 July 2001].

20. Transcript of House Democratic Leader Richard Gephardt's 28 June 2001 Press Conference, *U.S. Newswire*.

21. See chapter 4.

22. David B. Magleby, ed., "Dictum Without Data: The Myth of Issue Advocacy and Party Building," report presented at the National Press Club, Washington, D.C., <www.byu.edu/outsidemoney/dictum>, November 2000 [accessed 15 August 2001].

23. Jordan, interview by Magleby.

24. See chapter 10.

25. Barry Rundquist, "The 2000 Illinois Tenth Congressional District Race," in "Outside Money," ed. Magleby.

26. Early in 2000, we hosted four regional seminars on soft money and election issue advocacy for reporters in states and congressional districts likely to see substantial outside money activity.

27. Magleby, *Outside Money*, 72–74.

28. Linda Lipson, Association of Trial Lawyers, interview by David B. Magleby, Washington, D.C., 13 December 2000.

29. Ibid.

Appendix A

List of Interviews Conducted by David B. Magleby and BYU Research Associates

Name	*Organization*	*Date Interviewed*
Ackerman, Karen	AFL-CIO	9 November 2000
Adams, Tiffany	National Association of Manufacturers	29 February 2000
Adams, Tiffany	National Association of Manufacturers	10 November 2000
Baker, Charlie	Gore 2000	16 June 2000
Baran, Jan	Election Lawyer	21 March 2000
Basu, Saundra	Congressional Quarterly	6 April 2000
Bauer, Bob	Election Lawyer	20 March 2000
Beale, Anne	Population Environmental Balance	27 January 2000
Benenson, Bob	Congressional Quarterly	6 April 2000
Berring, Helle	Washington Times	22 March 2000
Blancato, Bob	Matz, Blancato & Associates	27 January 2000
Bowman, Karlyn	American Enterprise Institute	10 April 2000
Broder, John	New York Times	22 March 2000
Budde, Bernadette	Business-Industry Political Action Committee	10 April 2000
Budde, Bernadette	Business-Industry Political Action Committee	10 November 2000
Burch, Jr., J. Thomas	National Vietnam & Gulf War Veterans Coalition	29 February 2000
Burns, Martin	AARP Vote	14 December 2000
Caroline, Glen	National Rifle Association	15 November 2000
Cino, Maria	Bush Campaign	29 June 2000
Collins, Mary Jean	People for the American Way	11 December 2000
Cuff, Courtney	Friends of the Earth	11 December 2000
Cunningham, Chuck	National Rifle Association	12 April 2000
Cunningham, Chuck	National Rifle Association	11 December 2000
Dal Col, Bill	Forbes 2000	3 March 2000
Dal Col, Bill	NRSC	9 July 01
Davis, Rick	McCain 2000	14 June 2000
Dogherty, Suzanne	Congressional Quarterly	6 April 2000
Donaldson, Anita	Citizens for Sound Economy	25 May 2000

Name	*Organization*	*Date Interviewed*
Dowd, Matthew	Bush Campaign	15 June 2000
Dunn, Anita	Bradley 2000	15 May 2000
Easton, John	American Medical Association	13 December 2000
Elar, Tony	AmeriComm Direct Marketing	15 May 2000
Elisabeth, Mary	National Education Association	10 April 2000
Fletcher, Roy	McCain 2000	6 June 2000
Ginsberg, Ben	Bush 2000 National Council	6 July 01
Giraux, Greg	Congressional Quarterly	6 April 2000
Glantz, Gina	Bradley 2000	21 March 2000
Glaser, Susan	Washington Post	27 January 2000
Guzik, John	NRCC	1 March 2000
Guzik, John	NRCC	13 November 2000
Hanahan, Mike	Voter Contact Services	25 May 2000
Hansen, Dave	NRSC	12 April 2000
Hansen, Dave	NRSC	8 December 2000
Hansen, Dave	NRSC	2 July 01
Hazelwood, Dan	Targeted Creative Communications	1 June 2000
Johansen, Karin	DCCC	15 November 2000
Jordan, Jim	DSCC	9 November 2000
Kamark, Elaine	Harvard University	6 June 2000
King, Tom	Ben and King	23 May 2000
Kranowitz, Alan	National Association of Wholesale-Distributors	1 May 2000
Laguens, Dawn	Laguens, Hamburger & Stone	15 November 2000
Lipsen, Linda	American Trial Lawyers Association	13 December 2000
Lutz, Will	NARAL	12 January 2000
Lutz, Will	NARAL	14 December 2000
Lux, Mike	Progressive Strategies	14 December 2000
Lyons, Rachel	Planned Parenthood Action Fund	13 December 2000
McClellan, Scott	Bush Campaign	21 June 2000
McGee, Christi	National Restaurant Association	12 January 2000
McInturff, Bill	Public Opinion Strategies	10 April 2000
Miller, Bill	U.S. Chamber of Commerce	18 December 2000
Miller, Mark	Republican Leadership Council	13 January 2000
Mings, Mike	Human Rights Campaign	13 December 2000
Mitchell, Denise	AFL-CIO	16 July 01
Mix, Mark	National Right to Work Committee	13 December 2000
Murray, Barbra	Congressional Quarterly	6 April 2000
Norquist, Grover	Americans for Tax Reform	12 January 01
Norquist, Grover	Americans for Tax Reform	13 January 2000
Pacheco, Jack	National Education Association	10 April 2000
Pacheco, Jack	National Education Association	7 December 2000
Paul, Jon	Seniors Coalition	12 January 2000
Petro, Michael	Committee for Economic Development	22 March 2000
Piass, Naomi	Handgun Control, Inc.	15 November 2000
Pierce, Emily	Congressional Quarterly	6 April 2000
Polidori, Jack	National Education Association	7 December 2000
Potter, Trevor	Wiley, Rein & Fielding	21 March 2000

Quinn, Richard	McCain 2000	14 June 2000
Ray, David	Federation for American Immigration Reform	15 June 2000
Rosenthal, Steve	AFL-CIO	28 June 2000
Rothenberg, Stu	Roll Call	11 April 2000
Ryan, Tim	Citizens for Better Medicare	14 May 01
Schneider, Bill	CNN	21 March 2000
St. Martin, Darla	National Right to Life Committee	13 January 2000
Thoren, Don	National Restaurant Association	12 January 2000
Totten, Gloria	NARAL	12 January 2000
Totten, Gloria	NARAL	14 December 2000
Van Loihouzen, Jan	Voter Consumer Research	21 June 2000
Wade, Lisa	League of Conservation Voters	13 November 2000
Walker, Kevin	American Medical Association	13 December 2000
Weaver, John	McCain 2000	14 June 2000
Weiss, Dan	Sierra Club	14 January 2000
White, Deanna	Sierra Club	14 December 2000
Willis, Derrick	Congressional Quarterly	6 April 2000
Wolff, Sharon	National Association of Independent Business	12 January 2000
Wolff, Sharon	National Association of Independent Business	14 November 2000

Appendix B

Election Advocacy Database (Description and Notes for Tables)

DATA COLLECTION

Each group of academics was responsible for collecting and cataloguing campaign-related communications in their respective race. They recorded these observations into a database through a password-protected Web site interface. The data can be divided into two major groups: unique communications observed in various media and ad buy data collected from television and radio stations.

Observed Communications

It is not feasible to gather and quantify the exact breadth and depth of any organization's activities in terms of total number of mailings sent or phone calls made. However, it is possible to track and estimate an organization's number of unique ad campaigns, that is, how many unique, different mailers it created for distribution. The academics recorded observed activity in the following media: banner ads on the Internet, e-mails, mail pieces, newspaper/magazine advertisements, person-to-person contacts, phone calls, radio advertisements, and television advertisements.

Collected Ad Buy Data and the Campaign Media Analysis Group

Participating academics visited radio and television stations to retrieve ad buy data: number of spots aired for each commercial and money spent for those spots. Although some stations were wholly unwilling to cooperate in providing data, the data in this study constitute the most complete existing tally of money spent by organizations and parties in the seventeen sample races. The Campaign Media

Analysis Group (CMAG) also provided very useful data on organization activity in the top media markets within the races. However, in terms of cost analysis, CMAG uses a price averaging method to determine the approximate cost of the detected commercials. Because costs escalate as election day approaches, the CMAG estimates are conservative. For a more complete explanation, see Jonathan S. Krasno and Daniel E. Seltz, *Buying Time: Television Advertising in the 1998 Congressional Elections* (New York: Brennan Center for Justice, 2000).

EXPLANATIONS FOR ALL TABLES USING THE ELECTION ADVOCACY DATABASE

Data Exclusions

Unless otherwise indicated, all data totals contained in this monograph exclude all data from the presidential, Oklahoma 2 Primary, and Oklahoma 2 Runoff races. However, any communications that endorsed or opposed a presidential candidate *and* a candidate from one of the sample races remain in the totals.

Ad Buy Deficiencies

The collected television and radio ad buy data may contain extraneous data due to the difficulty in determining the content of the ads. The parties or interest groups that purchased the ad buys possibly ran some ads promoting presidential candidates, other house or senatorial candidates not in our sample but still within that media market, or ballot propositions. Unless the participating academics were able to determine the exact content of the ad buy from the limited information given by the station, the data may contain some observations that do not pertain to our House or Senate races. To help adjust for this problem, we have incorporated the CMAG data into the study's analysis of airwave spending. With its technology, CMAG is able to better determine the content of political advertisements.

Allied Interest Groups

Interest groups have been classified as either Democratic or Republican allies. In many cases, organizations are openly supportive of a certain party, or ideology, and its candidates. Certain organizations, however, publicly maintain neutrality, such as Citizens for Better Medicare, the National Education Association, and the National Rifle Association. Upon further examination of their communications, it was possible to categorize many of them as a partisan ally due to which candidates they supported or attacked or whether their communications were anti- or pro- conservative or liberal.

Affiliate Consolidation

Data that are collected from multiple races will contain observations from state-level organizations and their national affiliates. In our samplewide totals (tables 3.2 and 3.3), all state and local chapters or affiliates have been combined with their national affiliate to better depict the organization's overall activity. For instance, the Montana Education Association data have been included in the NEA totals.

Index

About the Contributors

Anna Nibley Baker earned a bachelor's degree in political science from Brigham Young University. She helped manage research and editing on this book and currently works as a case manager at The Road Home.

David C. Barker is assistant professor of political science at the University of Pittsburgh. He is the author of the forthcoming book, *Rushed to Judgment? Talk Radio, Persuasion, and American Political Behavior.*

Jason Richard Beal graduated with a master's degree in public policy from Brigham Young University. He worked on the research project in Washington as the liaison with interest groups, parties, and other governmental contacts. He is currently pursuing a career as a consultant in Washington, D.C.

Adam J. Berinsky is an assistant professor of politics at Princeton University.

Christopher Jan Carman is an assistant professor of political science at the University of Pittsburgh. His research focuses on the dynamics of political, particularly legislative, representation.

Sue Carter, J.D., is the executive assistant to the president and secretary of the Board of Trustees at Michigan State University. She is also a member of the School of Journalism faculty.

Todd Donovan is professor of political science at Western Washington University. He is coauthor of five books, including the forthcoming *Electoral Reform and Minority Representation.*

Robert Dudley is associate professor of government at George Mason University. His most recent publication is *American Elections: The Rules Matter* (coauthored with Alan R. Gitelson).

Eric Freedman is a Pulitzer Prize-winning reporter and assistant professor of journalism at Michigan State University.

Robert Holsworth is the director of the Center for Public Policy at Virginia Commonwealth University. His recent writings include work on the Clinton presidency, race and politics, and Virginia political issues.

Scott Keeter is professor of government and politics at George Mason University. His research interests include civic engagement, religion and politics, and survey research methods.

Susan S. Lederman, professor of public administration at Kean University, is a former president of the League of Women Voters of the United States. She serves on the New Jersey Election Law Enforcement Commission.

Drew A. Linzer is a graduate student in political science at the University of California at Los Angeles. He is studying campaign strategy, elections, representation, and political institutions.

David B. Magleby is dean of the College of Family, Home and Social Sciences, distinguished professor of political science, and director of the Center for the Study of Elections and Democracy at Brigham Young University. He was the principal investigator on this project. His books include *Direct Legislation: Voting on Ballot Propositions in the United States*; *The Money Chase: Congressional Campaign Finance Reform*; and *Outside Money*.

Stephen K. Medvic is assistant professor of political science at Old Dominion University. He is the author of *Political Consultants in U.S. Congressional Elections* (Ohio State University Press).

David Menefee-Libey is the author of *The Triumph of Campaign-Centered Politics*. He teaches politics at Pomona College in Claremont, California.

Charles Morrow is a master's student at Western Washington University. He has served as a research associate with the Coalition for Human Dignity and the Center for Democratic Renewal.

Eric A. Smith graduated magna cum laude with his bachelor's degree in economics from Brigham Young University. He helped manage research and data on this project and is currently pursuing an entertainment career in Los Angeles.

Michael W. Traugott is professor of communication studies and a senior research scientist at the Center for Political Studies in the Institute for Social Research at the University of Michigan.

Craig Wilson is a professor of political science and chair of his department at Montana State University-Billings.

Harry L. Wilson is associate professor of political science and director of the Center for Community Research at Roanoke College. His current research deals with gun control and elections.